Sexual Harassment and the Law

LANDMARK LAW CASES

AMERICAN SOCIETY

Peter Charles Hoffer
N. E. H. Hull
Series Editors

AUGUSTUS B. COCHRAN III

Sexual Harassment and the Law

The Mechelle Vinson Case

UNIVERSITY PRESS OF KANSAS

Published by the University Press of Kansas (Lawrence, Kansas 66049), which was organized by the Kansas Board of Regents and is operated and funded by Emporia State University, Fort Hays State University, Kansas State University, Pittsburg State University, the University of Kansas, and Wichita State University

Library of Congress Cataloging-in-Publication Data

Cochran, Augustus B., 1946–
Sexual harassment and the law : the Mechelle Vinson case / Augustus B. Cochran.
p. cm. — (Landmark law cases & American society)
Includes bibliographical references and index.
ISBN 0-7006-1322-6 (cloth : alk. paper) — ISBN 0-7006-1323-4 (paper : alk. paper)
1. Sexual harassment — Law and legislation — United States.   2. Vinson, Mechelle — Trials, litigation, etc.   I. Title.   II. Series.
KF4758.C63 2004
344.7301′4133 — dc22   2003022976

British Library Cataloguing-in-Publication Data is available.

Printed in the United States of America

10 9 8 7 6 5 4 3 2 1

The paper used in this publication meets the minimum requirements of the American National Standard for Permanence of Paper for Printed Library Materials z39.48–1984.

CONTENTS

In this authoritative study of the rise of sexual harassment law, Augustus Cochran rightly begins with the connection between employment and law. Whereas Americans once defined themselves by where they lived, they now greet newcomers with, "What do you do for a living?" Whereas all hiring was once "at will," and the employer held the high cards, now local, state, and federal agencies and courts all have a hand in supervising fair employment practices. With the Occupational Safety and Health Administration looking for unsafe working conditions, the Equal Employment Opportunity Commission ensuring compliance with the Civil Rights Acts' ban on discrimination in employment, and myriad child labor, workers' compensation, and other statutes on labor conditions, employment and law seem inevitably bound together. But until the 1970s, the law primarily supervised only the tangible environment of the workplace. Could the law also peer into the intangible personal relationships among bosses and employees? Could courts determine when unwanted sexual advances and insensitive sexual innuendos made a workplace inhospitable? That was the question raised by the landmark case that Mechelle Vinson brought against her boss and the bank that employed them both in 1978.

When Vinson filed her suit, the law was hazy. Title VII of the Civil Rights Act of 1964 prohibited discrimination on the basis of sex, but the casual if pervasive power that employers and their agents had over the everyday lives of their employees was a gray area of law. What rights did employees have against the quid pro quo offer of sex for promotion or the more subtle forms of harassment that created a hostile environment for them? What did the victim have to do, or not do, to assert her rights? Was the corporate employer liable as well if it did not have notice of the harassment? What remedies might courts or legislatures order if the employee quit on her own?

Vinson and her counselors would have to "make law," the most difficult of all efforts in our system. They would have to persuade the courts to reach beyond the precise language of statutes and the holdings of earlier cases, for Mechelle Vinsion had not been fired for resisting and may even have contributed to the alleged unwanted sexual advances of her immediate superior Sidney Taylor. The facts, too, were murky. Had he demanded sexual favors for the support he had given her early in her career? Did she entice him with seductive words or dress styles? Even the term *sexual harassment* was new at the time, its meaning contested by the parties to the suit and by scholars watching it move through the courts.

Cochran's thorough, scholarly essay puts the human story in its larger context. These were heady times for the women's movement, when women were gaining a voice in training programs, mass media, higher education, government, and even locker rooms. Consciousness-raising groups and feminist publications urged women not to accept the "boys will be boys" rationale for untoward sexual conduct. Cochran uses a wide variety of social science studies to document the existence of sexual harassment and how it diverged from genuine, mutual romantic relationships. He masterfully synthesizes as well the scholarly literature on sex discrimination. Finally, he encapsulates the case law and the emerging statutory provisions relating to sexual harassment.

All these came together in Vinson's case as it moved from the federal district court all the way to the U.S. Supreme Court and back to the district court. Cochran explains clearly and precisely the rulings of the district court judges and the opinions of the appellate justices along the way. The case had a surprise ending, but the law of sexual harassment continues to evolve. In the last three chapters, Cochran traces that evolution through the courts, in the pages of scholarly and legal journals, and in the workplace itself. This is the definitive work on sexual harassment and the law.

ACKNOWLEDGMENTS

Any man who undertakes to write on sexual harassment necessarily embarks on an enterprise of self-education. In my project, I was fortunate to have many astute and generous teachers. In addition to the sources cited in the text and countless others that had to be omitted because of space limitations, I would like to thank my colleagues Cathy Scott and Beth Hackett, my friend Will Reid, and Peter Hoffer, Michael Briggs, and two anonymous reviewers with the University Press of Kansas for their valuable editorial advice. At Agnes Scott College, Linda Gray, Sala Rhodes, Susan Dougherty, Amy Whitworth, Courtney Frierson, Doug Talbott, and Neta Counts lent able assistance, and students in FYS and PS360 contributed to my understanding of sexual harassment law. In Washington, Calvin Craney of the U.S. District Court Clerk's Office and Laura Khare of the Equal Employment Opportunity Commission helped with documents. Many of the attorneys in the *Vinson* case provided invaluable information, especially Charles Fleischer, Pat Barry, Bob Troll, and John Meisburg. I am grateful to the faculty of Georgia State University's College of Law, especially my employment and labor law professors Mary Radford and Steven Kaminshine, for an absolutely first-rate education in the law, and to the attorneys at Stanford Fagan, who taught me how to practice it. To my family, especially Miller, Molly, and Mildred Cochran, the debts are simply too numerous to recount.

Mechelle Vinson felt grievously wronged by her boss and by the company for which she had worked for four years. The job as a bank teller, which she had taken at age nineteen, had started promisingly enough. Befriended by Sidney Taylor, who had hired her to work in the branch bank he managed in Washington, D.C., she had received positive evaluations and several promotions in her "first real job." Beneath this placid surface, however, Vinson claimed that she had had to cope with an ugly underside of her employment. She charged that the cost of keeping her job had been submitting to the sexual demands of Taylor, her direct supervisor.

According to Vinson, after initially playing the part of helpful mentor, Taylor had propositioned her, pressuring her to have sex with him in a local motel. She had acquiesced to sex with Taylor only because of his threats, out of fear of losing her job. The demands, however, had only escalated, and over the course of two and a half years, the sexual requests had turned into constant harassment, forty to fifty incidents of sexual assault, and even rape. Finally, after four years of outstanding job performance accompanied by nightmarish sexual harassment, Mechelle Vinson took extended sick leave and was then fired by the bank for excessive absenteeism.

Believing that her rights had been violated, Vinson sought a lawyer and filed a lawsuit against Taylor and the bank in federal court. But at the time Vinson sued, in September 1978, it was anything but clear that the wrongs she said she had suffered were illegal. However reprehensible sexual harassment might be, no law expressly forbade such outrageous practices in the workplace. Several legal prohibitions might be stretched to cover these types of harms, but a perfect fit was lacking. Potentially the most effective legal tool against sexual harassment was Title VII, the federal law against sex discrimination in employment, but only a few recent cases had tested this legal theory, with decidedly mixed results. Federal judges were quite reluctant to find that *sexual harassment* was the kind of *sex discrimination* that Congress had intended Title VII to prohibit. If such interpretations seem shocking today, we should recall that the very term *sexual harassment* was not coined until 1975, although the practice itself had a long, unseemly history.

"There oughta be a law" is a common refrain among people who feel unjustly wronged, and Vinson joined this chorus of plaintiffs seeking legal remedy. But many acts that may be wrong are not illegal. Had Mechelle Vinson been incorrect in believing that the alleged actions of Sidney Taylor were illegal as well as immoral, she would have been in good company: most Americans vastly overestimate their legal rights at work. U.S. employment law does not contain a blanket prohibition against employers abusing their authority, nor does law protect employees from unfair treatment generally. Many wrongs perpetrated in the workplace lack legal remedies; only a few specifically enumerated wrongful practices are prohibited by law. Despite a spate of legal changes protecting employees in recent decades, employers enjoy incredible discretion in exercising their authority over their employees. When Vinson sued, no law explicitly stated that sexual harassment was specifically forbidden; thus, however morally wrong such conduct might be, there was genuine doubt that it was illegal conduct that entitled Vinson to a legal remedy. In the field of employment, except for certain types of discrimination, U.S. law typically defers to the private, market solution: find another job.

Perhaps in retrospect it appears obvious that the law should attempt to protect employees from abusive sexual misconduct at work and, failing that, compensate them for their injuries. But reflection on this scenario may reveal questions about the merit of legal remedies for sexual harassment. Should the legal system get involved in this kind of "she said, he said" dispute? What rules of evidence and standards for truth should be applied in sorting out these tangled workplace conflicts? Is sexual harassment any different from other forms of discrimination prohibited by law, or is this the type of messy relational conflict that is best left to interpersonal skills or the internal rules and policies of private businesses and organizations? If the law tries to protect workers from sexual harassment, will the government inevitably be drawn into the trap of overriding social norms and legislating morality? Will, as the harshest critics contend, the government become a kind of "morality police," regulating the sexual etiquette between men and women and, indeed, coworkers of the same sex at work? Or are these ingrained but inegalitarian social customs and everyday practices exactly the kind of barriers to opportunity and full citizenship that the law ought to rectify in a democratic society? However muddled these questions may be today, they were much murkier when Mechelle Vinson sued Sidney Taylor and the bank in 1978.

Inevitably, the case raised questions of fact and credibility that are almost always present in lawsuits. Taylor answered Vinson's allegations of sexual harassment by claiming that he had never had sex with Vinson or acted improperly toward her, and the bank contended that despite its anti-discrimination policy, Vinson had never complained to higher bank officials or sought to alter her employment at the bank. The defendants implied that Vinson's suit was vindictive retaliation.

The reader is strongly advised to suspend judgment about the particular facts of this case and to treat all disputed facts as unproved. Typically, a jury or a judge acting as the trier-of-fact weighs the evidence supporting various assertions made by the plaintiffs and defendants to determine the probable truth of the allegations. In this case, however, a series of rulings, appeals, and remands left the factual issues ultimately unresolved; the truth or falsity of the parties' various versions of events was never definitively established by a court of law. The Supreme Court did not rule on the veracity of any version of the facts. Instead, playing its usual role in our judicial system, the highest court clarified the legal issues involved rather than resolving the factual disputes. In ruling on Vinson's case, the Supreme Court did not decide her claims; it decided the standards for sexual harassment law to be used in judging her and other plaintiffs' claims.

The Court's doctrinal focus was not surprising because, in Vinson's appeal, legal issues overshadowed the factual contentions. Most basically, is sexual harassment in the workplace illegal? Although several lower court rulings had anticipated the Supreme Court's decision, no national, authoritative answer had been given until the highest court spoke in Vinson's case. Second, the Court addressed what constitutes sexual harassment. If an employee is subjected to sexually harassing behavior but suffers no adverse economic consequences, such as discharge or denial of tangible job benefits, is such "environmental" sexual harassment illegal employment discrimination? Last, should employers be held legally liable for the sexual harassment of their employees, and if so, under what circumstances?

By pursuing her conviction that there ought to be a law against the harms she felt she had suffered, Mechelle Vinson initiated a series of legal battles that lasted well over a decade, producing hearings at all three levels of the federal court system. The treatment of sexual harassment by the law was hazy when this lawsuit commenced, but the arguments and legal maneuverings of the parties evoked a sequence of court rulings culminating in the Supreme Court's 1986 landmark decision, *Meritor Savings Bank v. Vinson*. Although *Vinson* left significant issues to be resolved by future decisions, it went far toward clarifying the standards for prohibiting sexual harassment at work. More fundamentally, the highest court authoritatively confirmed that sexual harassment in the workplace is indeed illegal sex discrimination in the United States.

This first Supreme Court decision on sexual harassment graphically illustrates how legal changes occur in tandem with larger social changes. This litigation cannot be understood in isolation but must be considered within its historical and social setting. Key aspects of that social background are the long-term changes in the nature of women's roles in the economy and their status in society, as well as contemporaneous efforts by activists in the women's movement that helped put the issue of sexual harassment on society's agenda. Evolving notions of gender relations are both reflected in and shaped by the courts' decisions on sexual harassment. And subsequent developments in political and social arenas, such as the Anita Hill–Clarence Thomas hearings and the Tailhook scandal, as well as intense if not sensationalized media coverage and a sharp barrage of critical backlash, have kept the issue of sexual harassment on the front burner of public attention. The immense attention given to sexual harassment since the Supreme Court's ruling in *Meritor Savings Bank v. Vinson* in the legal community, in business and other organizations, in the media, and among the public at large indicates the momentous impact a landmark Supreme Court decision, in conjunction with other influences, can have on society. The controversies that still surround sexual harassment in multiple settings, ranging from law reviews to proverbial office water-cooler conversations, also demonstrate that this impact is subject to widely varying assessments of its efficacy and legitimacy.

This book tells the story of Mechelle Vinson's lawsuit in the broader social context in which issues of sexual harassment arose in the United States. To highlight the threat posed by sexual harassment at work, chapter 1 notes the importance of work to human well-being and traces how women have increasingly become engaged in paid jobs over the years, often in occupations segregated by sex. Since the late nineteenth century, American jurisprudence has considered the relationship between employers and their employees a private, contractual agreement; however, the growing number of women employees was one of several factors that pressured government to regulate facets of the employment relationship, including eventual bans on select forms of discrimination. This chapter traces how sex discrimination came to be included in the legal prohibitions against certain types of employment discrimination enacted by Title VII of the Civil Rights Act of 1964 through curious legislative maneuverings. Chapter 2 sketches the history of sexual harassment at work and an overview of its current prevalence. Although sexual harassment is enduring and pervasive, in the 1970s, feminist activists and lawyers sought to end this long history of abuse in the workplace. This chapter narrates the story of their struggles to have workplace sexual harassment declared illegal, their early failures and tentative victories in forcing the law to recognize sexual harassment as a form of illegal employment discrimination.

Mechelle Vinson's suit against Sidney Taylor and the bank is the centerpiece of chapter 3, which dissects the alternative factual and legal assertions of the parties and their competing strategies during the dispute. Vinson's allegations about Taylor's conduct toward her and her legal claims that Taylor's actions amounted to illegal sexual harassment failed to persuade the trial judge, who ruled in favor of the defendants. Plaintiff Vinson's legal arguments fared better before the court of appeals, which rendered interpretations of the law favorable to her case. This ruling, however, merely set the stage for the decision by the U.S. Supreme Court. Chapter 4 describes the litigation as it was heard and decided by the country's highest court, laying out the arguments of the parties and the Court's rulings on the legal questions presented. The aftermath of the decision includes reactions to it and the further proceedings on remand in the district court. Chapter 5 analyzes subsequent developments in the law of sexual harassment, including the changes wrought by the Civil Rights Act of 1991 and later court decisions clarifying the threshold of illegal sexual harassment, employer liability, and same-sex harassment. Chapter 6 draws a fuller picture by recounting the extension of sexual harassment law to education and the evolution of the law on a number of corollary issues: sexual favoritism, consensual relations between employees, free speech in the workplace, and compulsory arbitration of employment disputes.

Chapter 7 then turns to an assessment of the impact of this landmark Supreme Court decision and its ramifications for remedying gender inequality in employment. Commentators and social scientists vehemently dispute the social consequences of the *Vinson* decision and the legal prohibition of sexual harassment in the workplace. No consensus exists on whether the laws prohibiting harassment have had significant effects, much less on whether the consequences are salutary or deleterious to the health of society. This chapter examines that controversy, considering possible effects on employees, businesses, gender relations, and popular consciousness. The conclusion considers the enduring debate about the role of law in social change. Reformers have long tried to cure social ills by changing the law, but skeptics have charged that legal developments, far from causing and directing social reformation, merely reflect social change or, at best, legitimate transformations that have other, nonlegal origins. Examining this instance of legal change can perhaps yield tentative answers in this long-standing debate, or at least more nuanced ways to formulate the questions.

CHAPTER I

Work, Women, and the Law
Sex Discrimination Becomes Illegal

The socioeconomic context that framed Mechelle Vinson's lawsuit in the late 1970s reflected decades of change that affected the social roles of women in the United States. The legal landscape in which issues of sexual harassment were fought out in court also changed, at least partly in response to an economy shaped by industry and the market. This chapter surveys the crucial role that work plays in individual and social life, the evolving place of women in the paid workforce, and the changing approaches to the legal regulation of employment.

Working Life

Sexual harassment at work ranks as an egregious social problem partly because of the fundamental value of work for human well-being. American popular culture often casts work as a necessary evil, toil as punishment for our ancestors' transgressions in the Garden of Eden. Besides alternative theological interpretations of people as workers fashioned in the image of the Creator, other philosophical traditions understand work not as a bane of human existence but as a thoroughly human need. Creative work, although often not achieved, is a necessary component of a full and satisfying life. Despite society's glorification of leisure, increases in unemployment are accompanied by correlative rises in the death rate, and work satisfaction is the strongest predictor of longevity.

Life without work is intolerable because of the key functions that work fills in our individual and social lives. Work, "activity that produces something of value for other people," provides for our livelihood. By working, humans make, either directly or by earning the money to buy these necessities, the goods and services needed to sustain existence. In the process of "making a living," we also make ourselves. Ideally, work offers an arena in which people can develop talents, skills, and knowledge, contributing to a sense of mastery and self-realization. When this opportunity for personal growth is wasted, it is a tragic dissipation of human potential, a privation denounced by social critics as diverse as Karl Marx and Adam Smith. Noting the influence of work on human development, Smith observed that a worker trapped in a meaningless job "becomes as stupid as it is possible for a human to become."

Work connects individuals to life and to society. Daily tasks, far from enervating people, lend vitality to existence by establishing "the regularity of life, its basic rhythms and cyclical patterns of the day, week, month, and year." Without the stabilizing function of work, time seems amorphous and stifling, and individuals may suffer symptoms of anomie: rootlessness, normlessness, powerlessness, lifelessness, and disassociation. Work serves to connect individuals to others and to society. Work both brings contact with others and forces people to cooperate to accomplish complex tasks. Working links individuals' activities to the satisfaction of others' needs, contributing to the larger social good.

Small wonder, then, that work is so crucial for self-esteem. When work is worthwhile and satisfying, it buttresses a sense of competence and personal efficacy. Work bestows status; job titles give important hints of position in the social order. Even if individuals' parts pale in comparison to the overall endeavor, work ideally should win recognition of their contributions to humanity. The denial of recognition to millions of workers who make organized social life possible — from garbage collectors to nurses to farmworkers to teachers — is one of contemporary society's genuine shames. As the steelworker in Stud Terkel's classic *Working*, a collection of "workers talking about their work," lamented: "Someone built the pyramids . . . these things just don't happen. . . . Picasso can point to a painting. What can I point to? . . . Everybody should have something to point to." Our very identities depend to an extraordinary degree on the work we do. Introductions implicitly recognize this link between who we are and what we do: "I'm a doctor," "I'm a salesperson," or "I'm a student." Many surnames are derived from ancestral occupations, such as Gardner or Cook, a derivation often unrecognized because the jobs are archaic (for example, carter, smith, or steward) or designated in languages other than English.

Sexual harassment or other discrimination that interferes with the enjoyment of work threatens a social good and personal interest of the highest order. Women's acute vulnerability to sexual harassment at work subjects them to deprivation and discrimination in the enjoyment of one of life's most important aspects. Studies find that women lacking employment suffer from problems of low self-esteem, depression, and other health problems more than working women do. Although we should take care not to limit the definition of work to paid employment, any barrier to productive work for women, including sexual harassment, constitutes a major detriment to women's well-being.

Women Have Always Worked

Conflating work with paid employment reflects the dramatic transformations occurring since the capitalist and industrial revolutions, changes influencing the working roles of women as well as the nature of work. For much of human history, most production took place in the home as cottage industry, and fieldwork provided most goods and services to sustain human life. In this "family economy," husbands, wives, and children worked side by side, figuratively if not literally, although in traditionally gendered tasks amid inegalitarian social relations. In 1780, 64 percent of the non-native population of the United States lived in self-employed families. Only 16 percent were wage earners or indentured servants; another 20 percent were slaves. By 1890, wage workers outnumbered the self-employed by two to one. Today, nine out of ten Americans work for someone else, investing the problem of sexual harassment in the workplace with heightened significance. Besides the loss of economic independence, the advent of market economies also entailed a spatial transformation, as particular tasks were subjected to more minute division of labor and as bosses' desire to control their workforces, as well as the later invention of ever more powerful productive technologies such as the steam engine and the spinning jenny, made it profitable to concentrate workers in workplaces outside the home, epitomized by the modern factory.

The marketplace and factory exerted their tug on social groups differentially. Between 1830 and 1930, most men and a substantial number of single women were drawn into paid employment, while married women tended to stay home working at their traditional household tasks. This disparity partly reflects the different rates at which various work was commodified and mechanized, but it also reflects social prejudice and discrimination. Despite the lingering image of women as housewives and mothers, many women, especially those of less privileged race, ethnicity, or class, have worked in paid employment as well as in the home. Different types of labor systems existed in different regions of the country before the advent of a national labor market; for example, there was the plantation system, based on slavery, in the South, tribal systems in Native American territories, hacienda systems in the Southwest, and contract labor that imported workers from Europe and Asia. Women of different regional, racial, ethnic, and class backgrounds entered the labor market at different rates. In 1920, for example, Native American women had the lowest labor force participation, with 12 percent engaged in paid labor, while 39 percent of African American women held jobs. European American women fell in between, with 20 percent engaged in paid work.

Especially among upper- and middle-class European Americans in the nineteenth century, the ideology of domesticity glorified the role of women as wives and mothers while reinforcing the privileged position of men as protectors, household heads, property owners, and earners. Although women were valued as "nurturers of children and civilizers of men," this domestic ideal excluded them from the workforce and left them dependent on men for economic support. Men, in contrast, were identified with economic and financial power and competence. In 1900, men constituted 82 percent of the labor force, reinforcing the image that wage work is a masculine activity and establishing a link between "work" and successful manhood. Unmarried women were seen as only temporary workers, a view that justified deprivations in education, training, and pay. Single women who worked outside the home long term were called "spinsters" (a woman who spins thread for a living) and deemed unfit for marriage (often with the implication of loose morals as well). Women of color or lower class held jobs at greater rates, but this disparity simply reflected and perpetuated the social stigma attached to married women working outside the home. Despite the unreality of the ideal of domesticity, at least two-thirds of the married women in all groups worked in the home, and married women were much less likely to work outside the home than were single women, ranging from a differential of 7 versus 45 percent for European Americans to 33 versus 59 percent for African American women.

Although continuing to perform most of the unpaid reproductive and household work, married women moved into the labor market in rising numbers in the twentieth century. Two world wars elicited dramatic pleas to women to contribute to the war efforts through industrial production. New appliances and convenient utilities (less than 20 percent of households had electricity in 1910) helped reduce the labor required for housework (although, in actuality, housekeeping standards rose rather than the hours devoted to it falling) and increased the demand for income to pay for the new inventions. More services were available in the market, including food preparation, laundry, cleaning, and care for children, the sick, and the elderly, but these services required purchasing power. Soaring consumption stressed family budgets and encouraged more family wage earners, while burgeoning production to meet escalating consumer demands boosted the demand for labor. Women were both pulled into jobs by the economy's escalating need for workers and pushed into earning income to help pay for their families' expanding desire for consumer goods. Greater educational opportunities for women qualified them for jobs and made many discontent with remaining at home. These trends contributing to the entrance of married women into paid employment produced the most dramatic changes for European American married women, whose labor force participation rate rose from 3 percent in 1900 to 58 percent in 1990. Rates still varied among racial and ethnic groups, with two-thirds of African American married women holding paid jobs, for example, but differences in labor force participation rates had lessened markedly between racial and ethnic groups and between married and single women by the end of the century. By 2005, 62 percent of women (compared with 72 percent of men) are projected to be in the labor force, and in 1996, women accounted for 46 percent of paid employment.

Changing family patterns likewise nudged women into paid jobs. The improvement in birth control technology, especially the invention of "the pill" in the early 1960s, enabled families to plan their child conception and rearing patterns, allowing women to control their careers with more predictability and assurance. The divorce rate rose fivefold during the century, and single-parent households, the vast majority headed by women, increased sharply, while married-couple families fell from 74 percent of households in 1960 to only 56 percent in 1990. By 1990, female-maintained households (families, unrelated individuals, and loners) amounted to 28 percent of the total, up from 18 percent in 1960, requiring female income earners. Jobs could be cause as well as effect by allowing economically independent women to live on their own. As the economy stalled in a sea of stagflation and slowed growth after 1973, even so-called traditional families needed women as well as men to work to attain middle-class status. American families maintained their real incomes through the 1980s and 1990s only by having more family members employed and by working longer hours. By 2002, only 20 percent of children lived in classic *Leave It to Beaver* families, with father as chief breadwinner and mother as stay-at-home mom, glorified in 1950s television sitcoms.

The women's movement contributed a political impetus to the mix of motives for women's increasing participation in the labor force. In the latter third of the twentieth century, women's aspirations for liberation focused on increased choice and participation in all areas of social life; paid employment for women, as for men, was a central concern in this emancipatory vision. In writings culminating in her 1963 *The Feminine Mystique*, Betty Freidan questioned the postwar ideal of wife- and motherhood within the traditional nuclear family. Liberal feminist organizations such as the National Organization for Women (NOW) portrayed careers in the paid workforce as liberating paths to economic self-sufficiency, personal fulfillment, and equality with men. Although many women entered the job market with strictly pragmatic goals of supporting themselves or boosting family incomes, the impact of liberal feminism's ideal of equal treatment unquestionably bolstered the impetus for equal pay for equal work and the removal of barriers to women's full enjoyment of employment opportunities.

When women were drawn into paid employment outside the home, they were originally limited to certain job niches, an occupational segregation that has proved remarkably durable. One study found that the index of dissimilarity, which measures the percentage of women who would have to switch careers to match men's occupational pattern, declined only from 74.3 in 1910 to 67.5 in 1970. Although more change has been evident in recent years (1980's index was 59.7), the rate of decline appears to be slowing (the index dipped only to 53.9 by 1997), with a changing occupational structure producing more of the movement than the integration of job categories. In 1985, more than two-thirds of employed women worked in jobs that were 70 percent or more female, a statistic that did not change appreciably in the 1990s. The number of women employed as paid domestics fell dramatically; for example, 30 percent of European American and 44 percent of African American women worked as domestics in 1900, but those percentages were less than 1 percent and about 2 percent, respectively, by 1990. However, the high percentage of women working in service industries (15 percent of European American and 23 percent of African American women in 1990) meant that many women performed functions such as cooking, laundry, health care, and day care, but now through paid employment. During the twentieth century, women doubled their share of professional jobs, from 20 to 48 percent. This trend will no doubt continue as education becomes available to women on a more egalitarian basis; in 1960, women earned only 5.5 percent of the medical degrees and 2.5 percent of law degrees, but by 1991, these percentages had risen to 36 and 43 percent, respectively. But much professional employment remained concentrated in careers historically open to women; in 1994, 48 percent of female professionals were employed as teachers, nurses, librarians, dieticians, or social workers, jobs filled two-thirds or more by women.

Given the operation of supply and demand in the labor market, the "crowding" of women into limited fields artificially inflated the supply of potential workers in those occupations, depressing the cost of labor (that is, women's wages). Historically, some occupations, such as teaching and clerical jobs, have shifted from being almost exclusively male to mostly female work; when women begin to predominate an occupational category, wages for that job decline. In 1963, when the Pay Equity Act legislated equal pay for equal work, women earned only 63 cents on the average dollar earned by men. Despite progress in closing the pay gap, movement has been slow — half a cent per year — and in 2002, women still earned slightly less than 78 cents for each dollar earned by men. Estimates of the impact of occupational sex segregation vary; a low estimate attributes 14 percent of the gender gap in wages to sex segregation, whereas another study estimates that occupational segregation accounts for at least 20 percent of gender disparities, with sex segregation across broad industrial categories contributing an additional 16 percent.

Some economists posit a "dual labor market" composed of different tiers of jobs of varying quality and remuneration, staffed in various proportions by different racial, ethnic, and gender groups. Primary-sector jobs offer higher salaries, secure employment, and opportunities for career advancement. White men historically enjoyed almost exclusive access to these jobs, which often require education and connections. They still dominate the upper tier of primary jobs, such as managerial, professional, and supervisory positions and self-employment, holding 61 percent of these jobs in 1990, but white women have made significant inroads, with a 31 percent share. Jobs in the lower tier of the primary sector are even more male dominated, with 30 percent of males of all racial-ethnic groups in jobs such as crafts, driving, and protective services. Although some traditionally female jobs fall into this category, only about 11 percent of women in most ethnic groups hold jobs in this sector. Secondary labor market jobs offer lower pay, fewer or no benefits, little chance of advancement, and unstable employment prospects — much work is part-time or temporary. It includes many traditionally female jobs, and roughly 46 percent of women continue to work in this sector. Lower-tier secondary jobs include service workers, laborers, farmworkers, and domestics; women of color disproportionately hold these jobs. Although women and minorities have succeeded in gaining access to better jobs, with members of all ethnic, racial, and gender groups represented in significant numbers at every tier of the occupational ladder, economic opportunities are not equally available. In addition to the well-recognized "glass ceiling" preventing the achievement of top executive status, more workers are affected by a "sticky floor" that thwarts the efforts of many minorities and women to escape dead-end secondary-sector jobs.

Discrimination in a multitude of forms has contributed to the maintenance of gender segregation and employment disparities. Educational opportunities have been offered on a disparate basis to men and women, limiting women's access to many occupations. Discriminatory hiring and promotion practices, as well as invidious differences in the terms and conditions of various occupations, have served to maintain gender barriers to some jobs. Historically, male workers and sometimes their unions have contributed to the disparities. Feeling threatened by the early "family industrial system" in which women and children were employed alongside male family members, male workers and male-dominated unions, instead of organizing women, generally sought to exclude women and children from "men's work" by multiple means, including so-called protective legislation. Sexual harassment has played a key role in maintaining gender inequality by keeping women out of the labor force entirely or relegating them to less desirable jobs. Despite this legacy of inequality supported by many pillars of discrimination, the massive entrance of women into the paid labor force has ratcheted up pressure for change in recent years.

Employment at (Whose?) Will

Despite the growing participation of women in the paid labor force and the increasing embrace of equal treatment ideals, women's employment equality faced a twofold hurdle (in addition to the unequal burden of domestic duties borne by women in the patriarchal household division of labor). First was sexist discrimination itself, which had historically blocked women from access to paid work, relegated women to certain occupations, and treated women unequally within the jobs they managed to attain. The second barrier was less visible because it was deeply grounded in ideological views of the market economy: the American tradition of treating employment as a private relationship largely beyond the purview of government regulation meant that few public remedies existed for the social problem of widespread discrimination against women in private employment.

The private labor market has not always been considered beyond the pale of public law. Traditionally in Anglo-American law, employment was treated as an important status that required protection in the name of a perceived public interest. In England during the Middle Ages and into the early modern era, although common law was the chief method of employment regulation, statutes periodically supplemented this judge-defined law. For example, Parliament had passed the Statute of Laborers in 1349 (amended in 1389), capping wages to limit workers from reaping windfalls in the wake of the bubonic plague and the resulting shortage of labor. In 1563, the Elizabethan Statute of Artificers attempted to modify traditional principles to fit changing industrial realities by prescribing facets of the employment relationship, such as the duration of apprenticeships, the hours of labor, and the setting of wage rates. Employment continued to be regulated under the traditional rubric of the law of master and servant even into modern times. For example, under English law, an employment agreement that did not specify its duration was assumed to last for one year. As Blackstone's *Commentaries* stated the proposition: "If the hiring be general, without any particular time limited, the law construes it to be a hiring for a year; upon a principle of natural equity, that the servant shall serve, and the master maintain him, throughout all the revolutions of the respective seasons, as well when there is work to be done as when there is not." Reflecting the seasonal imbalances of farmwork, this one-year presumption made sense in a largely agricultural economy. Controversy clouds the extent to which this so-called English rule survived the trip to the New World, but regardless of its prevalence in earlier times, by the late nineteenth century, American courts had abandoned the one-year rule for a strong presumption of at-will employment contracts. Judge Horace G. Wood's widely recognized *Treatise on the Law of Master and Servant*, published in 1877, plainly stated the predominant rule that has since then guided the interpretation of employment contracts: "in the United States, the rule is inflexible that a general or indefinite hiring is, prima facie, a hiring at will; and if the servant seeks to make out a yearly hiring, the burden is upon him to establish it by proof."

As interpreted by American courts, at-will employment had huge implications for the substantive power of employers over employees. Although workers gained some freedom of choice and mobility, they were now vulnerable to being fired at any time on the whim of their employers. As one court baldly phrased it, under at-will employment, employers may discharge employees "for good cause, for no cause, or even for bad cause."

Statutory reforms to protect workers' interests ran afoul of American courts' interpretation of constitutional limits on the power of legislatures to regulate employment conditions. For example, when New

York passed a law limiting the working day of bakers to twelve hours to protect the health of the public as well as of bakers, the Supreme Court, in *Lochner v. New York* (1905), struck down the law as an impermissible infringement on the freedom to contract, which the majority of justices found to be protected under the Fourteenth Amendment's due process guarantee of liberty. Under this contractual conception of the employment relationship, bargaining power was the exclusive protection of workers against discriminatory or abusive treatment. If at-will contracts authorized employers to exercise virtually unlimited freedom to hire and fire workers at their discretion, mutuality ensured that workers were "free" to agree to any terms and conditions of employment they could extract from employers or to seek work elsewhere at any time.

The Great Depression of the 1930s and the reforms ushered in by Franklin Roosevelt's New Deal made limited but significant inroads on the power of private employers. In the harsh landscape of economic blight, with one-fourth of the workforce unemployed, the myth of mutuality was punctured; threats to depart for greener employment pastures were plainly idle. In an effort to better balance the bargaining power of employees with their employers, as well as to contain employment conflicts and stimulate the sagging economy by bolstering workers' purchasing power, Congress enacted the National Labor Relations Act in 1935. This legislation guaranteed employees' right to "self-organization," primarily by forming unions. The Fair Labor Standards Act passed in 1938 established a minimum wage, overtime pay past a normal forty-hour week, and other basic items to ensure a floor of minimally decent employment conditions. Above this bare foundation, however, the New Deal left the substantive terms and conditions of employment to private negotiations between employers and employees, expecting many to be organized and represented by unions in collective bargaining with management.

This private ordering within public parameters benefited many workers in some sectors. The system, however, fell far short of attaining equal bargaining power for employees and employers or of remedying all the problems of private employment. Subsequent judicial rulings and legislation, especially the Taft-Hartley Amendments of 1947, limited labor's power. Even at their height in the early 1950s, unions never organized more than about a third of American workers, and many unions were too weak to win favorable contracts for their members. Finally, union representation was skewed: discrimination was actively practiced by some unions, and in other cases it was passively institutionalized by nepotism or favoritism in hiring and membership.

Title VII: "Don't Forget the Ladies"

Ending discrimination in employment was a key goal of the civil rights movement. Although demonstrations and court cases to remove Jim Crow segregation from the statute books of the South received the most national attention, leaders of the civil rights movement recognized that genuine equality and full participation in American life would require overcoming private discrimination along with public, legally sanctioned segregation. Many rights, such as access to public accommodations or freedom of speech and association, mean little without adequate resources to exercise them fully. Nondiscriminatory employment opportunities offered the means of acquiring the requisite resources.

By the early 1960s, several civil rights measures had been enacted by Congress or by presidential order, but with limited impact. Southern segregationists, strategically positioned as leaders of key congressional committees because of their accumulated seniority, ensured that any bills with a realistic chance of passage were relatively toothless. With the election of John F. Kennedy, civil rights leaders hoped that the administration would back a stronger civil rights bill, but the measures first proposed by the administration were disappointingly cautious. Kennedy's original proposal failed to include a ban on employment discrimination because the administration assumed that it could not overcome the intense resistance in Congress. After the televised brutality of police dogs and fire hoses ravaging young civil rights demonstrators in Birmingham, Alabama, in the spring of 1963, however, the administration toughened its bill's proposed provisions.

In addition to sections designed to desegregate public accommodations and schools, Title VII of the strengthened bill aimed to remove the discriminatory barriers that kept African Americans from attaining equal employment opportunities. Reconstruction-era legislation to protect the freed slaves' freedom to "make and enforce contracts" and other rights had been construed so narrowly by the Supreme Court that they were useless in remedying discrimination in private employment. Under intense pressure from African American leaders on the eve of World War II, President Franklin Roosevelt had signed Executive Order 8802, establishing the Fair Employment Practices Committee to investigate charges of racial discrimination in defense jobs and to pressure federal contractors and other employers into ending discriminatory practices. President Kennedy issued Executive Order 10925, creating a Committee on Equal Employment Opportunities to ensure that government agencies and contractors took affirmative steps to employ and treat fairly job applicants of diverse backgrounds. But these measures were limited in scope or weakly enforced. Title VII proposed to extend the ban on employment discrimination to a much wider range of private employers and to create effective enforcement mechanisms. The critical section of the legislation declared it "an unlawful employment practice for an employer to fail or refuse to hire or to discharge any individual, or otherwise to discriminate against any individual with respect to his compensation, terms, conditions, or privileges of employment, because of such individual's race, color, religion, or national origin."

Debate on the proposed civil rights bill was passionate and protracted, dragging out for a year and thirteen days from its introduction in June 1963 to its passage in July of the following year. Two groups constituted the core of opposition: conservatives, who opposed federal regulation of discrimination by private persons and entities, which they viewed as dangerous government "intervention" in the private sphere and an infringement of private property rights; and southern politicians determined to preserve the region's segregated racial patterns.

The legislation took a startling turn on February 8, 1964, when a key southern opponent surprised his colleagues with a bold legislative maneuver. Democratic Representative Howard Smith of Virginia, influential chair of the Rules Committee and longtime foe of civil rights measures, offered an amendment that stunned the House: he proposed that the bases of illegal employment discrimination include "because of sex." Shock followed initial laughter as the import of the amendment sank in. At a time when many presumed it to be self-evident that women were justifiably treated differently from men in jobs, a prohibition against discrimination based on sex carried such sweeping implications that observers called it "one of the most radical civil rights amendments in U.S. history."

Although Smith had a track record of supporting women's rights, many suspected that his motives were to sink the bill by adding sex discrimination to its list of banned practices. He had warned that the civil rights act "was as full of booby traps as a dog is full of fleas," and now he was laying a wily trap designed to cause consternation among the bill's supporters. The bill's chief sponsor in the House, Emanuel Celler, immediately registered his opposition to Smith's amendment, both because he feared overloading a bill whose primary intention was to achieve equality for African Americans and because he recognized that state protective laws enacted to shield the "weaker sex" from the harsh realities of the workplace could be jeopardized by the amendment. Celler, moreover, like many pre–women's movement liberals, embraced traditional views of women's proper roles. But Smith may have "outsmarted himself" with his sly maneuver, because while the seventy-five-year-old Celler and eighty-year-old Smith debated the significance of biological differences between men and women, a bipartisan coalition of women legislators rose to the challenge of supporting Smith's sex discrimination amendment in all earnestness. As Representative Katherine St. George (R–N.Y.) argued, "we are entitled to this one little crumb of equality. The addition of the little, terrifying word 's-e-x' will not hurt this legislation in any way." When Representative Martha Griffiths (D–Mich.) contended that without the addition of "sex" to the bill, white women would be denied the protections afforded other groups, even Smith dropped his sarcastic tone and registered his sincere desire to add a ban on sex discrimination to the bill he opposed overall. With five women representatives speaking in favor, the Smith amendment passed the House by a vote of 168 to 133.

A myth has grown up surrounding the origins of Title VII's ban on sex discrimination — namely, that women were the "accidental beneficiaries" of an amendment "slipped in" as a joke by an opponent of the bill only to demonstrate the absurdity of trying to ban employment discrimination based on sex. This conventional wisdom, along with the paucity of legislative history or explicit congressional hearings or reports on the amendment, emboldened some opponents of gender equality to claim that the ban on sex discrimination in employment does not really reflect a seasoned congressional intent. More recent scholarship, however, makes it clear that the addition of sex to the list of banned forms of discrimination was no accident or sick joke. Although Representative Smith's original intent may have been to sandbag the civil rights bill, he and other southern conservatives came to accept the modification, in part because the largely white, middle-class National Woman's Party supported it. Their support, along with the fervent support of women in Congress and other women's groups, ensured that the addition of "sex" remained intact when the whole bill was passed 290 to 130 by the House. The bar against sex discrimination survived as the bill was debated and passed in the Senate by a vote of 73 to 27, after that body voted 71 to 29 for cloture to end the longest filibuster in history (just over 534 hours). President Lyndon Johnson signed the bill, including Smith's "radical" amendment, into law on July 2, 1964. Any lingering doubts that Congress fully intended to prohibit sex discrimination were laid to rest in 1972 when the amendments to the Civil Rights Act retained and extended legal prohibitions on sex discrimination.

———

Title VII Goes to Work

The ban on employment discrimination based on sex as well as race, color, religion, or national origin covers all employers engaged in interstate commerce (a prerequisite for federal regulatory authority that excludes few enterprises in today's integrated economy) employing at least fifteen people (a threshold that denies the protections of Title VII to approximately 21 million workers, or one-fifth of the workforce). Discrimination by employment agencies as well as by unions acting in their capacities as employers or hiring agents is also banned. Amendments in 1972 extended coverage to state and local governments. The act prohibits discrimination in almost all aspects of the employment relationship, defining as illegal employment practices discrimination in job advertisements, hiring practices, wages and salaries, promotions, and other terms and conditions of employment. As interpreted by federal courts, discrimination includes both intentional discrimination, in the form of disparate treatment of protected groups, and employment practices causing an invidious and disparate impact on groups defined by the protected categories. Discrimination against whites as well as racial minorities is equally prohibited if based on race, and men are protected from sex discrimination along with women.

To enforce Title VII, the act created the Equal Employment Opportunity Commission (EEOC). The EEOC, headed by a five-person independent commission appointed by the president, processes individual complaints, enforces the statute, and issues interpretive guidelines. An Office of General Council administers the agency and also litigates on behalf of the commission. Regional offices do much of the work of the EEOC. Employees who believe that their employers have discriminated against them may not initially sue directly but first must file sworn written charges with the EEOC within 180 days of the occurrence of the alleged discriminatory act. This statute of limitations may be less limiting if the discriminatory conduct is "continuing" or if charges are first filed with recognized state or local enforcement agencies.

Once timely charges are filed, the regional EEOC office notifies the charged parties of the name of the charging parties and the nature of the charges filed. The EEOC then investigates the charges and, if there is reasonable cause to believe that the charges are true, tries to end the discrimination by "conference, conciliation and persuasion." After thirty days of attempts to remedy the problem to the satisfaction of the parties, the EEOC may file suit in federal court, but the commission's attempts at reconciliation have no time limit. Charging parties may simply wait for the EEOC to resolve the matter or may request a "right-to-sue" letter. When the EEOC decides not to file its own suit in the matter, or 180 days after the charge is filed, the EEOC must issue such a letter even if it believes that no violation has actually occurred.

Aggrieved employees have ninety days from receipt of the right-to-sue letter to file suit in the appropriate court, usually the federal district court for that jurisdiction. The litigation proceeds de novo, that is, the charges of discrimination are litigated from the beginning, rather than being limited to a mere review of any administrative proceedings by the EEOC or state or local agencies. Although information developed during administrative processes as well as official agency findings may be admissible as evidence, they do not determine the verdict in the federal suit. Until 1991, Title VII suits were matters of equity, to be decided by federal judges with no right to a trial by jury. The Civil Rights Act of 1991, however, allowed plaintiffs to demand jury trials in employment discrimination suits seeking monetary damages. Outcomes of Title VII cases in district courts may be appealed under the usual federal rules of civil procedure to the appropriate circuit court of appeals and to the U.S. Supreme Court, although requests for hearings in the Supreme Court are rarely granted.

Since the passage of Title VII in 1964, Congress has also barred employment discrimination based on age (Age Discrimination in Employment Act of 1967) and disability (Americans with Disabilities Act of 1990). Other national legislation has added protections for employees, including worker safety (Occupational Health and Safety Act of 1972) and pensions (Employee Retirement Insurance Security Act of 1974). By 2002, some localities and virtually all states had passed laws prohibiting various forms of employment discrimination; many follow Title VII standards, although some schemes offer advantages to plaintiffs, such as extending coverage to smaller firms. In addition, some state courts have begun to nibble away at the common-law doctrine of at-will employment using several approaches, such as recognizing implied contracts in employment handbook policies or prohibiting discharges held to be in violation of certain public policies, such as cooperating with grand jury investigations. The spread of state court–spawned limitations on at-will employment has been uneven, with the extent of protection varying widely among states.

Legal Protections, or Left in the Lurch?

Despite these innovations in employment law over the past several decades, employers' power to manage, and mistreat, their employees remains formidable. Employers no doubt feel genuinely constrained by government "red tape" in personnel matters, a belief matched by employees' overestimation of their legally protected rights. Relative to comparable countries, however, American employees enjoy fewer rights at work and, conversely, American employers possess more unrestrained power over their workforces. Although marginally modified by sparse laws and court decisions, the at-will relationship remains the norm in employment, ensuring impressive discretionary power for employers. Employment law, rather than empowering employees or protecting them against the whole gamut of arbitrary or unfair employment practices, limits its reach to only the abuses that legislatures and courts specifically prohibit.

This hazy legal terrain is what Mechelle Vinson wandered into when she filed her lawsuit. No doubt she firmly believed that her rights had been violated, but a decade and a half after passage of the Civil Rights Act of 1964, whether this or any other law protected employees against sexual harassment was far from clear. Was the outrageous treatment Vinson claimed she had suffered the type of discriminatory employment practice Congress intended to prohibit under Title VII, or was it merely one of a host of uncovered wrongs that American employees are potentially subject to without legal recourse? Years of litigation would be necessary to settle this and related issues, and *Meritor Savings Bank v. Vinson* would prove to be the landmark Supreme Court ruling to clarify the law on sexual harassment. But the courts did not answer these legal questions in a vacuum. The economic and demographic changes surveyed in this chapter placed the issue squarely on society's agenda. Changes in family and employment patterns made urgent the removal of barriers to equal economic opportunity for women. In 1978, the year Vinson sued, for the first time, half of American women worked in paid employment. More directly responsible for bringing these issues to the forefront were women activists and feminist theorists, whose story is told in the next chapter, which also traces the prevalence of sexual harassment.

CHAPTER 2

Naming Sexual Harassment
Sexual Harassment
Becomes Sex Discrimination

Sexual harassment has doubtless always existed, but little is known about its history. One screen obscuring a clear view of the extent and role of sexual harassment in the history of work is that although the actuality is ancient, the concept is remarkably recent. The term itself dates only from 1975. Feminist activists discovered, or rather uncovered, sexual harassment in the mid-1970s when women began to speak out against mistreatment at work. Naming sexual harassment was a prerequisite for being able to see it and talk about it. Because it had been invisible for so long, the amount of historical information on the topic is limited. Before turning to the story of how sexual harassment was brought to light by feminists, I briefly examine what has been unearthed about sexual harassment by historical and contemporary research.

History of Sexual Harassment

A major obstacle to surveying sexual harassment in history is that many of its victims lacked the resources to compel the inclusion of their voices in the historical record. The women who were most likely to suffer harassment were likely the most vulnerable, the most lacking in money, economic security, literacy, fluency in official bureaucratic language, support from coworkers, personal confidence, and social credibility — the kind of coins that buy attention in the recorded memories of "mankind." Two long-standing myths further prevented sexual harassment from appearing in the narrative of public concerns. First, many considered sexual harassment to be a natural phenomenon, an inevitable by-product of the male libido. This "boys will be boys" attitude makes sexual harassment part of the social backdrop, not an event that deserves to be recorded. Second, women were often blamed for sexual harassment. If the natural urges of men were the passive explanation for sexual harassment, viewing the victims as sluts made women the active cause of the problem. This moralistic myth further undermined any notion of recording incidents of sexual harassment as a serious social problem or, if they were noticed, buried them under the rubric of prostitution.

Still, accounts have survived, even if a systematic record is missing. Unfree women workers were, understandably, especially vulnerable to sexual harassment. Women who worked as indentured servants, a common practice to finance passage to the British colonies, were frequent targets of abuse by their masters. Indentured servants were forbidden to marry without permission, and if they became pregnant, the master could extend the length of their indenture, displacing blame for their exploitation onto the women themselves. African slave women have left numerous accounts of abuse at the hands of slave owners and their sons, overseers, and hirelings. Considered chattel property by the law, women slaves had no legal redress for sexual harassment, assault, or rape. Legal disability was reinforced by the owners' sense of entitlement and by racist stereotypes that portrayed slave women as sexually voracious and unrestrained by civilized morality. The disparate power exercised over female slaves exacerbated the severity of the problem by diminishing resources for resistance. Nonetheless, women did resist with actions ranging from flight to murder in self-defense.

Women doing domestic work, even if formally free, are especially accessible targets for sexual harassment. Not only do domestics generally work in isolation from other workers and in the home of potential abusers, but the low pay and prestige of the occupation also make resistance tougher. As a teen, Louisa May Alcott, author of *Little Women*, took a position as companion to an English gentleman's sister. She soon fell prey to the unwanted attention of her employer, and when she protested that she had been hired to provide companionship to his sister, not him, he reassigned all housework to Alcott. She soon resigned. Many less fortunate women working as domestics or in other positions either succumbed to their employers' pressure for sex or were forced out of gainful employment. With extremely limited options for economic survival, the end of either line could be prostitution. Reversing the causation, this sequence often perpetuated the public image of "loose" working women, encouraging and legitimizing sexual harassment.

Because women entering the factories of the incipient industrial revolution were disproportionately drawn from the lower socioeconomic classes, this image comported especially well with social prejudices. This stereotype of working woman as slut explains the extraordinary measures taken in the textile industry in Lowell, Massachusetts, in the early 1800s. To attract the daughters of conservative rural families, mill owners advertised that their "girls" would be housed in supervised dorms and governed by strict regulations to protect their morality and "marriageability." Ironically, these regulations reinforced the bleakness of the young female workers' lives by compounding the drudgery of long days in the factory with tightly disciplined regimens during the few hours allowed them outside of work. This early experiment in preserving the "purity" of female virtue presaged a common response to threats to women workers' well-being: protecting women by limiting their freedom and opportunities, rather than restricting the threat or removing the source of the problem.

As America's economic expansion created escalating demands for scarce labor, immigrants were admitted to staff the burgeoning factories. Immigrant women were especially vulnerable to unscrupulous foremen and supervisors. Often isolated by language, perhaps undermined by traditional misogynist cultures, and always economically dependent on if not desperate for their paychecks, recent immigrants were often forced to submit to bosses' sexual demands or face dire consequences. Not only were female employees harassed, but supervisors coerced male employees to obtain sexual favors from the workers' wives and daughters. Exploited and oppressed male workers sometimes vented their frustration by sexually abusing their family members.

Male employees as well as employers often harassed their female fellow workers. Besides the sheer vulnerability of most women workers, the harassment reflected male resentment of what they viewed as competition for "their" jobs, and their jobs were often bound up with their identities as men. They feared that the increase in the supply of labor would drive down wages and worsen working conditions. Women might undermine male employees' solidarity, and because women tended to quit when they married, they seemed to have fewer long-term stakes in fighting for benefits, a concern reinforced by an image of women as "the weaker sex." Working violated the social stereotype of femininity and, in the minds of many men, threatened to destroy the family.

Despite their vulnerability and the frequent callous unconcern of male-dominated working-class institutions such as unions and urban political machines, women workers did resist. The sexual solicitations of bosses provoked strikes, and eliminating sexual harassment appeared in lists of strike demands. Some union leaders believed that this issue of sexual exploitation could effectively rally public opinion to the side of strikers. Other union leaders, however, refused to showcase sexual harassment in labor disputes. Some reasoned that the problem required a national solution. Others felt that moral issues should not displace economic demands and that decent wages and conditions would reduce the vulnerability of women employees. Some union leaders must have shared or at least recognized the attitudes that made charges of sexual harassment at best a double-edged sword, tending to stigmatize victims as well as harassers.

Social prejudice blamed the victims of sexual harassment and placed the burden squarely on female shoulders to resist untoward advances. A 1935 handbook of business etiquette for women warned those embarking on a career that "every young woman with a normal endowment of feminine charm is bound to exert just so much attraction . . . [that] she may become the wholly innocent cause of a situation packed full of dynamite and calling for the wisdom of the serpent to avert a disastrous explosion." The guidebook counseled that "it is part of a girl's business training to learn to handle situations of this kind" and that "the standard technique is to pretend not to see them, or else to continue to act as if they were not serious," relying on the assurance that "the rules of the game for his side provide that he should drop that line at once, without making it necessary for the girl to take up a stand against him." Although this advice sounds archaic, as recently as 1960, 30 percent of companies acknowledged the hiring of women based on their sex appeal.

Women in traditionally male blue-collar occupations faced especially severe harassment. Although women had been encouraged to support the war effort by participating in industrial work during World War II, these "Rosie the Riveters" were largely pushed out of blue-collar jobs to make way for the returning "boys" in the wake of victory. By the 1970s, the legal ban on discrimination encoded in Title VII, aided by a feminist organizing impetus, pushed to integrate the building trades, where women constituted only about 2 percent of craft workers. In New York City's construction industry, pressure to admit others besides white males pushed minority representation in construction and mechanical apprenticeships to 22 percent by 1974, but harassment dramatically stalled rates of change for women. Feminist organizations were effective in securing trade jobs for women but were not prepared to support female hirees' efforts to resist on-the-job harassment. Pervasive hostility took various forms: verbal harassment ranged from general profanity to sexist expressions to directly personal taunts; hostile conduct ranged from unwanted touching to threatening gestures to accident-inducing safety violations that risked bodily harm for women workers. These tactics succeeded in holding female participation in the New York construction industry to infinitesimally low levels, with women accounting for only 1.75 percent of all jobs and only 3.68 percent of apprenticeships in the early 1980s.

Prevalence of Sexual Harassment

Social science research on sexual harassment has produced widely varying estimates of its frequency. One of the earliest polls consisted of *Redbook* readers' responses to a 1976 questionnaire entitled "How Do You Handle Sex on the Job"? Of the 9,000 readers who responded, 8,100 reported experiencing some form of sexual harassment at work. More recent mail-in surveys by *Working Woman* magazine also found extraordinarily high rates of sexual harassment. In 1992, more than 60 percent of readers responding to the magazine's questionnaire said that they had been harassed, and more than a third knew a coworker who had been harassed. The magazine's survey of Fortune 500 human-relations managers in the late 1980s and early 1990s discovered that this group of personnel professionals took claims of sexual harassment very seriously, with 64 percent believing that most complaints were valid. Complaints were also frequent: 90 percent of these large companies had received complaints of sexual harassment in the year preceding the survey, and 25 percent had received six or more complaints; a third of the companies had been sued. In a survey of federal employees by the U.S. Merit System Protection Board covering 1978–1980, 42 percent of the women reported that they had experienced at least one of the six types of sexual harassment listed in the questionnaire, and this finding was replicated by later surveys taken by the Merit System in 1987 and 1991.

Government-sponsored surveys in Britain and Canada at about the same time turned up sexual harassment rates of 52 percent and 49 percent, respectively. Other cross-national data on sexual harassment from the late 1980s into the 1990s reveal varying frequencies, ranging from 17 percent of Swedish working women to 50 to 90 percent of working women in Britain. A survey conducted by the British Labour Research Department, for example, found a sexual harassment rate of 73 percent. Other studies, using divergent methodologies, reported sexual harassment of women at the following rates: Belgium, 30 to 34 percent; Finland, 34 percent; France, 21 percent; former Soviet Union, 36 percent; Netherlands, 50 to 60 percent; Norway, 63 percent; Germany, 70 to 75 percent; and Spain, 80 to 90 percent. A 2000 review of the literature suggests that sexual harassment affects roughly 50 percent of women employees in industrialized countries.

One 1999 overview of American studies on the prevalence of sexual harassment found that estimates of the frequency of harassment range from 28 to 90 percent of women, and a 1990 study concluded that the median rate of harassment found by the eighteen surveys it canvassed was 44 percent. Organizational development expert Freada Klein told *Working Woman* in 1988 that "every employee-attitude survey that we've conducted for the private sector shows at least 15 percent of female employees have been sexually harassed in the last 12 months," and Catharine MacKinnon estimated that "only 7.8 percent of women in the United States are not sexually assaulted or harassed in their lifetimes."

The frequency of sexual harassment appears to vary based on type of behavior, with the more serious forms of harassment being reported less often by survey respondents. One compilation of surveys found that reports of sexual commentary averaged 28 percent in these surveys, whereas sexual posturing (staring, following, gesturing) averaged 24 percent, sexual touching 17 percent, pressure for dates or relationships 13 percent, and sexual assault 1 percent. Another survey reported that of the 53 percent who recounted harassing incidents, 15 percent reported degrading or insulting comments, 24 percent sexual touching, 11 percent expectations to socialize, and 8 percent pressure for sexual activity.

Men, too, can be victims of sexual harassment. Reported rates of male sexual harassment range from 6.7 to 19 percent, but several authors note that males are often sexually harassed by other males. The phenomenon of women sexually harassing men catches the public's attention and predominates in fictionalized accounts of sexual harassment, such as *Disclosure*, a film starring Michael Douglas and Demi Moore based on Michael Crichton's novel, and *Oleanna*, a David Mamet play made into a movie starring William H. Macy. Actually, however, the problem of female harassment of males, although it no doubt occurs and can be disastrous for its victims, pales in comparison to the magnitude of sexual harassment experienced by females at the hands of males. Estimates suggest that 90 percent of sexual harassment is perpetrated by men against women, probably 9 percent is same-sex harassment, and only 1 percent is women harassing men. Because of this disparity, this book follows the usual convention of using language referring to harassers as male and victims as female when specific identities are not given.

Different groups of employees seem to experience sexual harassment at different rates, and some theories about the nature and cause of harassment correspond to these findings. Some authors assert that sexual harassment is more likely in traditionally female-predominant occupations. Although sexual harassment in disproportionately female jobs may seem counterintuitive, "sex-role spillover" may occur in "pink-collar jobs" that replicate the traditional roles of women in the home. Male bosses who expect female employees to fix their coffee, pick up their laundry, succor their emotional needs, and boost their male egos may easily slide into the habit of expecting women workers to fulfill their sexual desires as well. In a 1982 survey, more than 60 percent of nurses recounted sexual harassment, mostly by doctors, and a late-1980s survey found that of the 76 percent of nurses reporting sexual harassment, 87 percent were harassed by patients, 67 percent by physicians, and 59 percent by other staffers. Similarly, dentists were the harassers in 54 percent of the incidents related in a 1990 survey of dental hygienists, 26 percent of whom experienced sexual harassment. The trumping of organizational norms by more diffuse but pervasive and deep-seated cultural norms and role expectations may explain the phenomenon of contrapower harassment, the harassing of women superiors by their male subordinates. Evidence also exists for a seemingly contrary hypothesis: that sexual harassment is most common in settings where women are scarce. This "sex-ratio hypothesis" seems to hold true particularly when the few women are forging a path onto the turf of traditionally male occupations. Sexual harassment is sometimes portrayed as primarily a problem of women in the white-collar sector, especially professions. Surveyed in 1993, female attorneys recounted sexual harassment by other lawyers (56 percent), by clients (45 percent), and by judges (31 percent). Where masculinist norms define the nature of the work, women "pioneers" entering previously all-male occupational terrain experience sexual harassment that is especially intense. Male norms, rituals, and language stake out as male preserves some blue-collar jobs, such as construction or mining. In many cases, harassment may constitute conformity rather than deviance; wolf-whistling, for instance, may be performed for a male audience to demonstrate membership in the all-male club, with the harassed women serving merely as stage props.

Masculinist work culture helps explain the high levels of sexual harassment in the military, an institution tainted in recent years by several high-profile scandals such as the 1991 Tailhook affair. These incidents may be the tip of the iceberg. A 1992 survey of female navy officers found that about two-thirds had been sexually harassed; this was close to the 64 percent of women reporting harassment in a 1990 Defense Department survey, three-quarters of whom had experienced three or more forms of harassment. Police departments, where studies have found that two-thirds of female officers experience harassment, exhibit similar problems.

Other organizational characteristics encourage sexual harassment. Evidence suggests that so-called sexualized workplaces, where many employees pursue romantic relations, engage in informal sexual bantering, or routinely discuss sexual topics, also have a high incidence of sexual harassment, perhaps because the sexualized atmosphere provides constant reminders of society's pervasive stereotyping of women as sexual objects. Organizations rife with bickering, rivalry, and favoritism may evoke high rates of sexual harassment as yet another symptom of the professionalism absent among employees. Workplace alienation, such as stressful, boring, routine, tedious, inflexible, and unfulfilling work, may foster an organizational climate prone to problems with sexual harassment, as workers try to vent pent-up frustrations. Studies have also found that organizational policies and procedures, as well as the attitudes of leaders, can affect the rate of sexual harassment. Strict organizational hierarchy probably increases the likelihood of abuse, as well as the importance of leaders' attitudes.

The critical role played by power in sexual harassment means that the most severe sexual harassment — coercive demands for sexual favors backed by economic sanctions — tends to be initiated by men with formal authority over their targets. Less coercive forms, such as offensive joking or touching, are more widely used by coworkers lacking organizational power. Power differentials also illuminate why certain categories of vulnerable women employees are more likely to be harassed — for instance, the younger, single, less educated, economically dependent, and psychologically vulnerable and those in low-status positions or with less seniority.

Some researchers suggest that minority women are disproportionately targeted for harassment. Racial and ethnic minorities may be particularly vulnerable to harassment because minority status may indicate a lack of power, marginal status, and economic vulnerability. Cultural stereotypes of these women as sexually voracious or submissive may also fuel male misconduct toward them.

Sexual harassment is not confined to the workplace. Students at all levels tell researchers that they are sexually harassed by fellow students and by teachers and other school employees. A national study sponsored by the American Association of University Women of junior high and high school students unearthed an alarming rate of sexual harassment of young girls. Undergraduates face harassment from both fellow students and some professors. One estimate predicted that 50 percent of female university students will experience sexual harassment at some point, and graduate students are even more likely to be harassed than undergraduates are.

Modernization of the home and the purchasing of goods and services in the marketplace drew women consumers out of the home and led to their increasing sexual harassment in public places such as shops, restaurants, parks, and theaters. Urbanization trends may have heightened the problem, with the mobility, density, anonymity, and diversity of cities probably facilitating sexual harassment. Women who were vulnerable in their housing arrangements made ready targets for unscrupulous landlords, lenders, and real estate agents, a problem that, like street harassment, continues to plague women today.

Extrapolating sexual harassment rates to the 1980s female labor force of approximately 42 million, historian Kerry Seagrave estimates that each year, 21,000 women employees were victims of rapes or attempted rapes at work, and 164,000 women were coerced for sexual favors. Pressure for dates afflicted 325,000 women workers, 500,000 were subjected to unwanted touching, and another 500,000 experienced suggestive looks. Seven million were the targets of sexual remarks. Despite its current prevalence, Seagrave suggests that sexual harassment almost certainly was more widespread in the past, when workers enjoyed less power and fewer rights, although recent attention to the problem might have reduced incidents but increased reporting. Stephen Morewitz contends that sexual harassment has become more subtle and ambiguous over time, somewhat analogous to the transformation of some racism from raw to more symbolic forms. Changing social norms that brought more freedom in personal relations and an emphasis on romantic love contributed to the fluidity of gender relations. Sexual "revolutions" — periods of rapid change in sexual mores and morals that swept the United States primarily in 1915–1920 and again in the 1960s and 1970s — loosened traditional constraints on relations between the sexes and helped make sexual harassment more ambiguous. These sexual revolutions, along with the women's movement and broader social and ideological developments, transformed the nineteenth-century Victorian view of gender relations as private and natural to the modern-day model of relations between the sexes, which Morewitz characterizes as political and conflictual.

_____

Lies, Damn Lies, and Statistics

With widely varying estimates of the frequency of sexual harassment in the workplace, it is easy to miss the larger point: even at the lowest estimated rates, and despite contemporary constraints against it, sexual harassment is clearly a major social problem in the United States and elsewhere. Reflecting on why studies report different rates of sexual harassment and on the various hypotheses about its incidence is revealing.

Contrasting theoretical understandings of the nature and causes of sexual harassment explain some of the variance in findings. A biological theory conceives of sexual harassment as the inevitable result of male sex urges driven by testosterone, an immutable landmark on the social landscape. Psychological theories, in contrast, view sexual harassment as abnormal, limited to certain "sick" individuals, thus downplaying the role of organizations and society. Social exchange theory explains sexual harassment and women's reactions as by-products of relationships based on costs and benefits, while habituation theory views sexual harassment as simply so common that it is routinely tolerated. Sex-role spillover argues that some jobs are sexualized because they blend into domestic female sex roles. Sex-ratio theory focuses on the numerical superiority of males in some work settings as a contributing cause. Other studies emphasize power differentials to explain both who are the more frequent harassers and who are the typical targets. Finally, some theorists diagnose cultural norms as the root of the problem or conceive of sexual harassment as a discursive practice grounded in patriarchy and an overarching sexist hegemony.

This maze of models can be condensed into three main tendencies. The natural model approaches sexual harassment as individual behavior rooted in biological and evolutionary psychological imperatives. Driven by hormonal urges and the need to perpetuate the species, men and women evolved, through the process of natural sexual selection, different strategies for successful mating. Men often seek short-term as well as long-term sexual liaisons, maximizing the odds of successful reproduction. Women, however, saddled with rearing offspring, seek long-term commitment from men who are able to provide resources for the women and their young. Different reproductive interests shape different sexual strategies. Men, with their interest in casual sex, read sex into ambiguous situations and think, "There's no harm in asking." Women perceive sexual behavior as potentially threatening to their long-term well-being, have more negative reactions to being propositioned, and consider "passes" to be sexual harassment. This model offers an essentially "no-fault" explanation of sexual harassment: because of their differing sexual strategies, men and women often simply fail to communicate.

A more political, liberal model of sexual harassment comprehends it as the product of individual behavior that violates social norms, especially equality. This perspective tends to emphasize the underlying dimension of unequal power rather than sexual drives and to link harassing behavior to the reproduction of workplace inequalities rather than to biological offspring. From this point of view, sexual harassment is a form of deviance that social norms, particularly legal prohibitions, can prevent.

The third perspective encompasses different approaches that emphasize the social, sociocultural, or structural dimensions of the problem. It emphasizes the context of asymmetrical power relations and cultural stereotypes that reinforce inequality. From this perspective, sexual harassment is a manifestation of a patriarchal society, an instance of using male sexuality to reinforce male power. Dominance, which also shapes sexual desire, is the driving force behind sexual harassment.

Beyond these deeper philosophical and theoretical divergences, the usual methodological variations, such as populations surveyed, sampling validity, time frame, and other study design choices, can skew results. Three knotty methodological issues in particular ensure disparate research findings.

First, the research shares no established definitions. Without a standard definition of sexual harassment, respondents may report and researchers may classify different behavior as sexual harassment. Findings vary markedly, depending on whether a broad or narrow notion of sexual harassment is investigated.

A related problem with empirical investigations of sexual harassment is that a range of behavior is included under the rubric of sexual harassment, and these behaviors are categorized differently. Gruber categorizes sexually harassing behaviors into an Inventory of Sexual Harassment consisting of (1) verbal requests (sexual bribery, advances, subtle pressures), (2) verbal comments (personal remarks directed to a woman, rumors or comments about a woman, categorical comments about women in general), and (3) nonverbal displays (sexual assault, sexual touching, pervasive sexual materials). Fitzgerald and her colleagues have developed an integrated model of sexual harassment, combining Gruber's model with those of other researchers. In the tripartite integrated model, sexual harassment consists of (1) gender harassment — "a broad range of verbal behavior, physical acts, and symbolic gestures that are not aimed at sexual cooperation but that convey insulting, hostile, and degrading attitudes about women"; (2) unwanted sexual attention — "verbal and nonverbal behavior that is unwelcome, offensive, and unreciprocated"; and (3) sexual coercion — "extortion of sexual cooperation in return for job-related considerations." Gender harassment and unwanted sexual attention correspond roughly to the type of sexual harassment recognized by the law as hostile environment, and sexual coercion is the paradigmatic example of what the law terms quid pro quo harassment.

Finally, most research uses surveys as yardsticks for measuring sexual harassment, with all the usual pitfalls of polling, including sampling, wording, coding, and interpretation. The validity of surveys depends on the willingness and ability of respondents to report accurately on their experiences. This assumption leads to worries about overreporting and underreporting. Consultant Kathleen Neville asserts that false claims of sexual harassment are rare but acknowledges that they can occur. She suggests that they are more likely in certain identifiable situations: when employees despise their superiors, when employees feel rejected by superiors, when employees have been made to feel inferior, when employees hate their employing organization, and when employees believe that they can win financial gain from false claims.

Research confirms plausible expectations that underreporting is a far bigger barrier than overreporting to accurately registering the frequency of sexual harassment, not only through official reporting channels but also in confidential surveys. Surveys find that 60 percent of women respondents who report experiences that researchers define as sexual harassment do not themselves label the reported behaviors as such, even though they judge the conduct offensive, stressful, or otherwise negative. Some women workers may prefer "educated ignorance," emphasizing their identities as workers or professionals at the expense of their consciousness as women. Others may fail to recognize sexual harassment for what it is because they are inured to occupational expectations that pigeonhole working women in the role of "office wife" and consider sexual advances to be part of the implicit job description. Furthermore, society endorses male sexual initiatives toward females; this pervasive gender norm permits even aggressive sexual advances by males to be interpreted as healthy and normal or, at worst, merely gauche misjudgments of proper gender etiquette or impatient outbreaks of overly exuberant libido. Hegemonic masculinist views about sex, gender relations, and social mores ensure that much abusive treatment is not perceived as sexual harassment by the perpetrators or by the victims themselves, but rather is considered normal sexual behavior, horseplay, miscommunication, or "just life."

The concept of hegemony expresses how "a certain way of life and thought is dominant, in which one concept of reality is diffused throughout society in all its institutional and private manifestations." Hegemony suggests that the ideas, values, and views of dominant groups become so suffused throughout society's institutions and customary ways of thinking that they become the unquestioned "common sense," defining "what is legitimate, reasonable, sane, practical, good, true, and beautiful."

Law, along with other social institutions such as schools and churches, sustains hegemony not only by inculcating dominant values and censoring challenges but also by "defin[ing] the parameters of legitimate discussion and debate over alternative beliefs, values and world views." By not recognizing "subjugated knowledge" — the experiences and viewpoints of the less powerful — law delegitimates claims of wrong and arguments for reform. The law's long-standing silence on sexual harassment made public recognition and discussion of the problem, as well as its solution, less likely.

Mass media constitute an especially powerful force in shaping perceptions and maintaining hegemony. Content analysis of prime-time entertainment discovered that sexual harassment saturated television: 84 percent of sampled shows featured at least one incident of sexual harassment, averaging 3.4 incidents per episode. Incidents were not usually portrayed as serious problems of harassment, but rather were treated humorously or trivialized; 60 percent of scenarios involving kidnapping or sexual bribery were accompanied by laugh tracks. Story lines also downplayed the seriousness of harassment by ignoring power dynamics. Many incidents involved less powerful actors as harassers: 24.4 percent of workplace harassment was initiated by subordinates, and in 7 percent of the incidents, children and adolescents harassed adults. The victims were usually unharmed and, in any event, readily handled the problem themselves. Victims rarely showed realistic emotions such as fear or anger, although they might express irritation, and the favored response was a quick retort, pictured as an effective means to end the exchange and put the harasser in his place. Virtually no victims took any formal action against the harassers. The study's authors concluded that sexual harassment is highly "visible" (very prevalent) yet simultaneously "invisible" (unlabeled) on television in a way that is likely to silence victims by depicting sexual harassment as "legitimate, normal, and acceptable."

Many researchers claim that the genders' views on sexual harassment issues differ markedly, although some evidence indicates that gaps are closing. Men file fewer complaints than women do and are less likely to label behavior as harassment. In a 1980 survey, only 8 percent of men versus 24 percent of women believed that a man eyeing a woman up and down constituted harassment. Men also assess the problem as less extensive; two-thirds of men but only one-third of women agreed that sexual harassment at work was greatly exaggerated. Some suggest that men and women inhabit "two worlds" because not only do men's and women's experiences diverge dramatically, but also men's perceptions of sexual harassment are colored by their higher probability of being harassers, or accused harassers, while women are far more likely to be targets. Power differentials also influence the perception gap, with organizational higher-ups tending to estimate the amount of sexual harassment as vastly exaggerated. Men's typically superior organizational and physical power, as well as the long history of violence against women, explains how conduct that many men might interpret as simply a harmless "pass" could prove threatening to many if not most women. But some researchers question the significance of the supposed gender gap in assessing sexual harassment. A 1995 review of studies found only small, although consistent, differences between men and women in evaluating workplace conduct, and differences within each gender were as large as or larger than those between the genders.

Not only do dominant social institutions, norms, and customs tend to ignore and trivialize sexual harassment, but deep-seated popular myths also undermine attempts to treat the problem seriously. Some researchers contend that a "just-world syndrome" works to suppress the recognition of sexual harassment; victims so badly want to believe that the world is fundamentally a just and good place that they reduce cognitive dissonance by ignoring injustices that cast doubt on this ideal. An ideology of "exit" reflects the larger cultural reliance on individualism. The American belief in the efficacy of individual choice leads society to perceive that a victim's appropriate response to a problem is simply to exit the situation, a remedy that society judges both possible and effective. Sexual harassment targets are seen as having numerous exit options: they can simply avoid the harasser, transfer to another position or department, or, if all else fails, simply quit. The myth of exit blinds observers to the constraints on choices and the limited number of realistic options available. More subtly, the exit myth militates against perceiving the existence of a problem. Failure to exit is presumptive evidence against the credibility of the victim, the seriousness of the problem, and the necessity of a social response. If the offensive conduct is really sexual harassment, the myth implies, why didn't the victim just "exit," avoiding the problem through individual initiative?

The combination of dominant sexual mores and individualistic ideologies easily leads to blaming the victim in sexual harassment cases. The tendency to attribute responsibility to the target rather than the harasser creates subtle but enormous social pressures working to silence complaints. Victims may assume the blame for their own harassment, perhaps failing to acknowledge, much less report, misconduct. Even when sexual harassment is recognized for what it is, tangible obstacles block it from surfacing. Sober anticipation of negative responses of coworkers or officials may deter victims from complaining. Embarrassment and loss of privacy are inevitable, and these detriments are often accompanied by shame. Victims voicing complaints face the prospect of not being believed and risk being branded troublemakers, a label that can haunt victims after they leave the organization. Victims must consider whether their harassers are in a position to retaliate or continue to make their lives miserable.

These disincentives are neither fanciful nor inconsequential. One survey found that 25 percent of women respondents described being fired or forced to resign after complaining of sexual harassment, a finding backed by a second study in which 24 percent of sexual harassment victims reported being fired after lodging complaints and an

{ *Sexual Harassment and the Law* }

additional 42 percent relinquished their positions because of their employers' retaliation or failure to stop the harassment. More than 20 percent of women say that they have quit, been transferred, been fired, or dropped their application for a job because of sexual harassment. Outcomes of charges filed with the California Department of Fair Employment and Housing confirm the fears recounted in surveys. Between 1979 and 1983, almost half of the complainants to this state agency were fired, and another 25 percent quit because of fear or frustration. It is no wonder that 60 percent of victims who failed to report sexual harassment feared being blamed themselves.

When victims do file complaints, their assessment of the results is not encouraging. One survey found that only 20 percent of complainants felt that their cases were handled justly, and 60 percent reported that the charges were ignored or that the punishment dispensed to their harassers was token. In a survey of government personnel, only 5 percent of sexual harassment victims formally reported the harassment, and most were dissatisfied with the results. These attitudes may closely coincide with actual outcomes, even when victims are credited and harassers punished. A 1988 survey of 160 large corporations discovered that eight out of ten offenders were merely given verbal or written reprimands. Transfer, suspension, probation, and demotion were meted out in less than 6 percent of the cases, although two in ten offenders were eventually discharged.

Whether for broad sociological or ideological reasons, for personal psychological motives, or based on prudent calculations of the likely costs and benefits, much sexual harassment goes unreported. Despite likely underestimation, the frequency of sexual harassment of working women found by studies averages 44 percent, with estimates ranging from 28 to 90 percent (and from 6.7 to 19 percent for men). This prevalence indicates the severity of the problem, which is better appreciated when its effects are examined.

Effects of Sexual Harassment

The harms sexual harassment causes to its victims are varied, multi-faceted, and potentially profound. Economic costs are both tangible and enormous. Many women are forced to transfer, pass up promotions and opportunities, or quit to escape harassers. Less severe job-related harms are also frequent by-products, including lower morale, absenteeism, declining job satisfaction, deteriorating job performance, and damage to interpersonal relations. Other financial costs result from disrupted work, including diminished benefits such as lost health coverage, life insurance, and pensions, and fractured child-care arrangements. Other monetary costs are not directly related to the job — for example, legal expenses, medical bills, or psychotherapy costs. Psychological and emotional problems often result from harassment. Reported reactions to harassment include feelings of depression, helplessness, fear, loss of control, and decreased motivation. Research into the psychological consequences of sexual harassment finds that between 21 and 82 percent of victims encounter emotional deterioration, a result exacerbated by the fact that many women feel doubly victimized when they try to use organizational or legal channels to counteract their harassment. Physical distress and illness caused by sexual harassment include symptoms such as headaches, sleep loss, eating disorders, gastrointestinal problems, nausea, weight fluctuations, and crying spells. Seventy-five percent of victims suffer at least one symptom of emotional or physical distress. Clinicians have identified a "sexual harassment trauma syndrome" characterized by "shock, emotional numbing, constriction of affect, flashbacks, and other signs of anxiety and depression." Empirical research deflates the myth that targets of sexual harassment who claim to suffer such symptoms are merely hypersensitive or whiners; the effects of sexual harassment are real, not the result of targets' oversensitivity, generalized job stress, or negative predispositions.

As severe as the consequences are for the victims, they are not the only ones harmed by sexual harassment. Sexual harassment costs American companies and organizations astounding amounts, even if incidents never surface. A 1988 study estimated that sexual harassment cost the typical Fortune 500 company $6.7 million per year in absenteeism, lower productivity, and employee turnover. Of course, if the conflict becomes public, organizations can expect further financial detriments incurred because of expensive litigation or settlement, diverted executive time and attention, and damage to jealously protected corporate images.

What's in a Name?

Despite the long history of sexual harassment, its shocking contemporary prevalence, and its high costs to victims and organizations, sexual harassment remained nearly invisible until relatively recently. It took a revitalized women's movement to uncover and name the sexual harassment that many women were experiencing as they entered the paid labor force in growing numbers. Feminist activists also played a crucial role in raising public awareness of the problem and in convincing courts that sexual harassment should be illegal.

The second wave of feminism, rising after a long period of diminished visibility and activism following the success of the suffrage movement in 1920, swelled in the wake of the civil rights and student antiwar movements of the 1960s. Although women played vital roles in the social movements of the 1960s, many women activists found their contributions sharply limited by widespread stereotyping of women and outright sexism among male activists and leaders in movements proclaiming their dedication to social equality and justice. Converging with these activists' heightened sensitivity to previously unremarked sex discrimination were the experiences of women entering the job market, where their duties and earnings were starkly inferior to men's. Ironically, the 1950s ideal of the stay-at-home housewife and mother masked great discontent among increasing numbers of women, who were more educated than any previous generation and felt confined and frustrated in cramped suburban homes. These confluences did not produce a monolithic movement; rather, the movement was united on the overall goals of equality and liberation for women but divided on both the meaning of these goals and the means of their attainment.

Liberal feminists were closest to mainstream American ideology, stressing individual choice and fulfillment, rights, and equal treatment based on merit. Rather than blaming fundamentally flawed institutions, they located the source of women's unequal social position in individual prejudices and the exclusion of women from otherwise healthy structures. The solution was to integrate women into the various facets of American life while demanding that they receive the same rights and treatment as men. As the 1970s slogan proclaimed,

"A woman's place is in the house — and in the senate." Despite social-ist feminists' sharper critique of capitalism, their stress on economic inequalities and exploitation reinforced liberal feminists' emphasis on integrating women into the labor market and overcoming barriers to attaining equality within the paid economy. Radical feminists shared with socialist feminists a deeper critique of social institutions but placed more weight on patriarchy as the source of structural inequal-ities. With their insight that "the personal is political," radicals emphasized sexual exploitation more than other feminists did, bring-ing to light power differentials between men and women in the home and in the bedroom, as well as in the workplace and the boardroom.

These early debates among feminists shade into theories of the nature and causation of sexual harassment and its remedies. The indi-vidualism of liberal feminism tends to emphasize stereotypes, preju-dice, and individual misconduct as the sources of sexual harassment and to privilege education and laws as the foremost remedies. Social-ist and radical feminisms stress the structural inequalities, especially power differentials, skewing society to the disadvantage of women; they argue for the necessity of deep cultural and structural transfor-mations to dismantle patriarchy. Other debates in contemporary fem-inism influence perspectives on sexual harassment. "Sameness" feminists reject stereotypical views of gender differences and divisions of labor and advocate equal — that is, same — treatment of the gen-ders. To talk of different traits, cultures, or even attitudes between men and women always runs the risk of essentializing gender dif-ferences, that is, seeing them as inherent in the nature of men and women rather than in the way societies are organized and how they inculcate values in their members. "Difference" feminists, in contrast, worry that treating men and women the same inevitably means treat-ing them according to male norms, which ensures that women will never measure up. To fail to recognize the real differences between the genders is to ignore the myriad contributions of women and to denigrate women's values, needs, and priorities. For example, differ-ence feminists might argue that using a "reasonable person" legal standard to judge what constitutes sexual harassment merely renames the traditional "reasonable man" standard but retains the male view-point as the standard for reasonable behavior. Sameness feminists remain skeptical, however, of adopting a "reasonable woman" standard and of other attempts to acknowledge male-female differences and incorporate them into different rules or standards. As long as society believes that women are from Venus and men are from Mars, they contend, Earth will continue to be dominated by men.

While these ideological debates swirled in the background, much common ground was staked out by the feminist movement in the late 1960s and early 1970s. Millions of women found themselves influenced by feminist ideas, and thousands more were moved to act to overcome the sexism identified by feminist theories as hindering their control over their own lives. All theoretical orientations contributed to shaping the elements of sexual harassment law, but the most immediate influence stemmed from a political practice shared across the spectrum of the women's movement: consciousness-raising groups. MacKinnon has called consciousness-raising "the method" of feminism and defined it as "the collective critical reconstitution of the meaning of women's social experience, as women live through it." Typically, women met in small groups to discuss their common experiences and reflect on them in light of feminist theory. The object of these sessions was to raise awareness, to integrate theory and practice, and to spur activism to improve women's lives. According to one early participant, consciousness-raising groups "cloned themselves," spreading like wildfire. Excitement permeated discussions because "we listened to each other and didn't judge the material. In other words, people said the truth."

One such consciousness-raising session occurred in conjunction with a class on women and work being taught on an experimental basis at Cornell University in 1974 by Lin Farley, a twenty-nine-year-old activist. When discussing their summer jobs, the students discovered a common pattern of unwanted advances that had forced them to leave their work: "Each one of us had already quit or been fired from a job at least once because we had been made too uncomfortable by the behavior of men." By 1975, concern about the issue of sexual harassment at work had galvanized the creation of a group called Working Women United, formed under the auspices of the Human Affairs Program at Cornell. One focal point of the group's energies was the sexual harassment case of Carmita Wood. Wood was a forty-four-year-old administrative assistant who finally walked off her job after becoming physically ill from fending off the advances of a world-renowned Cornell physicist. When she applied for unemployment insurance, the board denied her benefits. Voluntary quits are routinely denied payments intended to aid workers forced into unemployment through no fault of their own, and the credibility of an office worker was no match for that of a university professor of such vaunted reputation that his name still does not appear in accounts of the Wood case.

The term *sexual harassment* did not exist before these mid-1970s events. Although the precise origins of the term remain unclear, Farley, along with Susan Meyer and Karen Sauvigne, invented the term to characterize Wood's claims. Meyer and Sauvigne also established the Working Women's Institute in New York City as a clearinghouse and database to support public policy initiatives aimed at remedying sexual harassment. Although Wood lost her case before the unemployment insurance appeals board, which held that her reasons for quitting were personal, it sparked efforts that placed the issue of sexual harassment on the public agenda. The Cornell activists sponsored a Speak-Out on Sexual Harassment, encouraging women to voice their grievances about this experience, which was turning out to be startlingly common among women employees. They also designed and implemented the first survey that explicitly used the term *sexual harassment* to gather more systematic information on the phenomenon. The 155 responses did not represent a random sample, but the results were shocking nonetheless. Seventy percent of respondents reported having been personally harassed, 56 percent physically, and respondents were almost unanimous (92 percent) in considering sexual harassment to be a serious problem.

On the heels of these events, other stirrings of activism and attention served to raise the issue of sexual harassment to public consciousness. Farley's testimony in the summer of 1975 before the New York City Commission on Human Rights, chaired by a sympathetic Eleanor Holmes Norton, a veteran of civil rights struggles, also elicited national attention for the issue. In June 1977, three women previously involved in rape crisis counseling founded the Alliance Against Sexual Coercion in Boston, another key group that was instrumental in activism against sexual harassment at work. An ad hoc group of United Nations employees had its questionnaire on the problem confiscated by UN management, but not before 875 staffers had responded, reporting that more than half the female UN employees either had been harassed or were aware of such pressures in the

UN Secretariat. In 1976, *Redbook* magazine conducted a survey of its readers on their experiences with sexual harassment, and over 90 percent of the more than 9,000 respondents reported that they had been the recipient of one or more forms of unwanted sexual attention on the job. An article by Letty Cottin Pogrebin in *Ladies' Home Journal* that year used the term *sexual harassment* in print in a high-circulation magazine. In 1977, *Ms. Magazine* conducted a speak-out and published a cover story on the issue. Farley published *Sexual Shakedown: The Sexual Harassment of Women on the Job* in 1978— but only after twenty-seven publishers had rejected the manuscript. Several other books on the subject appeared in the late 1970s, including MacKinnon's *Sexual Harassment of Working Women* in 1979, and by the end of the decade, articles had appeared in every women's magazine. In 1980, the movie *9 to 5* presented a comedic yet critical look at the disrespect endured by countless female office workers in a lighthearted tale of revenge kidnapping. Karen Nussbaum, a clerk-typist who founded an organization of women office workers with the same name as the movie, was the film's inspiration. She turned to her friend from the antiwar movement, Jane Fonda, to produce the movie, which costarred Fonda along with Dolly Parton and Lily Tomlin. The commercial success of the movie ensured that a large audience was exposed to the previously unacknowledged travails of countless women workers.

The success of these feminist activists in bringing the issue to the forefront of public consciousness was little short of miraculous. Farley tells the story of a sexy secretary joke placed on New York Telephone's Dial-a-Joke on September 30, 1976. Although this joke was typical of the genre prevalent in "polite society" of that period, this time, the reaction was not giggles or slight blushes. The New York City chapter of Women Office Workers paid an "unsmiling visit" to the official in charge of Dial-a-Joke, which spelled the end of "sexytary" jokes in that venue. Farley writes that "it was almost as if America went to bed one night laughing its collective head off only to wake up and find it had insulted two-fifths of the work force. Sheer numbers began to force a new sensibility about female workers; it was strengthened by the impact of ideas spilling over from the women's movement."

The importance of naming sexual harassment can hardly be overstated. Without a name to express the concept, "sexual harassment was literally unspeakable," as MacKinnon noted. If language, by defining human experience and ways of knowing, frames how we understand our world and our place within it, failing to name something denies its very existence. "While sexual harassment has always occurred, until recently it was not named and, thus, had no *social* existence." One study found that when women faculty members and graduate students were asked if they had experienced any of thirty-one situations meeting the legal definition of sexual harassment, 88.8 percent of the respondents had experienced at least one form of sexual harassment. Only 2.8 percent of the graduate students and 5.6 percent of the faculty respondents answered affirmatively, however, when asked explicitly if they had experienced sexual harassment. Without a name, the reality is not recognized.

Women's "denotative hesitancy" to name and legitimate their experiences, a "discursive political tool of oppression" identified by Robin Clair, condemned them to suffer sexual harassment in silence as a personal travail. Without a shared, socially intelligible label, harassing conduct was viewed as normal behavior, barely recognized or, if noticed, easily trivialized as slightly humorous, generally good-natured, or, at worst, a breach of social etiquette, and dismissed as "boys will be boys." Naming sexual harassment was a necessary step toward transforming a "private trouble into a public issue." British feminist Sandra McNeill captures the empowering effect of speaking publicly of sexual harassment; at a 1980 workshop on women and work, when the subject of sexual harassment was broached, "We discovered we had all suffered from this, plumbers or University lecturers. As woman after woman cited incidents we breathed out a sigh of relief. We had (almost all) been so isolated. Felt nutty almost in complaining, blamed ourselves for reactions we 'had provoked,' or suffered in confused silence. Now we knew it was a common problem." The feminist strategy succeeded in "nam[ing] sexual harassment into public consciousness."

———

Catharine MacKinnon and the Theory of Sexual Harassment

Feminists enjoyed less early success in the legal system than in the court of public opinion. Sexual harassment was not the basis for a legal claim under the common law, and no statute passed by American legislatures or Congress had expressly prohibited sexual harassment. Consequently, judges in the first sexual harassment lawsuits were prone to dismiss the harassing conduct as perhaps boorish, offensive, and morally wrong, but not a violation of the law.

The work of a young legal scholar, Catharine MacKinnon, played a critical role in defining sexual harassment not only as a social wrong but also as a legal offense with a remedy in law. Her book *Sexual Harassment of Working Women* has exerted so much influence that Margaret Crouch wrote that "it might with justice be said that everything written on sexual harassment since is a footnote to MacKinnon." The book was published in early 1979, but drafts of the manuscript had circulated for years among activists and feminist lawyers and helped shape the legal analysis of sexual harassment claims in early court cases. Her work also importantly influenced the guidelines on sexual harassment developed by the EEOC, which in turn would eventually feature prominently in the Supreme Court's analysis of sexual harassment. MacKinnon criticized the prevailing view of sex discrimination, propounded an alternative view of male dominance, identified sexual harassment as a tool for maintaining male power and privilege, and proposed a legal theory of sexual harassment as illegal sex discrimination under Title VII of the Civil Rights Act of 1964.

According to MacKinnon, the reigning view of discrimination assumed what she called a differences approach, which had originated with Aristotle. Under this theory, equality was defined as treating similarly situated individuals similarly and differently situated individuals differently. But treating dissimilarly situated individuals the same was a disservice to justice, because relevant differences were ignored. Based on this view, sexual equality demanded that men and women be treated the same when they were similarly situated. Because this standard approach accepted differences between men and women, however, and because these differences were sometimes relevant to their treatment, making distinctions when these differences were germane was not discriminatory. So separate bathrooms or benefits that reflected real biological differences between the sexes, such as pregnancy, were considered valid, and ignoring these differences was not only foolhardy but also unjust.

According to MacKinnon's critique, the differences approach overlooked that men and women were dissimilarly situated because of social inequality. Even biological differences attained their significance in a social context. She noted that "men's and women's roles are not only different; men's roles are socially dominant, women's roles subordinate to them. The imagery of hierarchy, not just of distinction, animates the [judicial] opinions." Her preferred inequality, or dominance, approach emphasized that women were not merely differently but also unequally situated, placed lower in rank and treated worse. Men were better situated because of social domination. By disregarding power differentials, the standard differences approach overlooked the very inequalities that discrimination law should aim to remedy.

MacKinnon placed sexual harassment squarely in the midst of social hierarchy, of "determinate acts, however unconscious, which preserve the control, access to resources, and privilege of one group at the expense of another." Sexual harassment was an exercise of male power to preserve the current biased distribution of power and privilege enjoyed by males partly because of their command of superior positions in the world of work and partly because of their sexual empowerment by unequal social roles of masculinity and femininity. MacKinnon defined sexual harassment as "the unwanted imposition of sexual requirements in the context of a relationship of unequal power. Central to the concept is the use of power derived from one social sphere to lever benefits or impose deprivations in another." Through acts of sexual harassment, males used their superior power to maintain women's social subordination. Sexual harassment, according to MacKinnon, was a double-edged weapon, simultaneously "undercut[ting] women's potential for social equality in two interpenetrated ways: by using her employment position to coerce her sexually, while using her sexual position to coerce her economically."

MacKinnon was also the first to make the distinction that would later figure so prominently in many court opinions: that between quid pro quo sexual harassment and hostile working environment as a form of sexual harassment. Quid pro quo (Latin, meaning literally "this for that") is characterized by a "more or less explicit exchange: the woman must comply sexually or forfeit an employment benefit." A sexually hostile working environment, in contrast, "arises when sexual harassment is a persistent condition of work." MacKinnon saw the two types of sexual harassment as two places on a continuum rather than as sharply distinct phenomena: "In the quid pro quo, the woman must comply sexually or forfeit an employment opportunity. . . . In sexual harassment as a condition of work, the exchange of sex for employment opportunities is less direct."

MacKinnon argued that these types of harassment against women constituted discrimination based on sex of the kind prohibited by Title VII. Because sexual harassment represented a barrier to women's full and equal participation at work, it was not a purely private matter between two individuals or a wrong for which the law provides only individual remedies. Women were not merely differently situated because of their sex, and harassing behavior was not the inevitable result of biological differences between men and women. Viewed properly from the inequality perspective, sexual harassment was behavior creating and reinforcing not merely difference but hierarchy, with women unequally subordinated to men in most work roles. Sexual harassers treated women not just differently but discriminatorily, making such conduct discrimination based on sex and a violation of Title VII.

The Early Cases

Federal judges were not quick to agree with the view that sexual harassment violated the law. (Recall that Title VII declared it "an unlawful employment practice" for an employer "to discriminate against any individual with respect to compensation, terms, conditions, or privileges of employment, because of such individual's race, color, religion, sex, or national origin.") Women began to bring sexual harassment suits at about the same time that feminist activists were first identifying the concept and mobilizing against the problem, but of the first seven actions brought in federal courts, women plaintiffs lost in five.

One barrier to using Title VII's prohibition against employment discrimination based on sex was judges' predisposition to view sexual harassment as misconduct directed against individual victims based on sexual desire, rather than abuse afflicting a protected group or category (women, gender) covered by the antidiscrimination statute. In *Barnes v. Train* (1974), the first sexual harassment case decided in a federal court, Paulette Barnes alleged that her supervisor had harassed her and abolished her job because she had refused his advances. Judge

John Lewis Smith Jr. disagreed that the reprisals were sex discrimination, concluding that Barnes's boss had retaliated against her not because she was a woman, that is, "because of sex," but because she had refused a sexual tryst.

Legal terminology's confusion over how to analyze *sex* as a gender category as opposed to *sex* as sexual activities plagued the treatment of sexual harassment in other early court opinions. Adrienne Tomkins sued her employer because of sexual harassment that commenced when her supervisor invited her to lunch, supposedly to discuss her prospects with the company. He made sexual advances and detained her against her will. When she complained to company officials, they penalized her, eventually discharging her fifteen months later. The judge in *Tomkins v. Public Service Electric & Gas* (1976) dismissed Tomkins's claim of sexual harassment. He viewed gender as irrelevant to this misconduct driven by lust: "In this instance the supervisor was male and the employee was female. But no immutable principle of psychology compels this alignment of parties. The gender lines might as easily have been reversed, or even not crossed at all. While sexual desire animated the parties, or at least one of them, the gender of each is incidental to the claim of abuse."

That same year, a federal district court rejected Margaret Miller's Title VII claim in *Miller v. Bank of America*, revealing another obstacle to using a statute that forbade employers' "unlawful employment practices" as a vehicle to prohibit sexual harassment. Miller's supervisor promised her a better job for sexual favors and fired her when she refused the proposition. Judge Spencer Williams found no Title VII violation, noting that the prohibition on sex discrimination was aimed at acts of employers. He regarded the acts of Miller's supervisor as "isolated and unauthorized sex misconduct" and refused to hold the bank liable for actions that were not a practice, much less a policy, of the bank.

In *Corne v. Bausch & Lomb, Inc.* (1975), Jane Corne and Geneva DeVane alleged that their supervisor, Leon Price, had harassed them verbally and physically until they were compelled to resign. The judge declined to interpret the harassment as violating Title VII because employment discrimination involved "employer designed and oriented" policies, resulting in "some advantage to, or gain by, the employer from such discriminatory practices." Judge Frey ruled that any misconduct was not company policy because it was not directed by the employer, nor did it redound to the employer's benefit: "Mr. Price's conduct appears to be nothing more than a personal proclivity, peculiarity or mannerism. By his alleged sexual advances, Mr. Price was satisfying a personal urge. Certainly no employer policy is here involved: rather than the company being benefited in any way by the conduct of Price, it is obvious it can only be damaged by the very nature of the acts complained of."

Williams v. Saxbe in 1976 was the first case to hold that sexual harassment constituted sex discrimination prohibited by Title VII. The defendants argued that harassment was not discrimination "because of that individual's sex" unless "the practice is applicable to only one of the genders because of the characteristics that are peculiar to one of the genders." Because "willingness to furnish sexual consideration" could apply to either men or women, the class of people discriminated against by sexual harassment was not primarily defined by gender, and victims did not suffer from discrimination based on sex.

Judge Charles R. Richey rejected this reasoning. The judge was persuaded that the plaintiff had been solicited for sexual favors only because she was a woman; she would not have been subjected to her supervisor's demands "but for her sex." Judge Richey also rejected the defendants' argument that the supervisor's request for sex was merely personal misconduct rather than discrimination by the employer. Because the supervisor exercised authority as an agent of the employer, his sexual harassment of the plaintiff amounted to more than the actions of one individual against another and constituted an unlawful employment practice of the employer.

In a 1977 appeal of *Barnes v. Train*, renamed *Barnes v. Costle*, the Court of Appeals for the District of Columbia Circuit reversed Judge Smith's 1974 decision for the defendants. In an influential decision written for the appeals court panel by Judge Spottswood W. Robinson III, the circuit court followed the "but for" reasoning of *Saxbe*. Judge Robinson wrote that "but for her womanhood, from aught that appears, her participation in sexual activity would never have been solicited. To say then that she was victimized in her employment simply because she declined the invitation is to ignore the asserted fact that she was invited only because she was a woman subordinate to the inviter in the hierarchy of agency personnel. In all of these situations, the objectionable employment condition embraced something more than the employee's gender, but the fact remained that gender was also involved to a significant degree."

In 1981, *Bundy v. Jackson* became the first decision to uphold a claim of sexual harassment based on a hostile working environment. Sandra Bundy charged that two of her supervisors had propositioned her, and when she complained to a third, he had responded, "any man in his right mind would want to rape you." Because the district court had found that Bundy's supervisors had taken no reprisals against her, the "novel question" raised by her appeal to the D.C. appeals court was whether she had been discriminated against in her "conditions of employment" even though her refusal of these propositions had not resulted in the deprivation of any tangible job benefits. The court accepted the plaintiff's argument that "conditions of employment" included "the psychological and emotional work environment" and that "sexually stereotyped insults and demeaning propositions to which she was indisputably subjected which caused her anxiety and debilitation . . . illegally poisoned the environment."

Although *Bundy* was the first court opinion to hold that sexual harassment without quid pro quo loss of tangible job benefits was sex discrimination, it followed a path blazed in Title VII cases based on racial and national origin discrimination. In *Rogers v. Equal Employment Opportunity Commission* (1971), the Fifth Circuit Court of Appeals had ruled in favor of a Hispanic plaintiff who claimed that her employer had created a discriminatory work environment for Hispanic employees by discriminating in its service to Hispanic clients. Reasoning by analogy, the *Bundy* court asked, if courts had held that workplace "pollution" based on racial slurs and sexual stereotyping constituted employment discrimination, "How then can sexual harassment, which injects the most demeaning sexual stereotypes into the general work environment and which always represents an intentional assault on an individual's innermost privacy, not be illegal?"

Another influential decision finding that sexual harassment created a hostile work environment under Title VII was the Eleventh Circuit Court of Appeals' 1982 ruling in *Henson v. City of Dundee*. Barbara Henson, a dispatcher for the Dundee, Florida, police department, alleged that Chief John Sellgren had created a hostile and offensive working environment by his "numerous harangues of demeaning sexual inquiries and vulgarities." Echoing *Bundy* and *Rogers*, the Eleventh Circuit reversed the district court that had dismissed her claim and held that hostile environments based on sex violated Title VII. The court outlined the prima facie case for hostile environment, the necessary elements that plaintiffs must prove to establish that the alleged sexual harassment violated Title VII:

1. The employee belongs to a protected group.
2. The employee was subject to unwelcome sexual harassment.
3. The harassment complained of was based upon sex.
4. The harassment complained of affected a "term, condition, or privilege" of employment.
5. *Respondeat superior* (a doctrine imposing vicarious liability on an employer because of the misconduct of its employee).

The *Henson* court held that the fourth element varied by type of harassment: for a hostile environment claim, the plaintiff must show that the harassment was "sufficiently pervasive so as to alter the conditions of employment and create an abusive working environment." Quid pro quo claims required the plaintiff to show that her reaction to the harassment "affected tangible aspects" of her terms or conditions of employment. *Respondeat superior* also applied differently: in quid pro quo harassment, the employer was strictly liable for the actions of its supervisors, but in hostile environment harassment, the employer was responsible only for those conditions that it knew or should have known about and failed to correct.

––––––

Sexual Harassment versus the Law

Although sexual harassment is a long-standing and shockingly widespread abuse in contemporary societies, not until the mid-1970s did the women's movement name the problem and bring it to public attention. Early campaigns to convince courts to declare sexual harassment illegal yielded decidedly mixed results. This rapidly changing social and legal scene provided the backdrop for Mechelle Vinson's case alleging sexual harassment. When the bank hired Vinson in 1974, the very term *sexual harassment* had not yet entered popular discourse. By the time she filed suit in 1978, a Washington district court and the

D.C. appellate court had ruled that quid pro quo sexual harassment violated Title VII. Federal courts were split, however, and no court would reach a conclusion on hostile environment claims until after the district court had ruled in Vinson's case in 1980. Her suit would be on the cusp of rapidly changing legal developments, and as the appeal wound its way to the Supreme Court of the United States, this case would lead the way in shaping sexual harassment law.

CHAPTER 3

Making a Claim

Mechelle Vinson's Day(s) in Court

A Cautionary Note to the Reader

Mechelle Vinson began working as a teller-trainee for Capital City
Federal Savings and Loan Association in Washington, D.C., at its
Northeast branch, managed by Sidney L. Taylor, on September 9,
1974. Over the course of the next four years, she received several
raises and promotions, eventually holding the positions of both head
teller and assistant branch manager. Almost exactly four years later,
on September 22, 1978, Ms. Vinson filed suit against Mr. Taylor and
the bank, alleging that Taylor had sexually harassed her. On November 1, 1978, the bank wrote to Vinson that it considered her employment terminated, the same day that she resigned by mail. What went
wrong in this seemingly successful employment relationship is anything but clear. Beyond this sparse outline of Vinson's employment
with Capital City (renamed Meritor Savings Bank after mergers),
almost all facets of the underlying events remain bitterly contested.

Readers should not assume that any particulars of this story are
verified truth and should be aware that the facts of this case, by and
large, have never been authoritatively established. The intricacies of
the appeals process meant that most of the disputed facts were never
definitively proved in a court after an adversarial trial, the usual legal
standard for settling questions of fact. Readers should remember that
virtually every aspect of the story rests on conflicting allegations of
the parties or assertions of participants with varying degrees of
involvement in the events described. Not surprisingly, versions differ
markedly.

Mechelle Vinson's Story

Nineteen-year-old Mechelle Vinson was looking for work when a casual street conversation with Sidney Taylor, manager of a neighborhood branch bank, produced a break. He suggested that she apply for a job, and on his recommendation, the bank hired her. She began working as a teller-trainee on September 9, 1974. Taylor continued to exhibit the same beneficence toward the new employee that he had shown in helping her get the job. He not only trained her but was almost fatherly in his concern for her welfare, even helping out financially so that she could rent her own apartment. With other branch employees, they sometimes ate lunch together and occasionally shared an early dinner after the branch closed for the day.

Vinson contended that this cordial relationship changed, however, in May 1975. On an occasion in mid-May, Taylor and Vinson went to a Chinese restaurant after the branch closed, and Taylor steered the conversation to how good he had been to her. Vinson noted that she had thanked him for his kindness, but he replied that he didn't want her simply to say thank you; he wanted her to go to bed with him. Vinson replied that she appreciated what he had done for her but didn't feel that she should have sex with him. Taylor blatantly stated that just as he could hire her, he could fire her. Fearing for her job, Vinson accompanied Taylor to a nearby hotel, although their disagreement continued during the ride, with Vinson repeating that she didn't feel she should go to bed with him and Taylor answering that she was a grown woman and that he wouldn't hurt her, that she "owed him" for being so good to her. After checking into a room, Taylor told Vinson to take off her clothes while he showered. When he came out of the shower, she had not undressed, so he told her again to remove her clothes. When he again reiterated, "Mechelle, take off your clothes," she replied, "Mr. Taylor, I'm not going to take my clothes off." He then unzipped her dress and had intercourse with her, although she maintained that she never consented to his advances.

Vinson charged that after that initial encounter Taylor made frequent demands for sexual favors at the Northeast branch. She estimated that during the next two years she was forced to have sex with Taylor approximately forty or fifty times during and after banking hours, in the bank vault, in a storage area in the basement, and in other rooms of the bank. She also maintained that Taylor had harassed her in other ways, often fondling her breasts and buttocks on the job, at times on a daily basis, and sometimes in the presence of coworkers or customers who could not see his moves because of their angle of vision. She charged that on several occasions Taylor had made suggestive or lewd remarks in front of other bank employees, even following her into the restroom, where he exposed himself to her. She claimed that Taylor had actually assaulted and raped her, so brutally on one occasion that she had to seek medical attention. Vinson said that this constant harassment dissipated only in 1977 when she acquired a steady boyfriend, although she alleged that Taylor had sexually harassed other female employees in his branch office. She also charged that Taylor had falsified her absence record and eventually threatened her life, forcing her to take extended sick leave. On November 1, 1978, she informed the bank by letter that "due to the level of harassment and the unprofessional atmosphere that exists in my direction at your Northeast office, I am forced to submit this letter of constructive resignation; to take effect immediately."

The Defendants' Version

Sidney L. Taylor was "something of an Eagle Scout," in the words of the bank's lead attorney. He was the father of seven, a deacon in his church, well liked and widely known in the community, and successful in a career path that seemed to validate the American dream of social mobility. He had, in fact, crossed the virtually unbridgeable if almost invisible gulf separating blue-collar and white-collar work, having risen with Capital City from janitor to manager of a branch office. Taylor denied almost all the assertions in Vinson's testimony about their relations and attributed her accusations to a personal vendetta against him.

Taylor denied ever having sex with Vinson. He testified that he had never fondled her, never made suggestive remarks, never engaged in any sexual relationship with her, and never asked her to engage in a sexual relationship of any kind. He acknowledged that he had taken Vinson and Christine Malone, another branch employee, to lunch occasionally, perhaps to a Chinese restaurant, but he denied dining with Vinson alone. Taylor alleged that Vinson had sued as retribution against him because he had rebuffed her sexual overtures. He claimed that he had had to send Vinson and Malone home to change clothes because "their form of dress was really wrong for the type of atmosphere that we were working under." Taylor also asserted that Vinson had brought sexual harassment charges against him in retaliation for a work dispute in the summer of 1978. Taylor had instructed Vinson that, while he was on vacation, she should train Dorothea McCallum to be the branch's head teller. Vinson, who at the time was head teller as well as assistant branch manager, instead attempted to train Karen Kirkland.

Matters came to a head that fall. Beginning September 1, Vinson failed to report for work. Taylor, who had written to Vinson on June 14 warning that she had taken more sick days than she was entitled to, wrote to her on September 15 advising her to correct her excessive absences and suggesting that she might need a medical examination "to determin wheather your condition is satifactory to continue in the capacity you now hold [*sic*]." On November 1, 1978, David Burton, vice president of Capital City, wrote to Vinson: "In as much as you have refused to meet with me to discuss this problem [of excessive absences], we assume that you have elected to voluntarily terminate your employment with the Association and we will consider you no longer employed as of this date."

The Lawsuit

In 1978, Mechelle Vinson had an interview with attorney Judy N. Ludwic to discuss a divorce from her husband. "Something just snapped," and she began weeping. Ludwic later told the *Washington Post*, "She wasn't hysterical, it was like it came from deep inside. The tears were just rolling down her face." When Vinson chronicled her harassment at the bank, Ludwic responded, "Do you realize you have a case?" and suggested that she see John Marshall Meisburg Jr., an attorney to whom her Georgetown firm referred employment cases.

Meisburg had just launched his solo practice, opening an office on Connecticut Avenue near the White House. He had several years' experience with the EEOC in Atlanta and the Justice Department in Washington, so he was familiar with employment discrimination law and the new cases on sexual harassment. Of his initial interview with Vinson he says, "I'll never forget it. She was very impressive, very tearful. The story she told me was amazing and credible." Meisburg told Vinson that if she could get sworn statements from two other women bank employees that they had experienced similar problems with Taylor, he would file her case. When she did, and after some agonizing and discussion with fellow attorneys about whether he could prove the allegations and find a valid legal theory to support Vinson's claims, he decided to pursue the case. He believed that the factual basis of her lawsuit was so strong that she would have to prevail based on some legal theory.

On September 22, 1978, Meisburg initiated a civil lawsuit against Sidney L. Taylor and Capital City Savings and Loan Association by filing a complaint in the U.S. District Court for the District of Columbia. Vinson lodged her complaint in a federal court because the conduct she complained of violated federal rather than state laws. The complaint alleged that Taylor's conduct violated three provisions of federal law: the Fifth Amendment to the U.S. Constitution; Title 42 U.S. Code Section 2000e, a designation referring to Title VII of the 1964 Civil Rights Act as it has been codified into the laws of the United States; and Title 42 U.S. Code Section 1985.

The Fifth Amendment claim was never vigorously pursued. The Fifth Amendment's due process clause states that "no person shall . . . be deprived of life, liberty, or property, without due process of law." The Supreme Court has held that this clause forbids discriminatory treatment by the federal government, but the bank was a private employer. Although savings and loan associations are federally chartered, this minimal "state action" offered a shaky foundation for seeking redress from the bank.

The complaint also alleged violation of Section 1985(3) (although a typographical error referred to subsection 2 rather than 3), a civil rights protection enacted by the post–Civil War Reconstruction Congress in 1871 to allow private citizens to sue for monetary damages when persons conspired to violate their civil rights. Although originally intended to guarantee the newly freed slaves' rights, Vinson's complaint contemplated using this civil rights provision as a vehicle to sue for sex discrimination because Section 1985, unlike Title VII, allowed for compensatory and punitive damages.

The heart of Vinson's complaint was the allegation that Sidney Taylor had sexually harassed her in violation of Title VII. The Federal Rules of Procedure have loosened the rigidity that once characterized civil procedure, so that instead of pleading her case "in all its particulars," a plaintiff merely had to plead facts with "sufficient particularity to notify a defendant of the violation alleged" and specify charges sufficiently concrete for the defendant to respond. Vinson's complaint did not detail all the harassing conduct she had accused Taylor of committing but merely stated the general charges: that she had "constantly been subjected to sexual harassment"; that Taylor "sought sexual favors and sexual relations with and from the Plaintiff, as an inducement for retaining her employment"; and that Taylor had "forced the Plaintiff to have sexual intercourse with him using the threat that if she refused she would be terminated from her employment." The complaint's wording was more indicative of quid pro quo than hostile workplace harassment. At the time Meisburg filed, a federal district court in Washington had recently ruled that quid pro quo sexual harassment violated Title VII, but hostile environment was an even more novel claim that no court had yet upheld.

Vinson also named her employer, Capital City Federal Savings and Loan Association, as a defendant in the case. She sought to hold the bank financially as well as legally responsible for her supervisor's alleged harassment. She based this claim on the contention that Taylor had harassed not only her but also numerous other female employees and that "said conduct constitutes a well-known pattern of behavior which has been known to the officials of the Defendant Association for many years, and which thereby and therefore has been condoned by the Defendant Association."

The clerk of the federal district court filed Vinson's complaint as civil action number 78-1793, initially assigning it to Judge George L. Hart Jr. Federal rules of civil procedure require that defendants respond, within twenty days after being served with a complaint, by filing a motion, an answer, or both with the court. On October 20, the bank moved to dismiss the charges "for failure to state a claim upon which relief can be granted," a standard procedural tactic contending that the facts alleged by the plaintiff do not constitute a legal offense. Meisburg responded on November 1, citing recent cases in which sexual harassment had been found to be a violation of Title VII for which the employer could be held liable. Judge Hart denied the bank's motion to dismiss. Sidney Taylor's answer to Vinson's complaint denied Vinson's factual allegations that he had sexually harassed her. On November 16, Capital City's lawyer, F. Robert Troll Jr., filed the bank's answer asserting multiple defenses to the complaint, the usual practice. It argued that Vinson had not pled facts to support her Section 1985 claim because she had not alleged a "conspiracy." It denied any knowledge of sexually harassing behavior by Taylor and disputed most of the other factual assertions in the complaint — for example, Vinson's statement that she had received high employee evaluations. The answer also raised serious procedural defenses, suggesting that by neglecting to first file charges with the Equal Employment Opportunity Commission and obtaining a right-to-sue letter, Vinson had failed to fulfill the statutory prerequisites to filing a Title VII suit in court.

Meisburg had filed first in federal court because, having worked for the EEOC, he believed that the agency's procedures would unduly retard progress in the litigation, and he did not consider that preliminary step necessary. Besides, the Section 1985 claim should support his access to the court, he felt. Nonetheless, he had Vinson file EEOC charges on November 22, 1978. The charges, mirroring the allegations in Vinson's complaint filed two months earlier, specifically stated that Taylor had "threatened to fire me if I did not submit to his sexual advances," "altered my personnel records by reporting me late or absent when I was not late or absent," and "threatened my life." The charge concluded that "as a result of the sexual harassment by Mr. Taylor, I submitted to his sexual demands. The pressure became so severe I was forced to resign, effective Nov. 1, 1978." On March 21, 1979, Meisburg requested a right-to-sue letter from the EEOC, which was issued to Vinson on March 28, 1979.

On December 11, 1979, Meisburg filed a motion for leave to amend the plaintiff's complaint and to add parties to the lawsuit. Vinson sought to join two fellow bank employees, Christine Malone and Mary Laverity, as fellow plaintiffs and to add David Burton, the bank's vice president, as a codefendant. The proposed amended complaint alleged that Sidney Taylor had sexually harassed Christine Malone on numerous occasions by demanding that she have sexual relations with him "as an inducement for keeping her job with Defendant Capital City." The new complaint also claimed that Taylor, in a phone conversation, had told Mary Laverity, whom he had just hired, that "inasmuch as he had done her the favor of hiring her, she should do him the favor of having sexual relations with him," and that she was later fired because she refused to have sex with him.

The request to add Burton as a defendant was justified, the plaintiff complained, because he had refused to refund Vinson's $2,500 accumulated pension benefits when her employment was terminated. This first amended complaint raised the amount of damages sought by Vinson to $400,000 and included requests for compensatory and punitive damages of $400,000 for Malone and $200,000 for Laverity, for a total of $1 million sought by the three plaintiffs from Taylor and the bank. Meisburg also filed a demand on December 12, 1978, for a jury trial.

The bank filed its opposition and motion to strike Vinson's proposed amended complaint on December 19, 1978, as well as its opposition to Vinson's demand for a jury trial. In opposing the amended complaint, the bank asserted that although courts typically grant leave to amend complaints before the defendants respond to a plaintiff's complaint by filing an answer or a motion, the plaintiff had failed to file an amendment before the defendants had answered her original complaint in mid-November. Courts may also allow amended complaints to take into account new information turned up in the discovery process, but the bank asserted that no new facts had been discovered by Vinson to warrant amending the original complaint. As for the jury trial demand, the defendants argued that the time had expired for making this demand. Title VII contained no provision for an automatic right to a jury trial, but instead envisioned a bench trial, a hearing in which a judge determines the facts and applies legal rules to reach a verdict.

Although Meisburg answered, rebutting the bank's arguments and asserting that the jury demand was timely if measured from the date of his motion to amend the complaint, Judge Hart was not convinced. On January 3, 1979, he issued orders denying permission to amend the complaint and striking the demand for a jury trial. Two months later, he issued his pretrial order. A standard procedure to refine and clarify the issues of fact and questions of law to be resolved before or at trial, this order required all parties to list documents and exhibits, witnesses and experts, and any other evidence they foresaw presenting at trial and to submit pretrial briefs detailing factual assertions and legal arguments.

Before the case went to trial, however, on April 24, 1979, Capital City filed a motion for summary judgment. Such motions are common in employment discrimination cases and represent a significant hurdle for plaintiffs. In a motion for summary judgment, the moving party argues that there are no genuine factual disputes necessitating a trial and that the judge can decide the case solely on legal issues. In deciding a summary judgment motion, the judge assesses the facts in the light most favorable to the party seeking a trial. But assuming that the party seeking a trial would be able to prove its allegations, the judge goes on to ask whether that party could win its case even based on these facts. If no legal basis exists for prevailing on these presumably true facts, the judge will grant the motion for summary judgment, saving the time and expense of a trial to establish the facts for a claim that has no legal merit.

The bank's argument for summary judgment amounted to the contention that none of the facts alleged by Vinson were sufficient to support a claim that the bank was legally liable for Taylor's sexual harassment, even assuming, for argument's sake, that he had done what Vinson charged. As the bank's motion stated, "no evidence exists to support plaintiff's claim that defendant, Capital City, authorized, acquiesced, or ratified the actions of defendant, Sidney L. Taylor." Legally, the bank contended, even if Vinson's allegations were true, the bank would not be vicariously liable for Taylor's misconduct unless there was evidence that the bank acquiesced in or condoned his wrongdoing. To support this position, the bank submitted an affidavit, a sworn statement, by Vice President Burton stating unequivocally that if Taylor had acted as Vinson alleged, his conduct would have contravened bank antidiscrimination policy. Burton further stated that no bank official had been informed of any alleged sexual harassment until Vinson initiated her suit.

The plaintiff's opposition to the summary judgment motion countered that a trial was needed to determine genuine issues of factual disagreement concerning the bank's liability. Christine Malone's deposition claimed that she had informed David Burton of problems at the Northeast branch that he should investigate. She also stated that when she was eventually discharged, her lawyer, John Verchot, wrote a letter to the bank complaining that she had been sexually harassed, slapped, and called a "bitch" by Taylor. Vinson also implied that she had believed that complaining to higher officials in the bank would have been futile. In her deposition, Vinson noted that she had seen how Malone's case had been handled when she reported the problems she was having with Taylor: "Nothing was done," and she was fired. Vinson claimed that Taylor had shown her Verchot's letter but had dismissed its effect, saying that he was so powerful that no one could do anything to him and calling Malone "crazy" for accusing him.

While the bank's motion for summary judgment was pending, changes in key personnel occurred. In April, defendant Sidney Taylor retained the services of his own attorney, Karen Smith Woodson. That summer, John Meisburg withdrew to take a job as a senior trial attorney with the EEOC in Miami, asking Patricia J. Barry, another solo practitioner with employment and civil rights law experience, to take over as plaintiff Vinson's attorney. He told Barry that he regarded the case as "very strong" and that she "should litigate it to the hilt." It is unclear whether he added what Barry recalls him saying: that the lawsuit was "an open and shut case, no problem." She concurred that it was a good case (she now adds, "But what did we know in 1979?"), although she worried that Vinson's admission of having sex with Taylor, even if coerced, would damage the credibility of her claims of sexual harassment. At this time, the case was also reassigned to create a docket of cases for Judge John Garrett Penn, a Boston University law graduate, former Justice Department attorney, and Washington superior court judge, who had been appointed to the D.C. District Court by President Carter in March 1979.

On November 19, 1979, Judge Penn denied the defendant's motion for summary judgment, ruling that the allegations were sufficient to create factual disputes that required resolution at a trial before the issue of the bank's liability could be determined. At a status call on November 29, Judge Penn scheduled trial for January 21, 1980. Barry requested permission to file another motion to amend Vinson's complaint, and the judge granted her until December 3 to submit the motion. Barry sought to amend the original complaint by adding claims of assault and battery and intentional infliction of emotional distress. She further alleged that Capital City knew of Taylor's actions, or should have known, and that its failure to protect Vinson was willful, malicious, or grossly negligent. She requested a jury trial on all issues triable by a jury. Assault and battery (harmful or offensive bodily contact that causes injury) and intentional infliction of emotional distress (outrageous actions that inflict severe emotional harm) are torts, a miscellaneous category of civil wrongs for which defendants can be held liable. The penalties imposed are generally monetary damages to compensate victims for costs incurred and injuries suffered and sometimes to punish the perpetrator and deter others. Punitive damages are generally imposed only if the wrongful conduct was malicious or grossly negligent. Tort claims are mostly matters of state law but can be heard in federal court under the doctrine of pendent jurisdiction.

Adding these tort claims to the original Title VII claim offered several strategic advantages to the plaintiff. If Penn granted permission, this new complaint would be filed after Vinson had received a right-to-sue letter from the EEOC, escaping the defendants' contention that she had failed to exhaust her administrative remedies before suing and adding alternative claims if the court agreed that she had not complied with the statutory scheme for leveling Title VII charges. The additional charges offered another advantage: if Judge Penn ruled that sexual harassment did not constitute sex discrimination under Title VII, these tort claims would provide other avenues for Vinson to claim that she had suffered harm because of Taylor's actions. And because Title VII (before being amended in 1991) allowed only remedial rather than compensatory or punitive relief, even if Vinson won on the Title VII claim, she would be entitled only to "make whole" relief—which could include reinstatement to her job and back pay, minus what she had earned or reasonably should have earned in the interim by way of mitigating her losses, in addition to injunctions from the court for the defendants to "cease and desist" from sexually harassing conduct. Tort damages, in contrast, could include compensation for any physical and possibly psychological harms suffered and would expose the defendants to punitive damages if their actions were malicious or grossly negligent. Tort claims are usually tried before juries, so by amending her complaint, Vinson could renew her request for a jury trial, which would now be timely if the amended complaint was considered the last pleading.

Both Taylor and the bank registered their opposition to Vinson's second attempt to amend the original complaint. They noted the late date and impending deadlines — December 30 for the completion of discovery, January 7, 1980, for the pretrial conference, and the trial date of January 21. Taylor's reply emphasized that Vinson had known the bases for the new claims since early in the litigation, and the bank's reply stressed the novelty of the amended complaint — namely, that the new claims changed even the basis of the court's jurisdiction, added new factual allegations, requested different relief, and renewed the request for a jury trial. To facilitate disposition of cases on their merits rather than by procedural maneuverings, federal rules state that leave to amend "shall be freely granted when justice so requires," a standard creating a strong presumption favoring amendments unless they are unreasonably dilatory, futile, in bad faith, or unduly prejudicial to the opposing party. The bank's opposition stressed the "undue prejudice" that would result from allowing the amendment. It emphasized that the new claim of emotional distress alleged that Vinson had suffered humiliation, psychic trauma, embarrassment, pain, and mental anguish — all allegations that would require extensive discovery to glean information on her state of mind. These and other new claims would require extensive and time-consuming research by the bank if it were going to defend itself, but that would be impossible under the current schedule of discovery and trial. Further postponement would be undesirable in a case filed more than a year previously. The bank noted that several claims would be barred by statutes of limitation if brought in state court and argued that the attempt to amend the complaint was an effort to circumvent the missed deadline for requesting a jury trial, which the plaintiff was not entitled to under Title VII anyway.

Barry replied that the defendants would suffer no prejudice from an amended complaint. Vinson had originally sought monetary damages under Section 1985, a claim now dropped because the Supreme Court in *Great American Federal Savings and Loan Association v. Novotny*, decided in June 1979, had held that Section 1985 could not be used by plaintiffs seeking to recover monetary damages for employment discrimination. Although Vinson's original Section 1985 damages were not viable after *Novotny*, the amended claims did not differ substantially, meaning that the defendants had been on notice all along to defend against these types of claims. Barry argued that she was attempting to amend the complaint at this late date only because she had waited until after Judge Penn's ruling on Capital City's motion for summary judgment; a motion granting summary judgment would have rendered moot any motion to amend the complaint. Finally, disputing the contention that the statute of limitations had run on several claims, she argued that the amended claims "related back" to Vinson's original claims because they arose from the same "conduct, transaction or occurrence," alerting the defendants to prepare to defend any legal claims arising from those transactions, not merely those stated in the original complaint.

On January 9, 1980, Judge Penn denied Vinson's second attempt to amend the complaint. The judge stated that the motion came too late; granting permission to add new claims would require postponing the pretrial conference and trial and reopening a prolonged period of discovery. The defendants were entitled to a quick resolution of the serious charges lodged against them, so he mandated that the original schedule be maintained.

Vinson lost on another critical issue before trial, this one an evidentiary ruling. Having failed to obtain permission to add Christine Malone and Mary Laverity as plaintiffs, Barry wanted to present them and several other female employees who had worked at the bank's Northeast branch to testify that Taylor had sexually harassed them, too. The defendants opposed allowing this testimony, arguing that it offered no evidentiary support for Vinson's claim that Taylor had sexually harassed her. Barry countered that their testimony would tend to support the existence of a pattern and practice of sexual harassment, making it relevant to the bank's liability by providing evidence that the bank knew or should have known about Taylor's misconduct and, by its failure to prevent or correct it, in effect condoned or even ratified the misconduct. Judge Penn, however, would not allow Barry to present this pattern-and-practice evidence as part of her case in chief, that is, during the part of the trial when the plaintiff seeks to directly establish her case. Instead, he limited the use of coworkers' testimony to rebutting possible claims that the bank might make about Taylor's proper conduct and the atmosphere at the Northeast branch.

Barry made one final attempt on January 18, 1980, to convince Judge Penn to reconsider his order denying Vinson permission to amend her complaint. She suggested that Vinson would not object to postponing the upcoming trial if the defendants believed that maintaining the original schedule would prejudice their defense. She also sought to amend the complaint to add yet another claim: that the bank, by firing Vinson because she had refused Taylor's sexual advances, had violated an implicit employment contract and should have to pay Vinson damages. This last claim was supported by reference to *Monge v. Beebe Rubber Co.*, a 1974 New Hampshire case holding that in firing the plaintiff because she had refused to date her foreman, the employer had violated an implicit covenant of good faith and fair dealing.

At Trial

Trial in *Mechelle Vinson, Plaintiff v. Sidney L. Taylor (Capital City Federal Savings and Loan Association of Washington, D.C.), Defendants,* civil action number 78-1793, began on January 21, 1980. The court began by considering motions, ruling on several. Judge Penn declined to reconsider his refusal to amend the complaint, so the only two legal claims to be tried were the alleged violations of Title VII and the Fifth Amendment. These allegations, however, involved numerous and complex questions of disputed facts, and the trial for which Judge Penn had set aside three or four days ended up lasting eleven days. The central witnesses were Mechelle Vinson and Sidney Taylor.

Vinson offered testimony that supported her main contentions: that Taylor had coerced her into having sex with him and that she had agreed to have intercourse with him, both at a hotel and on the bank's premises, only out of fear of losing her job; that he had eyed her, groped her, and made sexually suggestive and disparaging remarks to her, sometimes in front of coworkers and even customers; that he had followed her into the women's restroom and exposed himself to her on more than one occasion; and that he had raped her more than once. She testified that the bank had notice of Taylor's misconduct but failed to stop it. She also claimed that the bank had fired her because she resisted Taylor's continuing and constant pressure for sexual favors.

Taylor denied all these allegations, stating that he had never had sex with Vinson. He suggested instead that she was vindictive because he had rebuffed her sexual advances and because he had asked her to train another employee for head teller instead of her favored candidate for the position. He stated that the bank had discharged Vinson for excessive absences.

Several subsidiary issues besides the direct accusations and denials of sexual harassment arose during the course of the trial. One question involved the possible harm caused by the alleged harassment. No one disputed that during her employment with Capital City, Vinson had received several promotions, raises, and bonuses or that these were earned on any basis other than merit. The plaintiff introduced letters showing that Taylor had consistently rated Vinson a nine or ten on a ten-point scale on her employee evaluations. These facts were double-edged, because while they bolstered Vinson's credibility as a good employee and as a witness, they undercut her claim that she had suffered any employment-related harm from Taylor's supposed sexual harassment.

A related issue was Taylor's supervisory authority over Vinson. Although he was a branch manager and a vice president of the bank, such titles can be honorific, and the bank argued that Taylor lacked the authority to hire or fire employees, even those who worked at the Northeast branch. The bank implied that Taylor lacked the authority with which to coerce sexual favors from Vinson. Conversely, Vinson presented evidence that Taylor's recommendations about personnel at his branch, though perhaps formally mere suggestions, were invariably accepted.

Over Barry's strenuous objections, the court allowed testimony by several defense witnesses concerning Vinson's style of dress and her discussion of sexual matters at work. Dorothea McCallum, the employee whom Vinson allegedly refused to train as head teller, testified that Vinson's "dress wear was very exposive" and that "most of the days she would come in with, if not a third of her breasts showing, about half of her breast showing; and some days, short dresses; or if she did wear a skirt, something that had a slit in it. It would really be split up." She confirmed that Taylor had sent Vinson home to change her clothes. Fellow employee Ron Rose stated that Vinson wore open dresses with lots of chest and leg visible, while coworker Yvette Peterson said that Vinson wore low-cut blouses and extremely tight pants, acknowledging that tight pants were in style but contending that Vinson's were indecently revealing.

Dorothea McCallum also testified about Vinson's fantasies and sexual conversations. She opined that Vinson "had a lot of sexual fantasies." One particularly outlandish tale involved Vinson dreaming that her dead grandfather, in younger form, visited her and had sexual intercourse with her. McCallum also testified that Vinson "talked quite a bit about sex. I guess more than half of her conversation was related to sex." McCallum offered graphic examples of sexual references that she asserted permeated Vinson's conversations. Vinson vigorously disputed this testimony.

The trial subjected Taylor's sexual proclivities to scrutiny. Vinson stated that he had frequented a nearby "naked go-go bar" while she trained employees at the branch office and that he read pornography in his office. Wanda Brown corroborated that she had seen him reading "*Penthouse* or something like that," correcting her phrasing by saying, "well, looking at the pictures or whatever."

A major evidentiary clash concerned the bank's knowledge of Taylor's alleged misconduct. After Judge Penn ruled that Vinson's coworkers could not directly testify about their sexual harassment by Taylor to establish a pattern or practice about which the bank knew or should have known, sparse testimony was offered on rebuttal to support charges that Taylor had sexually harassed other female bank employees, despite pretrial sworn affidavits to that effect by Christine Malone and Mary Laverity. Malone testified that she had told David Burton, vice president of the bank, about "strange things" going on at the Northeast branch. Although she testified at first that she had specifically mentioned sexual harassment, she later admitted that she had not used that term. Burton not only denied any mention of sexual harassment but also disputed that Malone had spoken of any problems at the Northeast branch. The bank denied receiving a letter from Malone's lawyer, John Verchot, complaining of sexual harassment, and Malone did not have a copy. The lone letter from Verchot entered into evidence simply informed the bank that he had been retained to represent Malone in her employment dispute with the bank.

Judge Penn's Decision

The trial ended on February 4, with Judge Penn taking the matter under advisement. The parties did not have long to wait to learn his decision. On February 26, 1980, the judge issued his order entering judgment for the defendants and dismissing the case with prejudice, meaning that the defendants could not be retried on the same charges, and his opinion explaining his decision.

Judge Penn's opinion laid out the facts of the case — those that were undisputed, the allegations made by the plaintiff, and the denials of the defendants. The undisputed facts were few: the judge noted that Vinson had worked at the bank in a series of positions beginning in September 1974, that she had received several promotions, and that her promotions had been based solely on merit. He pointed out, "Plaintiff does not contend that she was required or asked to give sexual favors in order to obtain promotions." She took indefinite sick leave in September 1978 and was discharged in November of that year. He summarized the highlights of Vinson's allegations: that she had had sex with Taylor at his request because she feared for her job if she refused, that he had harassed her in numerous other ways frequently and publicly, and that he had raped her on several occasions. He rehearsed Taylor's denial that he had ever had sex with Vinson and his contention that she had fabricated the charges because she was vindictive. The judge duly noted that the bank likewise denied Vinson's allegations of sexual harassment but further argued that "in the event sexual advances were made by Taylor, they were not made with the consent or approval of the bank, and such activities were unknown to the bank." The bank maintained that no employee, including Vinson, had ever complained of sexual harassment.

Before assessing the contending factual claims, Judge Penn considered the defendants' challenge to the court's jurisdiction to entertain Vinson's Title VII claim. The defendants argued that Vinson's lawsuit was improper because she had not filed charges with the EEOC and obtained a right-to-sue letter before suing. This failure was immaterial, Barry had contended, because even if the original Title VII claim was invalid, Vinson could have amended her complaint to restore the Title VII claim after receiving the right-to-sue letter. Judge Penn acknowledged that the customary liberality in granting amendments supported Barry's argument, but he expressed skepticism; approving such a procedure would allow plaintiffs to bypass the EEOC. He doubted that Congress had intended to allow such an end run around the administrative process it had created as part of the statutory scheme for Title VII. Nevertheless, rather than issue a definitive ruling, Judge

Penn merely registered these comments, noting that this jurisdictional issue was not critical to the outcome of the case, since he was deciding against the plaintiff on other grounds.

The only factual dispute that Judge Penn weighed at length was the issue of the bank's notice of the alleged sexual harassment. The judge did not credit Christine Malone's testimony that she had notified Vice President Burton of misconduct at the branch office. He found no evidence that a letter mentioning sexual harassment from her attorney to the bank was ever written or sent. He found that Mary Laverity never gave notice to the bank of sexual harassment or other discrimination. Finally, he rejected the argument that since Taylor was a supervisor at the bank, his knowledge of sexual harassment, which he was committing, counted as the bank's knowledge of the harassment by virtue of Taylor's position of authority. Judge Penn doubted the reasonableness of holding an employer responsible for information known only to a supervisor who is the perpetrator of the misdeed. The judge contrasted cases in which the supervisor was acting as an agent for the employer with cases in which the supervisor was acting "to gratify his own desires." Judge Penn concluded that "the evidence presented by the plaintiff does not establish that notice to Taylor should amount to notice to the bank" and found that "the bank was without notice and cannot be held liable for the alleged actions of Taylor."

These conclusions were buttressed by the court's other findings of fact. Looming especially large in the court's conclusions was the existence of a nondiscrimination policy in the bank's employee handbook and, even more importantly, an informal as well as formal grievance policy. The judge found that Vinson had never filed any kind of grievance against Taylor using the handbook's procedures, had never complained to bank officials, and had never filed a grievance with the EEOC while employed by Capital City. Despite Vinson's denial, the judge credited the bank's assertions that Vinson had declined opportunities to transfer to other branches, moves that would have allowed her to escape from Taylor's supervision.

The court's findings rejected Vinson's contentions that she had been forced to have sex with Taylor as a condition of her employment. The judge found that her promotions, which were rapid, and her salary increases and bonuses, which were usual and customary, had been based on merit, not sexual favors. He concluded, "If the plaintiff and Taylor did engage in an intimate or sexual relationship during the time of plaintiff's employment with Capital, that relationship was a voluntary one by plaintiff having nothing to do with her continued employment at Capital or her advancement or promotions at that institution." Ultimately, Penn determined that "Plaintiff was not the victim of sexual harassment and was not the victim of sexual discrimination while employed at Capital during the period September 9, 1974 through November 1978."

Given these findings of fact, the judge's legal conclusion could be no surprise. He rejected Vinson's Fifth Amendment claim, noting that in addition to the claim's having no factual basis, she had not made a valid legal claim in light of the 1972 Supreme Court decision in *Moose Lodge v. Irvis*, ruling that no state action is entailed by virtue of a private employer holding a government license — to serve liquor, in that case.

Unlike some other federal judges who, only a few years before, had held that sexual harassment claims did not, as a matter of law, constitute a violation of employment discrimination prohibitions, Judge Penn did not dismiss the Title VII claim on the basis of law. Instead, he affirmed that "it is without question that sexual harassment of female employees in which they are asked or required to submit to sexual demands as a condition to obtain employment or to maintain employment or to obtain promotions falls within protection of Title VII." Judge Penn thus joined the small but growing number of federal judges who by 1980 were beginning to recognize that sexual harassment does amount to sex discrimination prohibited by Title VII. Having recognized that point of law, however, Judge Penn ruled that Vinson had not proved a valid claim of sexual harassment. But the judge's reason for this conclusion contained a crucial ambiguity. Did he simply disbelieve Vinson's allegations about Taylor's misconduct, or did Penn conclude that this misconduct was not illegal because it did not fit the paradigm of quid pro quo sexual harassment, since the sex was not coerced and she had not lost any job benefits? If the latter, Taylor's actions potentially constituted sexual harassment, but of the hostile environment rather than the quid pro quo type. Judge Penn had not considered that possibility; as of 1980, no court had ruled that hostile environment sexual harassment was prohibited as sex discrimination under Title VII, and Vinson's attorneys had not explicitly raised the issue. These questions remained to be argued and clarified on appeal to higher courts.

On Appeal

On March 18, 1980, Pat Barry filed for permission to appeal *in forma pauperis* (in the form of a pauper). This motion, if granted, would have excused Vinson from paying certain costs of appealing Judge Penn's decision to the circuit court of appeals. She also requested that the government pay for the trial transcript for use on appeal, a considerable expense for an eleven-day trial. Barry's notice of appeal asserted that the appeal would raise important legal issues, identified as the necessity of exhausting administrative remedies, the denials of the amended complaints, the requirement of employer notice, and Taylor's supervisory status. The admissibility of other female employees' testimony about a pattern and practice of sexual harassment would form the center of the evidentiary issue on appeal, but Barry denominated twenty-two specific errors of fact in the judge's opinion. Some were minor, such as the details of Vinson's hiring, but others disputed the factual bases of Judge Penn's decision. For example, she claimed that Taylor had never testified that Vinson had made sexual advances toward him; that Vinson had not testified that the harassment had stopped when she got a steady boyfriend, but rather that she had been able to resist Taylor's advances after she became involved in a relationship, even though the harassment continued; that she had accepted a pending transfer offer to manage a suburban branch office; and that she had utilized the grievance process, initiating the first step by complaining to her supervisor (who, of course, was Taylor, the alleged harasser).

The defendants registered their opposition to Vinson's motion, questioning Barry's restatement of the record. The bank's brief charged that she had mischaracterized testimony, relied on facts not admitted into evidence, blatantly misconstrued the court's opinion, and cited errors that were harmless and inconsequential.

On June 10, 1980, Judge Penn denied the request to appeal *in forma pauperis*, questioning whether Vinson lacked the financial resources to appeal. He also ruled that furnishing a transcript at public expense was not justified because the appeal did not present a "substantial question" warranting the expense. He maintained that he had implicitly ruled in Vinson's favor on the issues of Taylor's status as a supervisor and the EEOC's right-to-sue letter, making the issues a frivolous basis for appeal. He suggested that Barry could have presented more pattern and practice evidence and concluded that her assertions of factual errors presented versions of the facts that either differed insignificantly from the court's factual findings or were "harmless or obviously would not affect the result in the case."

Vinson appealed Penn's denial of her request to proceed *in forma pauperis* to the Court of Appeals for the District of Columbia. Her contention that the appeal presented an important issue was buttressed by an affidavit from Joan Vermeulen of the Working Women's Institute. Vermeulen presented research showing that sexual harassment was a major occupational health hazard to victims and an economic barrier for women. Because Judge Penn's exoneration of the bank from liability failed to conform with legal trends, appellate review of the district court's decision was critical, and "such a review should not be contingent on the appellant's ability to pay." Barry also filed exhibits establishing Vinson's indigence, including documents detailing medical expenses incurred because of a car wreck suffered while working. On August 20, 1980, the appeals court remanded Vinson's motion to Judge Penn to reconsider in light of the "changed circumstances." Although he still viewed the question as being "very close," on October 30, Judge Penn granted Vinson permission to appeal *in forma pauperis*, but he again denied her request to have a transcript provided by the government, reaffirming his belief that the plaintiff did not raise a "substantial question on appeal" and that she had "mischaracterized some of the evidence." Barry proceeded to appeal *Vinson v. Taylor*, which was assigned appeals court docket number 80-2369 on November 10, 1980.

Barry now renewed her attempts to circumvent the lack of a trial transcript. When the appeals court declined to have a transcript reproduced without cost to Vinson, Barry moved for permission to proceed with the appeal without a transcript, claiming that its estimated cost of $4,000 to $5,000 would be prohibitive. She contended that many issues on appeal would not require a transcript to decide, such as

Penn's denial of Vinson's amended complaints and her exhaustion of EEOC procedures. Robert Troll, on behalf of the bank, opposed this request, arguing that a transcript was necessary to decide if Judge Penn's findings were factually erroneous.

Troll and Barry sparred continuously on procedural matters, especially Barry's struggles with missed deadlines. When Barry was late submitting her brief to the court, Troll moved that the court dismiss Vinson's appeal. Barry requested frequent extensions; as a solo practitioner facing an established law firm, she asked the court to consider her limited staff support — one part-time typist — and also to extend the filing deadline until it had resolved the transcript issue. On May 1, 1981, the court granted Barry permission to proceed without a transcript and extended the time for filing her appellant's brief. After further extensions, Barry's August 26 brief asked the appeals court to reverse Judge Penn's judgment for the defendants and to remand to the district court for a new trial. It argued that Penn had abused his discretion by denying Vinson's attempt to amend her complaint to add tort claims and had committed reversible error by excluding testimony of other female branch employees about Taylor's sexual misconduct and by ruling that the bank could not be liable without knowledge of its supervisor's misconduct.

Troll filed his appellee's brief for the bank on November 11, 1981, arguing that the bank could not be liable without notice and, even more fundamentally, that Vinson had failed to establish a prima facie case for her claim of sexual harassment. Without establishing the necessary elements of her claim, the plaintiff was not entitled to present other witnesses to rebut defense testimony, and the bank certainly was not responsible for conduct that the plaintiff had failed to prove had occurred. Barry's reply brief, filed on December 31, charged that the bank's brief contained many factual mistakes, and it presented detailed rebuttals asserting her version of the actual record. More notable, however, was her harsh rhetoric condemning the overall climate of the trial: "What happened in Judge Penn's courtroom was not a rational, orderly attempt to get at the truth of what happened to Mechelle Vinson, but rather a ritualistic psychodrama based on enduring, but extremely hostile, and even possibly subconscious, notions of who woman is." At trial, "we had a throwback, a lapse, to the old defenses against a woman's charge of sexual abuse by a man. The defenses are she deserved it because she asked for it; we know she asked for it, because she is a temptress, a seductress, a lascivious woman."

What exactly had happened at trial was the subject of constant disagreement between the parties, who did not have a full transcript and could not agree on an appendix setting out a mutually acceptable record of the case. Barry moved to compel the defendant to meet and agree on a statement of record on appeal. Troll opposed this motion, arguing that Barry's version of the record conflated facts, inferences, arguments, and legal conclusions. Ruling for the appeals court, Judge Robinson denied Barry's motion but gave her an extension to file an appendix detailing the factual record. When she did, on January 19, 1982, Troll moved to strike it, contending that it included prejudicial material not in the official record of the district court. He had earlier informed the court that the bank was purchasing a partial trial transcript and entered his own appendix. With this issue unresolved as the time for oral arguments approached, the parties also disagreed over the participation of three amici curiae (friends of the court) who the previous summer had submitted briefs supporting Vinson: the Working Women's Institute, Equal Rights Advocates, Inc., and Women Employed. The bank opposed their request to participate in oral arguments, but the appeals court granted their motion and *sua sponte* (on its own initiative) allocated ten minutes for amici in addition to twenty minutes each for the appellant and appellee at oral arguments.

A three-judge panel of the Court of Appeals for the District of Columbia heard oral arguments in *Vinson v. Taylor* on February 16, 1982. On the panel were appeals court judges Spottswood Robinson III and J. Skelly Wright and senior district judge Edward S. Northrop. Sitting with appeals panels, although common practice, is considered a plum assignment that allows district judges to spotlight their legal talents, often by writing the court's opinion. Northrop, from the Maryland District Court, was reputedly somewhat conservative, so the defense team was encouraged by this draw. In contrast, Wright, a liberal with a national reputation, had authored the 1981 *Bundy v. Jackson* opinion, first recognizing hostile environment sexual harassment. Robinson, chief judge of the appeals court and also considered a liberal, had written opinions in several pioneering sexual harassment cases, including *Barnes v. Costle* in 1977, the first appellate decision holding that quid pro quo sexual harassment violated Title VII.

Barry argued Vinson's case, stressing that Judge Penn had ruled incorrectly in excluding testimony of other female bank employees alleging sexual harassment by Taylor. Ronald A. Schecter represented the Equal Rights Advocates and other amici supporting Vinson. He concentrated on trying to persuade the panel that the bank should be held absolutely liable for its supervisor's sexual abuse. Troll spoke for the defendants, urging the court to affirm Judge Penn's dismissal of the claims. The appellate judges, however, grilled Troll on the trial court's failure to consider whether Taylor had created a hostile environment, a theory of sexual harassment only recently upheld in the D.C. Circuit. Judge Northrop asked a friendly question: Should not evidence of the plaintiff's dress be admissible? Agreeing, Troll suspected that the judge's question was directed more toward persuading his fellow panelists than at the attorney — a not uncommon practice among judges on appellate benches. Troll did not have high hopes leaving that argument, however; based on the tenor of the judges' questions, it seemed to him that "the handwriting was on the wall." Barry, though not believing that the oral arguments had been a "slam dunk," felt that they had gone well and credited Schecter with doing a great job.

The Appeals Court Reverses

The court of appeals did not render its decision until January 25, 1985, almost three years after hearing oral arguments. Both lead attorneys feared the worst. Barry worried that the court was simply going to affirm and put the case on the back burner. Troll suspected that the liberal judges might be delaying the ruling until other appeals courts had joined the D.C. Circuit in upholding hostile environment claims. Although courts occasionally time decisions to avoid undermining their political support, the more likely explanation for the delay was the huge backlog of cases swamping Chief Justice Robinson at the time. Whatever the reason for the delay, however, the decision imparted a bold new direction to the case.

Robinson, writing for the court, began his opinion by identifying the major issue as "whether a corporate employer is accountable under Title VII . . . for its supervisor's sexual harassment of a woman employee notwithstanding the employer's lack of actual knowledge thereof." The appeals court concluded that the district court's ruling — that, absent knowledge of the harassment, Capital City was not liable even if Taylor had harassed Vinson — was "inconsistent with the intent of Title VII" and therefore reversed Judge Penn's judgment.

The appeals court sustained Judge Penn's refusal to dismiss the case because Vinson had obtained her right-to-sue letter after suing in district court, noting that later cases had established that "a timely filing with EEOC is not a jurisdictional prerequisite to suit." The appeals court also refused to reverse Penn's denial of permission for Vinson to add tort claims to her complaint, since such an amendment would have burdened the defendants with additional discovery and the prejudicial effect of further delay. The court declined, however, to express a view on whether Vinson should be allowed to amend her complaint on remand. With these additional claims precluded and the Section 1985 and Fifth Amendment claims in the original complaint dropped, the court focused on the Title VII claim.

Central to this claim was Penn's finding that if Vinson and Taylor had engaged in a sexual relationship, it had been voluntary, having nothing to do with her continued employment or advancement at the bank, leading to his conclusion that Vinson was not a victim of sexual harassment or sex discrimination. Rather than deciding whether Judge Penn's findings of fact were "clearly erroneous," the appeals court relied on two legal developments since Penn's ruling that undermined his conclusion. In April 1980, only months after Penn's decision in *Vinson v. Taylor*, the EEOC, chaired by Carter appointee Eleanor Holmes Norton, had issued its first guidelines on sexual harassment. Those guidelines included a definition of sexual harassment:

> Unwelcome sexual advances, requests for sexual favors, and other verbal or physical conduct of a sexual nature constitute sexual harassment when . . . submission to such conduct is made either explicitly or implicitly a term or condition of an individual's employment, [or] submission to or rejection of such conduct by an individual is used as the basis for employment decisions affecting such individual, or when such conduct has the purpose or effect of unreasonably interfering with an individual's work performance or creating an intimidating, hostile, or offensive working environment.

This definition incorporated MacKinnon's distinction between two types of sexual harassment: quid pro quo harassment, when submission is made a condition of employment or submission or rejection is used as the basis for employment decisions; and hostile environment harassment, when the conduct "has the purpose or effect of unreasonably interfering with an individual's work performance or creating an intimidating, hostile, or offensive working environment." The following year, 1981, the D.C. circuit court in *Bundy v. Jackson* had adopted the view that hostile environment harassment could constitute illegal sex discrimination.

Because no employment decisions affecting Vinson seemed to be based on her reaction to Taylor's alleged advances, Judge Penn deemed that she did not suffer from sexual harassment. The judge had apparently considered only quid pro quo harassment, however. The appeals court, mindful of the newer hostile environment theory, ruled that Vinson's allegations amounted to charges of environmental harassment. Drawing from *Bundy*, Judge Robinson wrote that the proper inquiry to assess this claim was whether Taylor "created or condoned a substantially discriminatory work *environment*, regardless of whether the complaining employees lost any tangible job benefits as a result of the discrimination."

The second legal development related to Judge Penn's damaging finding that Vinson had voluntarily acquiesced to the alleged sexual advances, assuming that any had occurred. The EEOC guidelines, however, had defined sexual harassment as *unwelcome* sexual conduct, not limiting harassment to conduct that was physically forced or otherwise involuntarily imposed on victims. Moreover, the *Bundy* court had ruled that "a woman employee need not prove resistance to sexual overtures in order to establish a Title VII claim of sexual harassment." If the victim's capitulation were allowed to establish that the relationship was voluntary, and if a voluntary relationship — no matter how unwelcome to the victim, who feared for her job — could never be sexual harassment, the court worried that victims of unwelcome sexual advances would be trapped in a set of cruel choices. This "cruel trilemma" identified in *Bundy* was the unsavory choice among acquiescing, resisting, or resigning, and "an even more hideous quadrilemma" would be formed by a fourth option: "to yield and thereby lose all hope of legal redress for being put in this intolerable position in the first place." Capitulation could not be allowed to demonstrate "voluntariness," negating a finding of sexual harassment. According to the appeals court, the correct test was not whether Vinson voluntarily submitted but "whether Taylor made Vinson's toleration of sexual harassment a condition of her employment."

Because Judge Penn's opinion failed to distinguish whether his conclusion that Taylor had not sexually harassed Vinson rested on incorrect legal criteria (ignoring hostile environment and using voluntariness as the standard for harassment) or exclusively on his reading of the facts of the case, the appeals court remanded the case to the district court for Penn to reconsider Vinson's claims in light of the legal standards enunciated by the higher court. The appeals court also issued two evidentiary rulings that contravened Penn's methods of considering evidence at trial. First, although Penn had not explained the reasons for his conclusion that any hypothetical sexual relationship between Taylor and Vinson had been voluntary, the appeals court worried that the judge might have relied on the "voluminous testimony regarding Vinson's dress and personal fantasies." Because voluntariness was not the correct question, but rather whether the employee's toleration of the harasser's conduct was "a condition of her employment," this testimony was inappropriate and should be inadmissible. As Judge Robinson put it, "Since, under *Bundy*, a woman does not waive her Title VII rights by her sartorial or whimsical proclivities, that testimony had no place in this litigation."

Conversely, the district court had excluded testimony by some of Vinson's coworkers about Taylor's alleged sexual harassment of them, except for the limited purpose of establishing whether the bank should have known about the misconduct. Judge Penn had ruled the testimony inadmissible for the purpose of proving whether Taylor had made sex a basis for employment decisions about Vinson. But although Taylor's treatment of other female employees was not admissible for establishing a quid pro quo harassment claim, the appeals court ruled that "evidence tending to show Taylor's harassment of other women working alongside Vinson is directly relevant to the question whether he created an environment violative of Title VII." Corroborating evidence from coworkers "could be critical to a plaintiff's case, for a claim of harassment cannot be established without a showing of more than isolated indicia of discriminatory environment."

Parenthetically, the court observed that "even a woman who was never herself the object of harassment might have a Title VII claim if she were forced to work in an atmosphere in which such harassment was pervasive."

But the most severe blow to the defense came when the court turned to what it considered the key question on appeal: employer liability. Judge Penn's ruling that Capital City could not be held liable for Taylor's conduct, even assuming that sexual harassment occurred, had hinged on the bank's lack of knowledge of misconduct. Penn had found that neither Vinson nor her coworkers had formally complained of Taylor's conduct nor informed the bank of their grievances through informal means. To impute knowledge to the employer "in these unusual cases of sexual harassment where notice to the employer must depend upon the actual perpetrator" struck Judge Penn as completely unreasonable. The appeals court, however, rejected Penn's conclusion and the rationale used to reach it.

Judge Robinson looked to the circuit's precedent, noting that in its two prior cases in which sexual harassment was found to violate Title VII, the D.C. appeals court had held the employers liable under the legal rule that "an employer is chargeable with Title VII violations occasioned by discriminatory practices of supervisory personnel." Robinson admitted that neither case was precisely analogous, so he undertook the task of determining congressional intent on this issue by employing multiple methods of statutory interpretation.

Examining the language of the statute, he found that the plain meaning of Title VII demonstrated an intent to hold employers liable for the discrimination of their supervisors. The statute defined employers covered by Title VII by various criteria, including that they employ a minimum of fifteen workers, and added the phrase "and any agent" of such employers. Defining employers to include their agents meant that discrimination by employers' agents was, in effect, discrimination by employers themselves. As branch manager, Taylor was beyond doubt the bank's agent with respect to the other employees of that branch.

Although finding little legislative history to support either side, Judge Robinson noted that some opponents of the bill had warned of employer liability for discrimination beyond its control or intent. He relied more heavily, however, on another basis for determining legislative intent: the interpretation of the statute by the agency charged with its enforcement. For Title VII, the EEOC's guidelines were unambiguous on employer liability for sexual harassment: "Applying general Title VII principles, an employer . . . is responsible for its acts and those of its agents and supervisory employees with respect to sexual harassment regardless of whether the specific acts complained of were authorized or even forbidden by the employer and regardless of whether the employer knew or should have known of their occurrence." Although administrative guidelines are not binding, courts have determined that they are "'entitled to great deference,' especially when they are supported by the statute and not inconsistent with its legislative history." Judge Robinson further noted that holding employers liable for sexual harassment by supervisors was consistent with Title VII cases holding employers liable for racial and religious discrimination.

The appeals court made it clear that it was basing its holding of employer liability solely on its interpretation of Title VII and was not imposing vicarious employer liability under the common-law doctrine of *respondeat superior*. The court noted that *respondeat superior* holds employers responsible for their employees' actions only when employees are acting "within the scope" of their authority. If sexual harassment by supervisors was considered their "personal proclivity" outside the scope of their employment, this limitation might result in employers being responsible "only if they explicitly require or consciously allow their supervisors to molest women employees," a plainly "ludicrous result" incompatible with Congress's purpose in passing Title VII to cure the evil of employment discrimination.

A general rule of employer liability for hostile environment as well as quid pro quo sexual harassment would better meet Congress's objective. To require notice for employer liability would create an incentive for employers "to remain oblivious to conditions in the workplace" and "open the door to circumvention of Title VII by the simple expedient of looking the other way." Such a knowledge requirement would introduce an "enormous loophole" in the statute. Citing the EEOC's guidelines that "prevention is the best tool for the elimination of sexual harassment," the court touted the positive effect of a rule of general employer liability. Not only would this interpretation cultivate "an incentive for employers to take a more active role" in maintaining a working environment free from illegal sex discrimination, but it also would promote realistic remedies when discrimination occurred. Noting that "only the employer can provide reinstatement, back pay or other remedial relief contemplated by the Act," the court observed that "much of the promise of Title VII will become empty if victims of unlawful discrimination cannot secure redress from the only source capable of providing it."

Having clarified the legal standards to be used in assessing whether conduct constituted sexual harassment, and having interpreted the statute to hold employers liable for both types of sexual harassment by their supervisors whether they had knowledge of it or not, the appeals court held that "Vinson alleged facts sufficient to state a claim of sex discrimination cognizable under Title VII, and that any discriminatory activity by Taylor is attributable to Capital City. Vinson is entitled to an adjudication of that claim on the evidence, considered in light of the legal principles applicable." Consequently, the appeals court reversed Judge Penn's judgment and remanded the case to the district court "for proceedings consistent with this opinion."

Drawing a Dissent

The defendants' defeat at the appeals court level was as total and devastating as their victory had been sweeping and unambiguous in the district court. The unanimity of the ruling underscored the magnitude of the reversal. Pat Barry found the ruling "incredible — I went 'Wow!'" But the depth of the defeat left the defense in a quandary as to how to proceed. Settlement was always an option, but the appeals court's favorable ruling had considerably strengthened Vinson's bargaining position. Defending themselves in the more hospitable venue of Judge Penn's courtroom was an option, but the new legal framework set by the appeals court would benefit the plaintiff. New standards defining unwelcome environmental harassment and admissible coworker evidence would help Vinson, and the exclusion of dress and fantasy testimony would disadvantage the defendants. Most discouraging, with the requirement of employer knowledge removed, the bank would be in a much more exposed position with regard to liability in a rehearing on the merits of the case.

The defendants could ask the appeals court panel to reconsider its decision, but in view of the panel's unanimity and the conclusiveness of Vinson's victory, this course appeared futile. An alternative was to appeal to the U.S. Supreme Court, but getting a hearing was a major hurdle to this strategy. Appeals courts decide about 28,000 cases annually. The Supreme Court is bombarded by requests to hear appeals of those decisions, but very few of the approximately 7,000 to 8,000 petitions are granted. Today, the Supreme Court agrees to hear only about 75 of the petitions filed each year, or approximately 1 percent. Although the odds were slightly better in 1985, when the Supreme Court typically heard about 150 cases a year, the defendants still had a less than 5 percent chance of having the Court agree to hear the case. A final alternative held hope of avoiding the pitfalls of the other options while maximizing the likelihood of winning a hearing before the Supreme Court. The defendants requested a rehearing, not by the original three-judge panel, but by the entire Court of Appeals for the District of Columbia sitting en banc, that is, with all the judges on the circuit court's bench hearing the appeal.

This strategy was a long shot, too. The court heard only six to ten cases en banc annually, less than 10 percent of the court's caseload, so the odds for a rehearing were only slightly better than those for an appeal to the Supreme Court. The D.C. appeals court also enjoyed a reputation as a liberal bench, with its judges known for their activism and innovative approaches to the law. Although by mid-1985 President Reagan's conservative "revolution" had reached the D.C. circuit court, with important Republican appointees added to the bench, the likelihood of receiving a hearing, much less of winning a reversal from the full court, appeared bleak.

With little hope of winning, the defense strategy was to at least draw a dissent from the conservative Reagan appointees, especially Judge Robert Bork. A well-known jurist and leader in the conservative judicial movement, Bork was widely rumored to be the president's favored pick for the next nomination to the Supreme Court (and Bork was nominated in 1987, only to have his appointment defeated in one of history's most contentious nomination battles). Even if a majority voted against a rehearing by the full court, Bork might be tempted to register a dissent. Dissenting would appeal to his philosophical values and contentious disposition; it would also showcase his opinion in a publicly visible forum and catch the attention of the conservatives on the Supreme Court, who might be favorably disposed to giving their fellow conservative jurist and possible future colleague a chance to have his views vindicated before the highest court in the land. Hoping to evoke at least a cry of conservative protest, the bank's lawyers filed a "suggestion" for a rehearing en banc on February 21, 1985.

The first step of the strategy worked admirably. On May 14, 1985, the U.S. Court of Appeals for the District of Columbia voted seven to three against rehearing the case en banc. Politically, the composition of the opposing groups was stellar. Those joining judges Robinson and Wright in voting against rehearing were, among others, Abner Mikva, a former liberal New York congressman, and Ruth Bader Ginsberg, a 1993 Clinton appointee to the Supreme Court. Bork indeed dissented, joined by Antonin Scalia, nominated to the Supreme Court by President Reagan in 1986, and Kenneth Starr, the future independent prosecutor whose investigation led to the impeachment of President Clinton in 1998.

Mincing no words, Bork staked out a combative reading of the appeals panel's opinion, attacking in his typically acerbic style those aspects that produced a result Bork deemed "unacceptable." First, Bork objected that by not limiting sexual harassment to involuntary sexual activities, the appeals panel ensured that "the supervisor charged may not prove that the sexual behavior, far from constituting harassment, was voluntarily engaged in by the other person, nor may the supervisor show that the charging person's conduct was in fact a solicitation of sexual advances." Bork equated the appellate panel's rejection of the voluntariness standard with "depriving the charged person of any defenses." The result, he argued, was that "sexual dalliance, however voluntarily engaged in, becomes harassment whenever an employee sees fit, after the fact, so to characterize it."

Bork maintained that this result was exacerbated because "the rules of evidence are rigged so that dalliance is automatically harassment because no one is allowed to deny it." He deplored the panel's exclusion of evidence "suggesting that the plaintiff wore provocative clothing, suffered from bizarre sexual fantasies, and often volunteered intimate details of her sex life to other employees at the bank." He acknowledged that such evidence is "hardly determinative" but contended that it is relevant to the question of whether sexual advances were solicited or voluntarily engaged in. Recognizing that "such evidence must be evaluated critically and in the light of all the other evidence," he found it "astonishing that it should be held inadmissible."

On employer liability, Judge Bork lamented that the panel's decision went well beyond past sexual harassment decisions in the circuit as well as the traditional common law. He differentiated sexual harassment from supervisory misconduct evoking *respondeat superior* by contending that this traditional common-law doctrine of vicarious employer liability applied only when the employee's intentional torts had the purpose "wholly or in part to further the master's business." The personal motivations of harassers not only made *respondeat superior* inappropriate but also distinguished sexual from racial harassment cases, implying that different rules of employer liability should apply. Racial discrimination and harassment inevitably benefited employers by lowering wages for minorities, but sexually abusive conduct advanced only supervisors' lustful desires, not company interests. Holding the employer automatically liable for sexual harassment in effect makes it "an insurer that all relationships between supervisors and employees are entirely asexual." In that position, employers can avoid liability only by "actually monitoring or policing his employees' voluntary sexual relationships," a policy as costly to employers as it would be outrageously invasive of employees' privacy.

In a final footnote, Judge Bork questioned the very foundation underlying the appeals court's decision, challenging the "awkwardness of classifying sexual advances as 'discrimination.'" He argued that "harassment is reprehensible, but Title VII was passed to outlaw discriminatory behavior and not simply behavior of which we strongly disapprove." To illustrate the "artificiality" of treating sexual harassment as sex discrimination, he cited the problem of the bisexual harasser, raised by Judge Robinson in *Costle*. A bisexual superior who insisted on sexual favors from both male and female employees would not discriminate because of sex, presumably not violating Title VII because he abused men and women alike. It was inconceivable to Bork that "only the differentiating libido runs afoul of Title VII, and bisexual harassment, however blatant and however offensive and disturbing, is legally permissible." This anomaly casts doubt that Title VII was intended to outlaw sexual harassment because "that bizarre result suggests that Congress was not thinking of individual harassment at all but of discrimination in conditions of employment because of gender." Although this argument is relegated to a footnote and Bork concludes not by rejecting Title VII coverage of sexual harassment but by calling for appropriate adjustments in subsidiary doctrines, Bork's challenge to treating sexual harassment as sex discrimination signaled that, despite the trend in various lower federal courts, sexual harassment had not yet been definitively established as illegal under Title VII.

Seven years after she had filed suit and almost ten years after the incidents complained of had allegedly occurred, the legal tide seemed to have turned in Mechelle Vinson's favor. The appeals court had refused to reconsider its ruling establishing legal standards and evidentiary rules that would be advantageous to Vinson in a remand to the district court. Yet in drawing a dissent from Judge Robert Bork, the defense had strengthened its position in seeking a hearing before the U.S. Supreme Court. Bob Troll now sought that appeal before the highest tribunal, filing the petition on June 21, 1985.

CHAPTER 4

Deciding the Case
In the Supreme Court of the United States

On October 7, 1985, the Supreme Court granted the bank's writ of certiorari, a request that a higher court hear an appeal from a lower court's decision. Although the Supreme Court agrees to hear few appeals, the process itself is simple. The justices assign their clerks to read and digest the particulars of the thousands of writs requested each year. Under the "rule of four," the votes of four justices are sufficient for the Court to grant "cert" and hear the case. The justices considered the bank's petition for cert in their conference on September 30 and decided to grant the writ over the lone dissenting vote of Justice Thurgood Marshall, who preferred to let the appeals court's reversal stand.

Written opinions rarely accompany decisions on cert, but certain factors predispose the Court to grant it. One factor may be the importance or urgency of the issue or the status of the parties involved. Contradictory appeals court rulings, making the law vary across judicial circuits, may also elicit cert. And sometimes the evolving legal standards are so murky or variable or displeasing to the Court that it seizes the initiative to clarify the law and establish a consistent direction for legal developments. When the bank petitioned for cert, only the D.C. appeals court in *Vinson* and the Eleventh Circuit in *Henson* had ruled on hostile environment sexual harassment under Title VII. These decisions were not fundamentally inconsistent; both had ruled sexual harassment actionable. But they differed in important respects, most significantly on the issue of employer liability. Taking *Vinson* on appeal gave the Supreme Court an opportunity to reconcile legal standards and to clarify the law in an area where new doctrine was evolving rapidly.

The clerk of the Supreme Court assigned docket number 84-1979 to the case and titled the action *PSFS Savings Bank, FSB v. Vinson et al.*

The change in name (and, before the Court heard the case, the bank's name would change again, to Meritor Savings Bank, FSB) reflected several developments since the original suit titled *Vinson v. Taylor.* The bank was undergoing a series of mergers and acquisitions that eventually absorbed the small, locally owned Capital City Federal Savings and Loan Association into the Philadelphia-based enterprise Meritor. This transformation was part of larger movements in the banking industry in the mid-1980s. The deregulation of the savings and loan industry not only resulted in a huge number of defaults and an industry bailout in which the U.S. government subsidized the owners of financially strapped savings and loans to the tune of half a trillion dollars; it also set in motion a merger movement in which savings and loans that had avoided fatal errors and done well in the less structured climate of deregulation found themselves the targets of takeovers by larger and stronger financial entities. The evolution of Capital City to Meritor Savings Bank mirrored the rapid transformations driven by the national savings and loan crisis.

The bank's name replaced Sidney Taylor's in the case name because it alone had appealed. Its name appeared first rather than Vinson's because it had sought the hearing. The bank, originally a defendant, was now formally designated the petitioner, seeking permission to have its appeal heard by the Supreme Court, and Vinson, the plaintiff in the lawsuit, was designated the respondent, responding to the bank's requested appeal. Taylor, too, was designated a respondent before the Supreme Court, although his role at this level was minimal.

———

The Parties' Briefs to the Court

Bob Troll remained the bank's counsel of record when he moved to the law firm of Ross, Marsh & Foster. Troll, senior partner Charles Fleischer, and associate Randall Smith drafted a brief arguing the bank's position, which they submitted to the Supreme Court on December 11, 1985. As they presented the issues, the case raised three questions: employer liability, admissibility of evidence, and hostile environment as a cause of action under Title VII. Party briefs seek to frame a case's legal issues strategically; which issues are raised, their ordering, and the phrasing all reflect jockeying for persuasive advantage. Seeking to define the priority issues and highlight its strongest arguments, the bank first presented the employer liability issue, leaving for last the logically prior but weaker argument about whether Title VII prohibited hostile environment harassment.

The bank's brief posed the key issue as: "Is an employer absolutely liable under Title VII of the Civil Rights Act of 1964, as amended, for sexual advances allegedly made by a male supervisor toward a female subordinate where the employer neither knew nor reasonably could have known of, had no opportunity to stop, and did not intend to permit the sexual advances?" This phrasing focused the Court's attention on the bank's key argument: "Congress did not intend to make innocent employers absolutely liable for Title VII sex discrimination." Title VII, the brief contended, banned only disparate treatment that intentionally discriminated, but the bank could not have intended discrimination that it knew nothing about. Although employer intent would frequently have to be imputed to the corporate entity from the actions of its agents, any automatic ascription of intent to the employer based on its agents' intents would effectively read intent out of the statute and might push harried employers toward drastic measures, including "policing personal relationships" of employees. Employer responsibility for discrimination by its agents required negligence: the plaintiff "must show that the employer knew or should have known of the harassment in question and filed to take prompt remedial action." But, said the bank, it had not known of any harassment and had taken "every reasonable preventative step." The law of agency did not treat notice to an agent as notice to the principal when their interests differed or the agent's actions were unrelated to its duties. Sexual harassers' knowledge of their own misconduct could not be considered notice to their employers, regardless of the perpetrators' position or authority, because harassers act on their own and hide their harassment to avoid disciplinary action.

Meritor's brief cited a second issue: "Is evidence of the complaining employee's workplace dress and voluntary conduct and her sexual fantasies and proclivities admissible in defense of her Title VII claim?" This evidence, the bank contended, was relevant for showing that "Vinson's involvement in alleged sexual activity with Taylor was entirely consensual and free from any job-related coercion." Vinson's discussions of her sexual fantasies proved that she "helped to create and was not offended by the very environment" her suit challenged. Her supposed fantasies could even indicate "whether the charges were fantasized here." This defensive evidence was crucial because sexual harassment differed from other types of harassment; unlike race-based workplace conduct, for example, sexual conduct at work is not inherently problematic. The brief quoted the concurrence in *Barnes v. Costle* written by Judge George MacKinnon (a lifelong Republican, Nixon appointee to the D.C. appeals court, and Catharine MacKinnon's father): "Sexual advances may not be intrinsically offensive, and no policy can be derived from the equal employment opportunity laws to discourage them. We are not here concerned with racial epithets . . . but with social patterns that to some extent are normal and expectable. It is the abuse of the practice, rather than the practice itself, that arouses alarm." Since personal relationships between supervisors and subordinates were not inevitably abusive, voluntariness was the critical issue, and evidence of plaintiffs' dress and fantasies was plainly relevant to determining "whether the subordinate welcomed or was offended by the invitations for sex."

The last issue raised in the bank's brief challenged the very notion that a hostile work environment could provide a basis for a sexual harassment claim: "Do allegations of sexual advances, without any loss or threatened loss of economic or other tangible job benefits, state a claim of employment discrimination because of sex in violation of Title VII?" The brief maintained that Title VII's purpose was to combat tangible economic discrimination, not to police the "purely psychological aspects of the workplace environment." Rejecting "sexual harassment, without more" would protect innocent employers from liability because the imposition of job sanctions inevitably requires the exercise of employer power, and the exaction of economic penalties would prove that the sexual relations involved coercion.

A basic tenet undergirded the bank's arguments: "Sexual activity is special because it is generally secretive and, in many circumstances, it is welcomed, desirable, and proper," requiring that "Title VII be applied in light of the special nature of the activity." The brief concluded with a broadside aimed at the very foundation of Vinson's claim that her harassment had been illegal, asserting that the uniqueness of sexual relations raised "the fundamental question of whether sexual harassment is cognizable at all under Title VII."

The brief filed on Vinson's behalf on February 11, 1986, cast the issues in starkly different terms. This brief was written by Catharine MacKinnon and reviewed by Vinson's attorney Pat Barry and by Sarah E. Burns, a former director of NOW's Legal Defense Fund who at the time was with the Sex Discrimination Clinic at Georgetown University's Law Center. Their respondent's brief raised four issues to the Supreme Court, beginning with a challenge to the Court's decision to hear the case. Vinson's brief contended that certiorari was "improvidently granted on this incomplete and ambiguous factual record." Too many factual issues remained unresolved, including the paramount issue of whether the sexual misconduct had occurred, to present crisp legal questions for the Court to settle. Strategically, this position sought to preserve advantages won on appeal by ensuring that further fact-finding on remand would be guided by the appeals court's favorable strictures.

Vinson's brief then addressed the same three issues raised by the bank's brief, but beginning on the territory most favorable to the respondent: "Whether sexual harassment as a condition of work, because it is sexual, is less discriminatory than other forms of employment discrimination." Criticizing the bank for advocating a "legal double standard," the brief maintained, "If a situation is found to be sexual harassment, it does not become *not* sex discrimination just because it is sexual. Rather, it presents a form of discrimination which is particularly personally invasive." Against the bank's broadest challenge to sexual harassment as Title VII sex discrimination because "sexual activity is special," the brief noted, "There is no disagreement before this Court that sexual harassment states a claim for sex discrimination under Title VII, a view which has been adopted by every Circuit that has considered the issue." On the specific question actually disputed in this case, whether hostile environment sexual harassment could furnish the basis of sex discrimination claims, the brief attacked the bank's contention that actionable harm had to involve tangible economic loss. Categories such as quid pro quo and hostile environment sexual harassment, as well as tangible and intangible job benefits, represented no sharp distinctions; "there is nothing ineffable about a daily gauntlet of vitriol" endured by victims of sexually hostile environments as part of their working conditions.

The bank's attempt to differentiate sexual from other forms of harassment also drew fire. Just as sexual activity or words did not necessarily create a "sexually derogatory workplace," discussions of race or ethnicity, including racial or ethnic words and jokes, were not always socially problematic. Context was critical, but "invective, slurs, and harassment," whether based on race, religion, or sex, are discriminatory "contextual harms." Courts had uniformly held that "citizens do not have to endure these atrocities to have an equal chance to make a living."

Vinson's brief recognized that "the unwelcomeness of a sexual encounter in employment is crucial to a sexual harassment claim." Voluntariness was too blunt an instrument for determining whether sexual conduct was harassment. Voluntary sex included not only relationships based on mutual desire but also unwelcome sex engaged in when facing "unsuccessful resistance" or "hopeless nonresistance." Requiring claimants to show that they successfully resisted and suffered tangible loss as a result would "protect all but those who need the protection the most: those who are so vulnerable that noncompliance is a physical impossibility or an unaffordable luxury."

Vinson's brief next addressed "whether employers are liable for sexual harassment by supervisors which creates a discriminatory working environment," designating this issue "the heart of the dispute." The debate was not "an abstract contest over whether sexual harassment is sex discrimination, which is undisputed. It is a concrete conflict over whether sexual harassment will be treated *as if* it is sex discrimination: whether the employer will be responsible so that its victims will receive relief." Courts should hold employers liable for discrimination by their supervisors because Title VII's statutory definition of "employer" included "any agent" of the employer. Hostile work environments implicated employer authority no less than quid pro quo sexual coercion did, because tolerating a discriminatory atmosphere as the price of retaining a job was "an implicit quid pro quo." Liability rules requiring employer knowledge of the harassment would create perverse incentives by rewarding employers that either remain ignorant and "look the other way" or establish reporting procedures on paper that in practice insulate them from complaints. The ineffectiveness of such sham procedures was amply illustrated in this case, where "the perpetrator was the procedure." Dispensing with a knowledge requirement would not unfairly expose employers to liability because of harassers' propensity to secrecy; supervisors practicing any type of discrimination would likely hide their misdeeds.

The bank's attempt to treat sexual harassment as exceptional discrimination reflected an implicit "archaic and stereotypic notion," namely, "that some women lie about sex for money." Such an overblown worry, however, could be adequately dealt with by courts, which should have no more difficulty in weeding out fabricated sexual harassment cases than in detecting other false claims. A second "deeper fear seems to be that if a woman can sue for forced sex at work, there will be no voluntary sex at work, because she could always lie about it later." But it is preposterous to believe that "if forced sex is actionable, voluntary sex will become too big a risk to take." The same issue could be raised about rape law, but rape statutes prohibiting coerced sex have hardly stopped consensual sex.

The final issue addressed in Vinson's brief was "whether evidence of plaintiff's dress and reported fantasies is admissible in a sexual harassment case." Analogizing to rape law, the brief noted that evidence even of prior sexual activity, unless with the defendant, would be excluded as "more prejudicial than probative." Vinson's brief conceded that "evidence showing that a relationship truly is voluntary would clearly be admissible" but contended that "apparel and reports of phantasms about others are *not that evidence.*" The sole purpose of introducing such evidence was "to provide a pornographic image of the kind of woman plaintiff is." The argument concluded, "Women simply do not volunteer to be sexually harassed by their clothing or the purported content of their voluntary conversation any more than by consenting to sex with others."

The brief closed by noting a paradox: women who had succumbed to coercive sexual advances were usually too intimidated and humiliated to air their grievances publicly. But such women, like Ms. Vinson, were most in need of judicial relief.

On March 14, 1986, the bank entered its reply brief, a short paper designed to rebut the opposing party's brief and reinforce the petitioner's major points. Meritor's reply countered Vinson's assertion that the factual record was too cloudy for Supreme Court review. Judge Penn's opinion had fixed the factual basis for the dispute, and, "having failed to attack the District Court's findings as clearly erroneous, Vinson is bound by them."

Revisiting the legal issues, the reply maintained that the phrase "and any agent of such a person" in Title VII's definition of employer was not intended to define an employer to include its agents but merely added agents as possible defendants. Holding employers automatically liable for their supervisors' sexual harassment would relieve victims of responsibility to complain: "The employee is thus privileged to accumulate grievances in secret preparation for suit." Excluding evidence of Vinson's "own sexual behavior at work" was tantamount to asking the courts to presume unwelcomeness, equating all sexual activity in the workplace with sexual harassment and making "a supervisor's advances toward a subordinate a *per se* violation." Although Vinson's argument that Title VII prohibits "conditioning economic survival on sexual submission" was accepted by all reasonable employers, it missed the point that Congress had not intended to regulate "private, one-to-one, voluntary activity." The question presented in this case was "whether the behavior described in this record is, without more, a discriminatory condition of employment."

Friends of the Court Speak Out

In addition to the briefs of the petitioner and respondent, several organizations filed amicus curiae briefs in *Meritor Savings Bank v. Vinson*. These "friend of the court" briefs allow nonparties to have a say in cases of particular interest to them by presenting information or legal arguments to try to influence the Court's decision. To file amicus briefs, organizations must obtain written permission from the parties or petition the Court for permission—which is usually granted.

The U.S. government and the Equal Employment Opportunity Commission submitted the weightiest brief in *Vinson*. The solicitor general, a presidential appointee, represents the official position of the U.S. government, and studies have found that the solicitor general's views often wield substantial influence with the Supreme Court, justifying the unofficial title of "the tenth justice." The name of Solicitor General Charles Fried, a conservative legal scholar appointed by President Ronald Reagan, appeared first on the government's brief. Other signers included Johnny J. Butler, acting general counsel of the EEOC, and

Reagan's assistant attorney general for civil rights, William Bradford Reynolds, known for his conservative views on civil rights.

The government-EEOC brief supported Vinson's claim that hostile environment sexual harassment violated Title VII's prohibition on sex discrimination, even if not tied to specific economic harms, when it unreasonably interfered with work performance or created "an intimidating, hostile, or offensive working environment." Beyond this bare agreement on the essential foundation of Vinson's claim, however, the Reagan administration's amicus brief lent far more aid to the bank's positions, including its philosophical premise that sex discrimination was unique: "sexual attraction is a fact of life, and it may often play a role in the day-to-day social exchange between employees in the workplace." Sexual advances and innuendo were ambiguous and likely to be private and unacknowledged. Rules governing this type of harassment must distinguish harassing sex from "consensual relationships that have taken a bad turn." "The gravamen of any hostile environment claim must be that the alleged sexual advances are 'unwelcome,'" and even unwelcome conduct must be sufficiently severe or pervasive to affect the general working environment. Evidence of the "totality of the circumstances" was relevant to determine whether the plaintiff participated in creating the environment she claimed was unwelcome, including testimony about her speech and dress. Judge Penn's unambiguous findings of fact "meant exactly what he said" and showed "appropriate sensitivity to the need to ensure that sexual harassment charges do not become a tool by which one party to a consensual sexual relationship may punish the other." Siding squarely with the bank, the government argued that the court of appeals had erred in remanding without overruling the trial court's factual findings as "clearly erroneous."

The most noteworthy feature of the administration's brief was its repudiation of strict employer liability for its supervisors' sexual harassment. The brief claimed to be an "elaboration" of the EEOC's guidelines, but unlike the 1980 guidelines framed during the Carter administration, the Reagan-era EEOC drew a bright line between quid pro quo and environmental harassment. Although supervisors use employer authority to coerce sex from quid pro quo victims, supervisors are not wielding delegated authority in creating hostile environments; their employers should not be liable for their nonauthorized abuse unless the employers actually knew or had reason to know of the hostile environment. In a slight nod to Vinson's claims, the brief acknowledged that the employer would have reason to know if it "turned its back on the problem, that is, if there is no reasonably available avenue by which victims of sexual harassment can make their complaints known to appropriate officials who are in a position to do something about those complaints." The brief stressed that this rule would help prevent sexual harassment by encouraging employers to promulgate and implement effective policies and grievance procedures. By contrast, "given the naturalness, the pervasiveness, and what might be called the legal neutrality of sexual attraction," the government worried that strict liability might generate perverse by-products by tempting employers to guard against legal exposure by "preventative measures—such as declining to hire women or regulating employees' personal relationships—so extreme as themselves to be offensive." The government concluded that the judgment of the appeals court should be reversed.

The Chamber of Commerce's brief supported Meritor on all issues but stressed its contention that supervisors' sexual advances toward subordinates, without threat or loss of tangible job benefits, did not constitute illegal discrimination. Also supporting the bank were amicus briefs filed by the trustees of Boston University, which, as an employer with 6,740 employees, was sensitive to the plight of employers that might be liable for sexual harassment committed by their supervisory personnel, and the Equal Employment Advisory Council, a private association of employers. Both briefs argued for variations of a knowledge requirement for employer liability, suggesting that holding employers accountable only for their own negligence was both the sounder legal rule and the better policy to encourage employers to implement preventive measures against sexual harassment.

More amicus curiae briefs were filed in support of Vinson. A brief by the Women's Legal Defense Fund and eighteen other rights advocacy groups—including the American Association of University Women; the Center for Constitutional Rights; the National Bar Association's Women Lawyers Division; the National Conference of Black Lawyers; the National Organization for Women; organizations representing Mexican American, Asian American, and women of color; and the National Board of the YWCA—urged the Court to endorse the EEOC guidelines and devoted extensive energy arguing against the admissibility of dress and fantasy evidence. Fourteen other amici, mostly women's rights organizations located in the Northeast and led by the Working Women's Institute of New York, entered a brief surveying data that documented that "sexual harassment is a substantial barrier to equal employment opportunity for women" and is prohibited by Title VII. The illegality of sexual harassment under Title VII, because of its adverse effect on the work environment as a "term, condition, or privilege of employment" apart from any other tangible job benefit, was argued by the Women's Bar Association of New York in a brief that supported Vinson on all the issues. Arguing for employer liability, the AFL-CIO's amicus brief pointed out that practically as well as legally, supervisors wield employer authority: "To an employee, the individual who directs his or her daily work, resolves grievances, and effectively decides upon his or her job security and advancement *is the employer.*"

Twenty-nine members of Congress, including six Republicans and twenty-three Democrats, and ten of the women in the Ninety-ninth Congress, submitted a brief marshaling evidence from the legislative history of the Civil Rights Act of 1964 and its 1972 amendments demonstrating that Congress had intended its ban on sex discrimination to be interpreted broadly to include hostile work environments and had not intended sex discrimination to be treated differently from discrimination based on race or ethnicity. The brief cited Title VII's language defining an employer as including its agents, the parallel interpretation of the National Labor Relations Act, court decisions, and the EEOC guidelines to support employer liability for supervisor sexual harassment. Practically, holding employers liable would ensure redress for victims from the only source able to remedy the harassment and would induce employers "to take an active role in eliminating all vestiges of discrimination from the workplace." The last point was also emphasized in a brief submitted by eight states (California, Connecticut, Illinois, Minnesota, New Jersey, New Mexico, New York, and Vermont) and the Pennsylvania Human Relations Commission. The briefs' authors, like players involved in other aspects of this case, included personalities of current and future political import: Hubert Humphrey III, attorney general and future gubernatorial candidate in

Minnesota and son of the former senator and vice president; and Joseph Lieberman, attorney general of Connecticut and future senator and Democratic vice-presidential candidate.

———

"And May It Please the Court": Oral Arguments

Arguing before the Supreme Court is the most fun a lawyer can have, according to Charles Fleischer, a member of the defense team. Robert Troll took the opportunity seriously, preparing assiduously for his day in the highest court. He worked through holidays and briefed fifty different issues anticipating the justices' questions. Yet prepared texts are of little value to attorneys before the Supreme Court, because the justices routinely interrupt with questions. Litigators' tricky task is to balance genuine responsiveness to the justices' queries with the need to bore in on points critical for their positions. Practicing law in the Washington area enabled him to visit the Court about twenty times to familiarize himself with the surroundings and observe the ritual of oral argument. His law partners staged moot courts, with nine colleagues playing the role of "the Supremes," bombarding Troll with questions and critiquing his answers. Pat Barry relied on a friend who had helped her prepare to argue a case before the Supreme Court five years earlier and also participated in two moot courts arranged by Sarah Burns. The moot courts proved very effective; Barry had already answered every question except one that the justices would ask in oral arguments. Troll and Barry confessed to feeling some nervous anticipation, but both lost any nervousness and concentrated exclusively on the issues once the justices began peppering them with questions.

The Supreme Court usually hears oral arguments from October through about mid-June each year. On March 25, 1986, the day of oral arguments for *Meritor Savings Bank v. Vinson*, Troll brought his children to see the big event, and Barry's mother attended. John Meisburg flew back from Miami to see the case he had initially filed being argued before the Supreme Court. The crowd was overflowing that day. Seating in the courtroom is limited, but a section is reserved for the parties and their invited guests. Another section contains seating for the bar of attorneys admitted to practice before the Supreme Court, separated by a literal bar from the main spectator gallery. The main gallery is open to the public on a first come, first served basis. Other visitors taking the building tour briefly enter the rear of the room to observe the proceedings in three-minute intervals. A section to the left of the room seats the press. The Supreme Court has retained its traditional rule barring television and photographs, so artists sketch by hand the action and the principal protagonists. The president has a reserved chair for observing cases of great interest to the executive branch, a seat that is rarely occupied. The nine justices sit behind a desk, or bench, at the front of the room, arrayed in descending order of seniority from the chief justice's position in the center of the bench, beginning with the most senior associate justice on his right, the next senior on his immediate left, and alternating sides until the least senior, seated on the extreme right end. Each justice sits in a high-backed black leather chair, adjusted in height to fit individual contours.

Attorneys arguing before the Supreme Court find on their assigned desks replicas of quill pens that they may keep as mementos of the august occasion, but the atmosphere connotes that much more than souvenirs is at stake in their visit to the nation's highest court. Attorneys register by 9:05 A.M. on the day of oral arguments and receive verbal and written instructions on procedure and protocol. For example, they are admonished not to waste the Court's time introducing themselves or simply rehashing arguments made in their written briefs. They are warned to address the members of the Court as "Justice," not "Judge," and to be cautious in their use of humor. Each side has thirty minutes allotted to make its arguments, which the petitioner may split to reserve time for rebuttal. Rarely is an attorney permitted to speak for more than a couple of minutes before being pelted with questions from the bench. Although disruptive to the attorney's train of thought, most attorneys welcome the justices' questions, both as an indication of what issues they should emphasize and as a chance to address the concerns that most trouble the justices. Questions and comments from the bench also present opportunities for the justices to debate issues and score points with their fellow jurists. A white light warns the attorney when only five minutes remain. When the red light appears, the attorney must finish that sentence and sit down, unless responding to a question.

The justices enter from the dressing anteroom behind a curtain as the marshal intones the traditional "Oyez, oyez, oyez. God save the

United States and this Honorable Court." On this Tuesday morning, at 10:12 A.M., Chief Justice Warren Burger called the case, announcing, "The court will hear arguments first this morning in Meritor Savings Bank against Vinson. Mr. Troll, you may proceed whenever you're ready." He invited Troll to elevate the lectern behind which attorneys stand, centered on the bench. After a brief pause, Troll began his argument for the bank, starting with the ritual phrase "Mr. Chief Justice, and may it please the Court." He immediately spotlighted "the primary question in this case," which he paraphrased from his written brief as "whether a corporate employer is automatically liable under Title VII for a supervisor's sexual advances toward a subordinate even though the employer did not know about the advances and never had a chance to stop them." He then recited the salient facts of the case and reviewed the decisions of the courts below, uninterrupted but for questions clarifying that Troll represented the bank alone and that Sidney Taylor was not before the Court.

Before he could return to the question of employer liability, Justice Sandra Day O'Connor broke in with a question going to the heart of Vinson's claim. Because Vinson had received raises and promotions, Judge Penn had concluded that she had suffered no quid pro quo discrimination, but O'Connor wanted to probe the bank's position on hostile environment as a species of sexual harassment. She asked, "Do you concede that the trial court simply didn't handle the case as one involving a recognition of a sexual harassment or hostile environment type claim?" Troll conceded that at the time of trial "that theory of law had not been applied to sexual harassment cases." Pressing the point, O'Connor asked, "Do you agree today that that is a valid claim?" Conceding again some territory on this question, the weakest link in the bank's defense, Troll suggested that hostile environment harassment was illegal "if the employee has sustained some form of tangible job detriment." He suggested that in passing Title VII, "Congress was concerned with tangible economic loss, not with psychological or emotional injury"; state tort laws constituted the proper remedies for the latter types of harms.

Bringing Troll back to his central concern, defending against employer liability, Justice Thurgood Marshall queried, "Do you rely fully on the point that the bank was not notified?" Troll responded, "Absolutely," which elicited a challenge from Marshall: "Where in the

{ *Sexual Harassment and the Law* }

statute or anyplace else do you get the need to notify the bank?" Troll maintained that Title VII required proof of intentional discrimination and that a "notice and opportunity to cure rule" was the clearest way to indicate intent. Marshall then asked whether notice had to be in writing. Troll acknowledged that "any form of notice will suffice" if given to an official with "sufficient authority to control the situation to stop the harassment in its tracks."

When Troll agreed that no notice was required in quid pro quo harassment because "a supervisor may act with the authority actually vested in it by the employer in making an employment decision," Justice O'Connor probed why the rule should be different for a hostile environment claim: "Isn't part of supervision the creation of a productive work environment and the proper management of the employees who are supervised?" Troll responded that in hostile environment cases, "the acts of the supervisor would be outside the scope, actual or apparent, of the supervisor."

Reaching for an analogy, O'Connor shifted the terrain to environmental harassment based on race. "Well, there certainly are a substantial number of lower court cases dealing with, for example, racial harassment by co-employees, that don't adopt your theory at all. And they go off on the theory that if the supervisor knows or has reason to know of the racial environment claims of co-employees, that's enough." Troll tried to distinguish those cases, claiming that "a close examination also shows in those cases that some form of management knew about what was going on and failed to stop the harassment." But O'Connor persisted: "Well, but some form of management, of course, is the supervisor. He's the person in place and who's in charge of trying to protect the work environment for the employees. That's part of his job."

Troll maintained that even in racial discrimination cases, the employee "has a duty to go forward to someone at the employer" that triggers the employer's duty to investigate and rectify the situation. Not only would "what the defendant does or does not do when the plaintiff complains" be "the best evidence and the clearest indication" of intent to discriminate, but a requirement for notice before finding employers liable would further the objectives of Title VII, according to Troll. "It encourages employees to speak up promptly, rather than to suffer in silence, and it permits the employer to end the problem before it worsens, and it encourages employers to address the problem because if they do they exonerate themselves from Title VII liability." It is also fair to the victim because "sooner or later she'll have to make a complaint to someone if she wants Title VII relief." And it is unfair to employers not to require notice, because that allows "hauling an innocent employer into court for a problem that it was unaware of and would have corrected voluntarily."

Troll summarized his argument: "Notice and opportunity to cure is consistent with the statute, it furthers the statute's goals, and it's fair. We believe that the Court of Appeals' decision must be reversed." He asked to reserve the balance of his time. The chief justice acceded to this request and called on Patricia Barry to speak for Mechelle Vinson.

Barry led off by suggesting that "the writ [of certiorari] was improvidently granted and should be dismissed by this Court" because, although the bank was challenging Vinson's hostile environment claim, the district court had not tried the case under that legal theory. Immediately, Justice O'Connor inquired: "Did the plaintiff and you on her behalf make clear in the proceedings below that you were proceeding on the basis of a hostile environment theory?" Barry responded that she "was going on the theory of pattern and practice. That is, evidence of how a supervisor treated other members of the protected class, other employees, is evidence that he treated this particular employee in a discriminatory fashion." She noted that case law had not yet established hostile environment as an illegal form of sexual harassment, but in response to questions by Justice Lewis Powell, she cited wording in the complaint and testimony that would support such a claim.

To the query, "What if we agreed that voluntariness is a defense to a suit like this?" Barry responded that hearing the evidence anew, with hostile environment now defined as harassment, "the trial court might just likely recast its findings of fact and determine that perhaps this aspect of voluntariness was no longer there." Interrupted by the observation that "well, the Court of Appeals ruled that voluntariness was irrelevant," Barry took this opportunity to shift to the firmer footing of arguing for unwelcomeness and was asked to differentiate the two standards. She ventured that in using unwelcomeness rather than voluntariness, the court of appeals seemed to be trying to avoid getting "caught up in this word game of, does it mean like, because she acquiesced, therefore she's capitulated her right to later legal redress?"

Responding to Justice O'Connor, she agreed that unwelcomeness was an element in a sexual harassment claim, endorsing the prima facie case outlined in the Eleventh Circuit's 1982 *Henson* decision.

Justice William Rehnquist broke in with a challenge: "That's hard to reconcile, Ms. Barry, with—your view of the unwelcomeness, with the Court of Appeals' ruling that evidence of the complaining employee's work place dress and voluntary conduct couldn't be admitted." This remark initiated a series of sharp exchanges between Barry and Justice Rehnquist. When Barry argued that such evidence had little probative value, Rehnquist queried, "Well now, is that for you as a lawyer to say, that no finder of fact could find that relevant?" Barry responded that because this evidence was "so subjective . . . the federal court has full authority to control the admission of evidence," and the justice retorted, "Yes, and the district court in this case controlled it by letting it in." Renewing her point that such evidence was prejudicial, Barry argued that "evidence of dress by itself standing alone is not admissible in a case of sexual harassment." Rehnquist quipped, "Well, of course it isn't standing alone here," but he gave her a chance to address another question: "What evidence can come in properly on the question of whether it's unwelcome?" Barry cited as "an excellent guidance" California's rules of evidence, stipulating that "work conduct related to the alleged perpetrator is relevant."

The direction of questioning shifted to the factual basis of the appeal. When Barry had to acknowledge that the appeals court had not overturned Judge Penn's findings of fact as "clearly erroneous," Justice Powell noted that among those findings was Penn's factual conclusion that "plaintiff was not the victim of sexual harassment or sexual discrimination." He then mused: "That puts this Court, it seems to me, in a rather difficult position, doesn't it?" Barry deftly turned the dilemma into an opportunity to return to the need for a remand to the district court because these findings of fact had been made without considering the possibility of hostile environment harassment. Noting that neither the EEOC guidelines nor court decisions upholding hostile environment claims had been available at the time of trial, she surmised that Penn "was not thinking in terms of, well, what about noxious environment, poisoned with sexual innuendoes, insults, aggressive behavior that was unwanted, that in this case led to a constructive discharge."

When Barry mentioned evidence of dress, Justice Rehnquist again latched onto this line of questioning. Barry renewed her attempt to argue that only evidence about the victim's behavior vis-à-vis the alleged perpetrator was relevant to proving welcomeness and that evidence of dress and fantasy was aimed at besmirching her general character rather than proving that her specific behavior was welcoming. She noted that this evidence would be excluded in rape trials, but Justice Rehnquist remained unconvinced. "This may be a good argument to make to the district court," he remarked, "but after the district court has resolved it against you, with all the discretion that a district court has in admitting evidence," excluding evidence was not the kind of decision appeals courts want to make. When Barry once again alluded to the California rules of evidence, Rehnquist manifested his impatience with her position, remarking, "Well, we're not governed by the California Rules of Evidence, Ms. Barry. We're practicing under federal rules of evidence."

Barry continued to argue that because "in this case the environment was the supervisor," how the employee acted toward the alleged perpetrator was all that was relevant to whether she welcomed the conduct, but a question about notice shifted the direction of the arguments. Barry reaffirmed her position in her written brief that notice was unnecessary because the statute defined the employer to include its agents, so "Sidney Taylor becomes the bank because he is a supervisor." But Justice Byron White read that definition of employer differently: "I agree that the statute defines an agent of an employer as an employer himself or herself," but "all that means is there are two employers in this case; one is Taylor and the other is the bank." When Barry replied that the single employer was the "collective entity called the bank, made up of individuals who perform the functions on behalf of this collective entity," White responded skeptically, "Well, that's quite a gloss on what the statute says, I must say." Barry also argued for employer liability for supervisors because "the bank or any employer is in the best position to control the actions of the supervisors," admitting that because employers "don't have that same kind of control over coworkers," a notice requirement would be sensible in cases of environmental harassment by nonsupervisory employees.

Chief Justice Burger posed a hypothetical: "Suppose Mr. Taylor was embezzling money from the bank regularly, unknown to anyone else in the bank. Would the knowledge of Mr. Taylor about his own embezzlements be imputed to the bank?" Barry responded by differentiating the hypothetical from the real case. "Here we're dealing with the employer-employee relationship," she contended, and "with respect to the Northeast branch of Meritor Bank Mr. Taylor was the bank for purposes of establishing the employer-employee relationship."

At this point, the chief justice interrupted, "Your time is expired now. The light is covered, but the red light is on." Troll returned to the lectern for his remaining two minutes of rebuttal.

Uninterrupted by questions, Troll zeroed in on the issue of notice. He argued that notice to Taylor was not notice to the bank because "notice to the actual perpetrator in and of itself can never constitute notice. The perpetrator is motivated to keep his conduct secret and to keep it concealed from his superiors, who may discipline him for it." He put the burden of reporting the harassment squarely on the employee: "The victim knows that notice will more than likely not come from her supervisor. If she wishes relief, she must complain."

Thanking the Court, Troll ended his argument. It was 11:11 A.M. Chief Justice Burger closed the oral arguments in the case by saying simply, "Thank you, counsel. The case is submitted."

The questions and repartee from the bench did not offer a clear indication of the likely decision in the case. Troll had managed to spend most of his time arguing against employer liability without notice of the harassment, the bank's primary concern. He felt that the oral arguments had gone well but could not hazard a guess as to the final outcome. Barry had been forced by Justice Rehnquist's aggressive questioning to spend the bulk of her time arguing against the admissibility of dress and fantasy evidence, the softest spot in her argument. However, friendlier questioning on the viability of hostile environment claims and unwelcomeness as the criterion for harassment seemed to indicate brighter prospects for the central tenets of Vinson's claim. The justices' questions and comments from the bench gave some indication of their thinking, but predicting the Court's final opinion based on these slim hints would have been a hazardous venture.

In Conference: Crafting an Opinion

Three days after hearing the oral arguments, on March 28, the justices gathered for their Friday conference. The justices use conferences to discuss the issues in the cases they have just heard argued; reach tentative decisions; and establish a preliminary alignment of votes, which serves as the basis for assigning the writing of opinions and dissents, if necessary, in the cases. The conference is one of the best-kept secrets in Washington; only justices attend, without clerks or secretaries. No transcripts or official records of the proceedings are kept, so historians, scholars, and journalists are left to infer or speculate about what occurs in these closed meetings. They base this speculation on the slimmest reeds of information, including secondhand leaks from clerks, who rely on tidbits of information gleaned from their bosses or other clerks, and, for older cases, the sparse memoirs and papers of retired justices.

On March 28, 1986, Justice William Brennan was making handwritten notes for his own use. Justice Brennan had devised a form allowing him to record both the tentative votes of his colleagues and their views on the merits of the cases. One sheet recorded basic case data, the justices' stances on certiorari, jurisdictional questions, the merits of the case, and any motions. A second sheet was divided, front and back, into quadrants, creating eight boxes, each labeled with the name of one of his fellow justices. In these quarter-page spaces, Justice Brennan jotted a few phrases summarizing the justices' remarks. Although schematic and filtered through the perception of a participant, Brennan's notes offer glimpses into the conference discussion of the *Vinson* case and an outline of the initial positions of the justices.

According to custom, the chief justice spoke first, laying out the issues as he conceived them. Warren Burger had been appointed chief justice in 1969 by President Richard Nixon. Chief justices have little formal authority beyond that of the other associate justices; they are first among equals mostly by dint of their persuasiveness or force of personality. Most accounts do not rate Burger highly as a legal mind or leader of the Court, but he did preside over the Court during an unusually volatile period. The 1970s and early 1980s were a time of balancing as the Court negotiated the transition from the liberal Earl

Warren Court of the 1960s to the conservative Court that would follow upon Burger's retirement in 1986, not long after deciding the *Vinson* case.

The chief justice seemed skeptical of Vinson's claims. He asked, "Shouldn't she have used grievance procedure? Credibility only issue—only unwelcome advances should be actionable." Burger's next recorded remark, "Can't believe voluntariness irrelevant," indicates that he either waffled or simply did not distinguish between involuntariness and unwelcomeness as the appropriate standard. The chief justice also identified the "core question" as strict liability without signaling his stand on the issue.

As senior associate justice, Brennan would have spoken next. Republican Dwight Eisenhower had nominated Brennan to the Supreme Court in 1956. Although the appointment expanded Ike's electoral appeal, the liberal justice's voting record had not pleased the president, who, according to some accounts, rated the appointments of Brennan and former chief justice Earl Warren as two of his worst presidential mistakes. Serving until 1990, Justice Brennan was, by the mid-1980s, one of the dwindling band of more liberal justices remaining from the Warren Court.

Brennan's conference notes did not record his own words, but his views are outlined in his file memo. On the basic issue of actionability, Justice Brennan wrote that the "plaintiff need not establish loss of a tangible job benefit" but need only "establish that he or she was subject to pervasive, on-the-job harassment that created discriminatory working conditions." Because "the district court did not try the case under an environmental sexual harassment theory," even though Vinson's "proof would appear to support such a claim," Brennan "would affirm the court of appeals' remand of the case to the district court for reconsideration." Equally decisive on employer liability, he wrote that "an employer should be held strictly liable for sexual harassment by a supervisor, even where the employer has no notice of and does not authorize such unlawful conduct," reasoning that "the employer gives the supervisor the authority that allows the supervisor to harass the employee." He also observed that this view coincided with the EEOC's guidelines.

Brennan did not interpret the appellate court's opinion as excluding evidence that Vinson might have consented to sexual advances by her supervisor, but rather as barring only "evidence that respondent may have *succumbed* to any unwelcome advances made by her supervisor, or evidence of her dress or discussions with coworkers." Brennan concluded that "*under the circumstances of this case*, I believe that such evidence should have been excluded" as irrelevant. He concluded, "I would therefore affirm this part of the decision below, making sure to clarify our understanding of the court of appeals' ruling."

Next in seniority, Justice Byron White spoke. White was a 1962 Kennedy appointee and holdover from the Warren Court, but the wary tone in White's remarks comported with his more conservative reputation. He agreed that "environmental harassment theory is available" but thought that the court of appeals was wrong if it said "voluntariness was irrelevant." Instead, he "would say that unwelcome would preclude voluntariness." White also seemed to favor the bank on the critical issue of liability: "EEOC says employer not strictly liable & should require employee to use grievance procedures." But Brennan records him as being in accord with the judgment of the appeals court to reverse Judge Penn and remand: "So disagree with much said by Ct of Ap but would affirm reversal."

Lyndon Johnson had appointed Thurgood Marshall to the high bench in 1967. Before joining the Court, he had headed the NAACP's Legal Defense Fund for years, arguing the famous *Brown v. Board of Education* school desegregation case in 1954. Considered one of the most liberal justices, in this case, Justice Marshall simply indicated "Agree."

That simple sentiment is also all Brennan recorded for Justice Harry Blackmun. Nixon had appointed Blackmun to the Court in 1970, shortly after naming Burger chief justice. Fellow Minnesotans, Burger and Blackmun were longtime friends, and Blackmun had been best man at Burger's wedding. Despite Blackmun's solid conservative credentials and initial voting record, which substantially paralleled Burger's (the two were often irreverently referred to as "the Minnesota Twins"), he had written the Court's *Roe v. Wade* decision legalizing abortion, and as the Court had moved rightward in recent years, he found himself more frequently in the less conservative wing.

Lewis Powell spoke next. Appointed in 1972 by Nixon, he had a reputation of being a "lawyer's lawyer," a great stickler for procedure and legal proprieties, as well as the swing vote in the finely balanced

Burger Court. Justice Powell was the only justice Brennan recorded as voting to reverse the appeals court at this point: "Findings of DCt are against her & I wouldn't give her second bite at the apple. No finding was held erroneous clearly. No one corroborated her evidence. No strict liability either."

William Rehnquist had been an assistant attorney general when Nixon appointed him to the Supreme Court in 1972. One of the Court's most conservative jurists, Rehnquist would be appointed chief justice by President Reagan upon Burger's retirement later in 1986. Rehnquist made extensive comments: "Finding of voluntariness (if took place, were voluntary) doesn't answer environmental theory. On strict liability, if there's a system for complaining, can't hold bank liable. Her voluntariness is admissible. I'd let it go back for retrial with understanding I don't agree with much of Ct of Ap." Rehnquist's position echoed that of Justice White; though voting to affirm the appeals court's remand of the case for reconsideration under a hostile environment theory, Rehnquist took fundamental exception with much of the substance of the appeals court's opinion.

Justice John Paul Stevens spoke next. President Gerald Ford had appointed Stevens to the Court in 1975. He seemed inclined to side with Vinson's positions, agreeing that there must be a retrial and that "hostile environment theory is available to her." He was more forgiving of Vinson's failure to complain than were Rehnquist and several other justices: "Significance of system of grievance very important but doesn't automatically defeat claim—woman would have good reason not to complain."

Speaking last was Sandra Day O'Connor, the Court's newest member and its first woman, appointed by Reagan in 1981. Characteristically, Justice O'Connor staked out a centrist position, a stance that would become a trademark of her jurisprudence. She agreed to affirm the remand to retry the case under a hostile environment theory and thought that the district court "must determine whether conduct unwelcome, not voluntary." She supported Justice Stevens's view that the mere existence of a grievance system did not insulate the bank from liability: "Adequate complaint system is significant but not conclusive—depends on whether the ave. employee would use." But on the issue of admitting dress and fantasy evidence of welcomeness, she sided with Justice Rehnquist: "Her conduct was relevant."

The chief justice's "single most influential function," according to former justice Tom Clark, is the power to assign the authorship of opinions. The chief justice normally keeps a rough tally of positions expressed in conference and assigns the writing of the Court's opinion to a member who reflects the position of the majority (unless the chief justice finds himself in agreement with the minority, in which case the senior justice in the majority assigns the opinion-writing task). If a minority disagrees, the senior dissenting justice assigns one of that group to write a dissenting opinion. In this case, the job of writing the Court's opinion fell to Justice Rehnquist. No record indicates why Justice Powell, despite his initial objections, endorsed Rehnquist's opinion rather than dissenting. Although the Court's judgment favored Vinson in affirming the appeals court, Rehnquist shaped an opinion for the Court that managed to keep potential dissenter Powell on board. Before the decision was announced, however, it had drawn disagreement from the other wing of the Court.

———

The Opinion Takes Shape

Within a month, Justice Rehnquist had produced a draft opinion in the *Vinson* case that, without significant revision, won unanimous endorsement for much of its reasoning and for its ultimate judgment affirming the court of appeals' reversal and remand of the district court's decision. The first draft of Rehnquist's opinion, fifteen typewritten pages, was circulated to all justices on April 22, 1986.

The opinion crafted by Rehnquist put the Court on record for the first time as endorsing the conclusion that lower courts had increasingly been gravitating toward: that sexual harassment was indeed illegal sex discrimination under Title VII. Because the bank had not directly challenged the illegality of all types of sexual harassment, the issue was not technically at stake, but Justice Rehnquist put any doubt to rest: "Without question, when a supervisor sexually harasses a subordinate because of the subordinate's sex, that supervisor 'discriminate[s]' on the basis of sex." The bank had argued that Title VII prohibited only quid pro quo harassment that resulted in "tangible loss" of "an economic character" and "not purely psychological aspects of the workplace environment," but Rehnquist ruled in Vinson's favor on this threshold issue. He noted that Title VII not only spoke of economic or tangible discrimination but also included "terms, conditions, or privileges of employment," language that "evinces a congressional intent 'to strike at the entire spectrum of disparate treatment of men and women' in employment." Rehnquist relied heavily on the EEOC's guidelines that declared environmental harassment illegal when "such conduct has the purpose or effect of unreasonably interfering with an individual's work performance or creating an intimidating, hostile, or offensive working environment." Citing lower court decisions prohibiting hostile environments based on race and national origin, Rehnquist concluded that "nothing in Title VII suggests that a hostile environment based on discriminatory sexual harassment should not be likewise prohibited."

But again drawing on lower court opinions, Rehnquist also noted, "Not all workplace conduct that may be described as 'harassment' affects a 'term, condition, or privilege' of employment within the meaning of Title VII." For sexual harassment to be illegal, "it must be sufficiently severe or pervasive 'to alter the conditions of [the victim's] employment and create an abusive working environment.'" Rehnquist ruled that Vinson's allegations—"which include not only pervasive harassment but also criminal conduct of the most serious nature—are plainly sufficient to state a claim for 'hostile environment' sexual harassment." He held that "since it appears that the District Court made its findings without ever considering the 'hostile environment' theory of sexual harassment, the Court of Appeals decision to remand was correct."

Rehnquist endorsed a remand for a second reason. He noted that the district court's failure to find illegal sexual harassment rested on its assessment that if any sexual relationship had existed between Vinson and Taylor, it had been a "voluntary" one. Like the appeals court, Rehnquist rejected this voluntariness standard: "But the fact that sex-related conduct was 'voluntary,' in the sense that the complainant was not forced to participate against her will, is not a defense to a sexual harassment suit brought under Title VII. The gravamen of any sexual harassment claim is that the alleged sexual advances were 'unwelcome.'" Rehnquist phrased the test for determining whether sexual conduct amounts to illegal harassment as "whether respondent by her conduct indicated that the alleged sexual advances were unwelcome, not whether her actual participation in sexual intercourse was voluntary."

In view of his harsh questioning of Patricia Barry at oral arguments, the setback dealt to Vinson on defensive evidence by Rehnquist's opinion came as no surprise. "While 'voluntariness' in the sense of consent is not a defense to such a claim, it does not follow that a complainant's sexually provocative speech or dress is irrelevant as a matter of law in determining whether he or she found particular sexual advances unwelcome. To the contrary, such evidence is obviously relevant." Despite Vinson's argument that testimony about her dress and sexual fantasies was unduly prejudicial, Rehnquist endorsed the EEOC guidelines' injunction that the trier of fact should consider "the totality of circumstances" and concluded that the appeals court's holding that such evidence "had no place in this litigation" was too categorical and simply erroneous. Rather than a rule barring such evidence, Rehnquist wrote that the decision on admissibility is properly one for trial courts, where judges can weigh the relative prejudice against the relevance of such evidence in the particular circumstances of each case.

On the critical issue of employer liability for sexual harassment, the opinion equivocated. Rehnquist discussed with approval the position taken by the EEOC's amicus brief suggesting that agency principles would not impute automatic liability to employers for hostile environment sexual harassment. Rehnquist acknowledged "some tension" between the EEOC's brief and its own guidelines, which held employers liable for their supervisors' sexual harassment regardless of notice, but he agreed with the EEOC's suggestion "that Congress wanted courts to look to agency principles for guidance in this area." In an ironic twist on Vinson's claim that Title VII defined an employer to include its agents, Rehnquist applied agency principles to deduce that the statute's use of the term *agents* implied a congressional intent "to place some limits on the acts of employees for which employers under Title VII are to be held responsible," presumably, only actions undertaken as agents, not for themselves personally.

Noting that many factual issues remained unresolved, giving the record a "rather abstract quality" in this case, the opinion said that the Court would "decline the parties' invitation to issue a definitive rule on employer liability." Although not spelling out precisely what he meant by the admonition to "look to agency principles for guidance in this area," Rehnquist ruled out several positions. In a major setback for Vinson, the opinion held that the appeals court "erred in concluding that employers are always automatically liable for sexual harassment by their supervisors." But Rehnquist also rejected the bank's position that "the mere existence of a grievance procedure and a policy against discrimination, coupled with respondent's failure to invoke that procedure, must insulate petitioner from liability." He noted that the bank's general nondiscrimination policies failed to address sexual harassment and that the reporting procedure began with the aggrieved employee's supervisor, the alleged harasser. Had the procedures been "better calculated to encourage victims of harassment to come forward," Meritor's argument would have been stronger.

Rehnquist's opinion concluded with the complex holdings of the Court: "In sum, we hold that a claim of 'hostile environment' sex discrimination is actionable under Title VII, that the District Court's findings were insufficient to dispose of respondent's hostile environment claim, and that the District Court did not err in admitting testimony about respondent's sexually provocative speech and dress. As to employer liability, we conclude that the Court of Appeals was wrong to disregard agency principles and impose absolute liability on employers for the acts of their supervisors, regardless of the circumstances of a particular case." The Court affirmed the judgment of the court of appeals reversing the judgment of the district court and remanded the case for "further proceedings consistent with this opinion."

––––––––

Concurrence: Disagreement within the Consensus

Despite his initial inclination to dissent, Justice Powell was the first to sign on to Rehnquist's opinion. On April 28, he sent a brief but formal letter, following the Court's customary practice, endorsing the draft opinion: "Dear Bill: Please join me. Sincerely, Lewis."

Although no justice dissented from the decision to affirm the appeals court's judgment, Justice Rehnquist's position on employer liability did split the Court. Justice Marshall's notation on Rehnquist's April 22 draft reads "Join??? But wait!!!" Soon, more formal disagreement was being expressed in a flurry of letters among several justices, each with "Copies to the Conference" to keep their colleagues on the Court abreast of the evolving deliberations. On April 24, Justice Stevens wrote to Rehnquist about his "serious reservations" concerning the draft's position on employer liability. Citing statutory law, agency principles, and practical considerations, he favored a rule that "the employer is strictly liable for the conduct of the supervisor concerning the environment and the employees that are directly under his or her supervision."

Later that day, Justice Rehnquist replied by letter that he was "willing to make a sixth vote, but not a fifth one" for Stevens's position; that is, he would change his draft only if a majority of the justices favored absolute employer liability. Rehnquist maintained that his draft position was aligned with "the normal principles of agency law" and commented, "I would think the draft would already satisfy you."

Also on April 24, Justice Brennan weighed in with a brief "Dear Bill" note to inform Rehnquist that he shared Stevens's reservations and urged Rehnquist to "consider accommodating this concern." Justice Marshall's one-sentence note on May 1 was more pointed: "I agree with John and Bill Brennan on the question of employer liability, and therefore cannot join your opinion as it is now written."

Despite these indications of growing disagreement among the justices, Rehnquist circulated a virtually unchanged second draft of his opinion on May 5. The only modification to the text was the insertion of the word "entirely" in characterizing the appeals court's disregard for agency principles. His conclusion now read: "As to employer liability, we conclude that the Court of Appeals was wrong to entirely disregard agency principles and impose absolute liability on employers for the acts of their supervisors, regardless of the circumstances of a particular case." Rather than accommodating the Stevens-Brennan-Marshall group, the simple one-word addition seemed to indicate a hardening of his position that the appeals court's rule of strict employer liability was at odds with agency principles.

On May 8, Rehnquist's opinion won the assent of Justice O'Connor, and on May 19, Justice White also wrote to Rehnquist, "Please join me." A simple "I join" on May 27 from Chief Justice Burger assured a majority for Rehnquist's opinion. But the next day, opposition jelled as Marshall notified Rehnquist in a curt note: "In due course, I shall circulate a dissent in this one."

Because he agreed with the Court's decision to remand, Marshall scrapped his dissent in favor of a concurring opinion that took issue with Rehnquist's analysis of employer liability. By June 6, Justice Marshall was circulating his concurrence, writing separately to "answer today the question the Court leaves to another day," namely, "the circumstances in which an employer is responsible under Title VII for sexual harassment in the workplace." Marshall's position rested heavily not on the EEOC's brief but rather on the agency's 1980 guidelines, which held employers liable for violations of their agents or supervisors while allowing employers' lack of knowledge of the misconduct to insulate them from liability for harassment only by coworkers. Title VII discrimination is generally effected through the actions of individuals and rarely is discrimination "carried out pursuant to a formal vote of a corporation's board of directors." Yet Title VII remedies, like those of labor law under the National Labor Relations Act, hold the employer as an entity accountable.

Marshall took issue with the government-EEOC brief's contention that supervisors exercised their employers' authority only when making personnel decisions. He insisted that supervisors also are "charged with the day-to-day supervision of the work environment and with ensuring a safe, productive workplace," making it reasonable to hold employers accountable when their supervisors make that work environment hostile. Although Marshall acknowledged that both the purposes of Title VII and agency principles supported some limitations on employers' liability for the acts of their supervisors—for example, when the harassing supervisor had no authority over the complainant because they worked in different departments—he maintained that neither Title VII nor agency law warranted a special notice rule for hostile environment sexual harassment that excused employers from liability until they were notified of such harassment by the victims.

Nor would the existence of grievance procedures alter the general rule of employer responsibility for supervisory misconduct. If the complaint were exclusively about hostile environment, the remedy would be injunctive relief, which the employer could avoid by curing the problem after EEOC notification of the charge during the conciliation period. If the plaintiff sought back pay, alleging that she had resigned to avoid the hostile environment, amounting to constructive discharge, the availability of company grievance procedures might affect not the company's liability but the remedies granted. If the plaintiff had failed to use complaint procedures without good reason, a court might be reluctant to grant either reinstatement or back pay, Marshall suggested. In contrast to the majority's reluctance to adopt a firm rule and its vague direction to "look to agency principles," Marshall stressed the simple rule that he believed the law supported: "I would apply in this case the same rules we apply in all other Title VII cases, and hold that sexual harassment by a supervisor of an employee under his supervision, leading to a discriminatory work environment, should be imputed to the employer for Title VII purposes regardless of whether the employee gave 'notice' of the offense."

As Justices Stevens, Brennan, and Blackmun joined his concurrence, Marshall circulated two additional drafts, adding the cosigners' names and making explicit his agreement with the majority's decision that "workplace sexual harassment is illegal, and violates Title VII." The third draft of June 16 explained that Marshall had written separately because Rehnquist's opinion left open the issue of employer liability, a question squarely before the Court.

Justice Stevens filed a one-sentence concurrence circulated to the conference on June 13, explaining that he joined both Rehnquist's and Marshall's opinions: "Because I do not see any inconsistency between the two opinions, and because I believe the question of statutory construction that Justice Marshall has answered is fairly presented by the record, I join both the Court's opinion and Justice Marshall's opinion."

Decision Day

On June 19, 1986, the Supreme Court announced its decision in *Meritor Savings Bank v. Vinson*, affirming the ruling of the Court of Appeals for the D.C. Circuit. The Court's opinion, given by Justice Rehnquist, and the two concurring opinions entered by Justices Marshall and Stevens were published as slip opinions, temporary copies immediately available to the press and the legal community until the opinion can be published in various "reporters," including the official *United States*

Reports, which records all opinions of the U.S. Supreme Court. The clerk of the Supreme Court, Joseph F. Spaniol Jr., entered the formal order in case number 84-1979: "ON CONSIDERATION WHEREOF, it is ordered and adjudged by this court that the judgment of the United States Court of Appeals for the District of Columbia in this cause is affirmed and that this cause is remanded to the United States Court of Appeals for the District of Columbia Circuit for further proceedings in conformity with the opinion of this Court."

Assessments of the Supreme Court's decision in *Vinson* varied widely, as they still do. Pat Barry "loved it," although she expressed some surprise that Rehnquist had written "that beautiful opinion." The *Washington Post* hailed the decision "a major victory for working women" and found "particularly welcome" the role of Justice Rehnquist, who two days before had been nominated as chief justice by President Reagan. Rehnquist's opinion gratified civil rights advocates, who had rarely found the conservative justice siding with them, and women's groups praised the decision. Eleanor Smeal, president of NOW, pointed out that *Vinson* "states definitively, for the first time, that sex harassment is discrimination and that it is definitely illegal." NOW attorney Kathy Bonk suggested that the ruling would strengthen the organization's hand in negotiating preventive measures with industry, which had taken a wait-and-see attitude after the Supreme Court had agreed to review the case. "What we can do now is say, 'okay gang, you have got to do it, read this decision.'" Legal scholars, too, deemed the decision a huge step forward. Cass Sunstein pointed out that although her arguments had seemed "bizarre and radical to many when initially put forward" in 1978, "remarkably, MacKinnon's basic position was accepted in 1986 by every member of the Supreme Court." Henry Chambers, though noting that it had taken thirteen years (since the first sexual harassment cases were filed) for the Supreme Court to announce authoritatively and definitively that sexual harassment violated Title VII's prohibition on sex discrimination, still judged the accomplishment nothing less than a paradigm shift, a major reconstitution of the way the law and, indeed, society viewed the problem of sexual harassment.

Others viewed the outcome more circumspectly. The *Washington Post* noted that Rehnquist's opinion had "sustained an interpretation of the statute that had been favored by the government" and had struck "a middle ground between the trial judge and an appeals court ruling."

Employer groups judged the decision as "substantially better for business than the appeals court opinion," and a Chamber of Commerce spokesperson suggested that the decision held "something for everyone." The bank's legal team was pleased with the decision, believing that it had won on two out of three issues (evidence of unwelcomeness and employer liability), losing only on the one it had never expected to win: whether hostile environment sexual harassment, "without more," is prohibited by Title VII. Bob Troll approved the decision's grounding in solid legal rules of agency and evidence. Charles Fleischer felt that the Court had "ducked" on the liability issue. But at the very least, even if the bank had not clearly won on this issue, which was its chief concern, neither had it lost. Furthermore, the Supreme Court's direction to "look to agency principles" in resolving liability would be applied in a forum, the federal district court in Washington, that was friendly terrain for the bank.

On Remand

The case was remanded to the D.C. court of appeals, which on October 14, 1986, remanded it to Judge Penn. At this point, both sides made substitutions in their legal teams. Meritor Bank replaced the twenty-seven-lawyer firm Ross, Marsh & Foster with Proskauer, Rose, Goetz & Mendelsohn, a large, prominent New York firm that represented the bank's parent company. Bob Troll, who had represented the bank from the beginning of the suit, left the case, continuing to practice law in suburban Maryland. Sidney Taylor's attorney, Karen Woodson, had moved to Atlanta, and defendant Taylor played virtually no role in the proceedings on remand. Patricia Barry, who had represented Vinson since June 1979, had moved to California in 1982. The burden of the *Vinson* case, which she referred to as her "personal Vietnam" because of its seemingly endless drain on the resources of her legal practice, had finally become too much, and she withdrew from the case when it was remanded. Barry filed for bankruptcy in February 1988, saying, "civil rights has destroyed me." Vinson, too, had filed for bankruptcy in 1980 and had returned to live with her parents. By 1986, she was working part-time as a temporary employee in a holistic health center. She also attempted a career switch, studying nursing at Marymount University in Arlington, Virginia, but eventually dropped out because of finances. To continue the case, she set up a Mechelle Vinson Defense Fund to receive donations, but she needed attorneys who could bear the burden of pursuing the case without requiring her to pay for ongoing expenses. Assuming the role as her legal representatives in February 1987 were Geoffrey Vitt and Joseph Sellers of the Washington Committee for Civil Rights Under Law, a group of volunteer attorneys that had played a prominent role in the struggle for desegregation in the South.

The sparring on remand proceeded at an agonizingly slow pace as the parties maneuvered to influence Judge Penn's conception of the remaining tasks necessary to decide the case, now guided by the Supreme Court's opinion. The remand merely ordered "further proceedings in conformity with the opinion of this Court," leaving much to the judge's discretion. The parties debated the issues to be reconsidered and the appropriate legal standards governing these issues, but their primary disagreements centered on what evidence would be needed. Vinson's attorneys wanted to fortify the factual basis of her claims now that the Supreme Court had given her a more favorable legal framework for assessing that evidence. They argued for a new trial to allow other bank employees to testify that the environment was hostile and that Taylor's conduct was unwelcome. They also sought to enter new evidence on the bank's liability. Meritor's attorneys, in contrast, attempted to contain the scope of new evidence, arguing that a new trial was unnecessary because Judge Penn had sufficient information to rule on all issues. They advocated that Penn simply review the factual evidence already on record in light of the legal standards upheld by the Supreme Court and make a judgment.

New motions reflected these strategies shaped by the Supreme Court's ruling. On December 12, 1986, before she withdrew from the case, Patricia Barry made a third attempt to amend Vinson's original complaint to add claims of intentional infliction of emotional distress, breach of an implicit contract, and negligent supervision. By adding these claims, Vinson could ask for relief in the form of compensatory and punitive damages beyond the equitable remedies such as reinstatement and back pay available under Title VII. She asked for $1.5 million each from the bank and Taylor. The plaintiff noted that the considerations that had led Judge Penn to deny earlier attempts to amend the complaint no longer applied, since no trial date was now pending.

Beyond opposing the new claims as too late and unfairly prejudicial to its interests, on January 12, 1987, Meritor responded with a motion asking Judge Penn to forgo a new trial and simply enter judgment based on amended findings of fact and conclusions of law, taking into account the new legal standards clarified by the Supreme Court. The plaintiff answered by noting that Judge Penn had never clearly decided even essential facts, for example, whether Taylor had engaged in sex with Vinson, and by arguing that the new legal standards enunciated by the high court required new evidentiary hearings. Evidence of sexual harassment would now be judged by whether a hostile environment existed at the Northeast branch, and the Supreme Court's standard of unwelcomeness rather than involuntariness was now the yardstick to measure hostile environment. Although the Supreme Court had not ruled out evidence of dress and fantasies, the plaintiff asked Judge Penn to exclude this testimony because it was more prejudicial than probative. To apply the agency principles mandated by the Supreme Court, the judge needed to hear more evidence on whether the bank had made available reasonable avenues for Vinson to report her abuse.

Penn, reputedly decisive in making in-court rulings but excessively slow in resolving out-of-court motions, took months to rule on Meritor's motion. In March 1987, the plaintiff filed a supplemental memo informing the judge of surprising new information: Sidney Taylor had recently been convicted on seventeen counts of embezzling from Meritor Bank and had received a sentence of eighteen to fifty-six months in jail. His crimes would be admissible in terms of weighing his credibility in denying that he had sexually harassed Vinson. The bank disputed whether Taylor's conduct ten years after the events at issue in the lawsuit was relevant and charged that the plaintiff was seeking to retry the case in its entirety. In November 1987, Barry, no longer actively involved but with a financial stake in the case, asked the appeals court to rule that Judge Penn was taking reprisals against her and Vinson by delaying his rulings in the proceedings.

At the end of February 1989, Judge Penn granted the plaintiff's attorneys' request, made the previous October, to discover new evidence on unwelcomeness and the harassment of other bank employees. Despite ongoing objections by bank attorneys, during the summer of 1989, Vinson's attorneys took depositions from Taylor, who had been paroled in March, in which he supposedly admitted that Vinson had dressed appropriately except on two occasions, that she had done nothing to suggest that his sexual advances would be welcome or that she would like to have sex with him, and that he had read *Playboy* and *Hustler* at the bank, but only for the articles. They also deposed witnesses who testified that Vinson's dress and behavior had been entirely professional when they had visited the Northeast branch, as well as a local dry cleaner who swore that he knew that Taylor was sexually harassing other female bank employees and that he had passed on money from Taylor to a neighborhood woman rumored to have had twins by Taylor. Not surprisingly, the bank argued that this kind of testimony was duplicative or mere hearsay.

On August 15, 1989, Judge Penn finally ruled on several pending motions. He denied Vinson's third request to amend her complaint. To permit the new claims would be "to allow the plaintiff to retry the entire case," an outcome inconsistent with the Supreme Court's limited remand. He also rejected Meritor's request that he dispense with a trial and simply amend his original opinion and enter judgment on the record, but he ordered that discovery be restricted to new witnesses and matters related to the two issues on remand—hostile environment and unwelcomeness.

Vinson's attorneys quickly moved for the court to reconsider its rulings, arguing that four issues required more information for a decision by Penn: Taylor's harassment of other women, the unwelcomeness of his advances, Vinson's dress and behavior, and Meritor's liability. They noted that the Supreme Court itself had observed that its failure to elucidate employer liability standards was the result of an inadequate factual record. A year later, Judge Penn summarily denied this request. Meanwhile, Bettina Plevan, the lead attorney for the bank, complained that Vinson's attorneys were conducting "extreme discovery" and proposed that the court bifurcate the issues, postponing discovery on employer liability until after ruling on the underlying sexual harassment charge. Unless Judge Penn reversed his findings against Vinson on the sexual harassment charge, he would not need to consider evidence on the question of the bank's liability. Vinson's attorneys opposed this suggestion, arguing that evidence might be lost by further postponing discovery. Without ruling on the bifurcation proposal, in March 1991, Judge Penn set the trial for October 22, 1991, and tentatively scheduled a second hearing on employer liability for December 3, 1991, if he later decided to bifurcate that issue.

<hr />

Resolution

That spring, both sides submitted memos outlining their positions for the trial, but before the trial date that fall, the parties settled the case out of court. The terms of the settlement are closed and remain secret to this day, because the parties and the attorneys are legally bound not to discuss the details of the agreement. Since the usual expectation is that companies prefer to settle claims before the adverse publicity of a trial, a settlement at this late date was somewhat puzzling. The various metamorphoses of the bank's ownership may have affected its calculations of the relative costs and benefits of continuing the litigation. Other developments during the remand period may have inclined the bank to settle. The Civil Rights Act of 1991, on the verge of passing, authorized compensatory and punitive damages for victims of discrimination prohibited by Title VII, raising the prospect of a larger monetary judgment against the bank should it be found liable in a retrial. Sidney Taylor's conviction for embezzlement would doubtless severely undermine his credibility, and his testimony, although not the bank's only hedge against liability, was surely its first line of defense.

From the plaintiff's perspective, the Supreme Court's decision allowing evidence of Vinson's dress and sexual fantasies kept the door open to challenging her character on retrial. She would have to endure the humiliation of having her sexual conduct, thoughts, and ethics, actual or invented, aired not only in the courtroom but also in the media, which could be expected to cover the trial more extensively because of the case's post–Supreme Court visibility. Already, the *Washington Post* had reported that Vinson's former boyfriend — a coworker whom she claimed was bisexual and had had a sexual encounter of his own with Taylor after a beer-drinking contest at the office — said that Vinson and other plaintiff witnesses had concocted the sexual harassment charges to make money, that "these are just totally malicious lies." Beyond the psychological costs of continuing the litigation, the

financial drain of a trial would be considerable, and although the 1991
Civil Rights Act held out hope for a damage award if she eventually
won, this would be severely limited by caps imposed on the amounts
awarded.

For whatever combination of reasons, the parties settled on August
22, 1991. Sixteen years after the alleged sexual harassment commenced, and thirteen years after Vinson filed her lawsuit, the long litigation was over. Judge Penn signed the stipulation and agreement
between the parties "that this action be dismissed in its entirety with
prejudice [with finality] and without costs or attorney's fees to any
party." Although the case can be considered a major achievement for
the women's movement in some respects, and at least a partial triumph
for employers in others, it is difficult to imagine that any of the parties directly involved could deem the results an unvarnished victory
for themselves.

CHAPTER 5

Filling the Gaps

Evolving Issues in the Wake of *Vinson*

Although the Court's *Meritor Savings Bank v. Vinson* opinion answered many questions about the illegality of sexual harassment, it left open many others, and many of its dictates have required clarification by lower courts and later opinions. Professor Rebecca Hanner White registers several important points that the *Vinson* opinion left unresolved:

> whether conduct of a sexual nature was unwelcome, whether such conduct was severe or pervasive enough to support a claim, whether severity or pervasiveness should be judged by a subjective or an objective standard, whether a "reasonable person" or a "reasonable woman" standard should govern assessment of severity or pervasiveness, whether a victim must establish psychological harm, and importantly, under which circumstances an employer may be held liable for sexual harassment engaged in by supervisors, coworkers, or even customers.

Critics assert that these unresolved issues reflect the Court's ambivalence toward sexual harassment's illegality, charging that although courts have opened the door to sexual harassment suits, they relegate them to the "back door" because courts harbor "unspoken disapproval" of these claims. Since 1986, this tension and new questions that were not raised in Mechelle Vinson's lawsuit have elicited new statutes, a spate of lower court decisions, and eventually new rulings by the Supreme Court itself. The complex and contested consequences of this legal evolution, debated in the media, public dialogues, and myriad law reviews, merit an examination of the broad outlines of the train of legal developments set in motion by *Vinson*.

Civil Rights Act of 1991

In its 1989 term, the Supreme Court decided eight employment discrimination cases with opinions unfavorable to the plaintiffs. In its notable *Price Waterhouse v. Hopkins* decision, the Court held that when the motives for adverse employment actions were "mixed," including some discriminatory animus as well as some legal considerations, an employer would not be liable for the negative decision if it could demonstrate that it would have made the same decision had it acted only on nondiscriminatory grounds. Thus, Price Waterhouse could defend against liability for failing to make Ann Hopkins a partner, a decision based partly on sexist stereotyping, if it could show that it would have denied her a partnership in any event based on her lack of interpersonal skills or other nondiscriminatory considerations. Another decision that drew critics' fire was *Wards Cove Packing Co. v. Atonio.* By raising the hurdles that plaintiffs had to overcome to prove that business practices inadvertently but systematically disadvantaged applicants or employees on the basis of race or other statuses protected by Title VII, the Court's opinion in this case reduced the viability of "disparate impact" discrimination suits. In *Patterson v. McLean Credit Union*, the Court narrowed the reach of Section 1981 of a Reconstruction-era civil rights statute, holding that the 1866 law's prohibition of racial discrimination applied only to contract formation and enforcement, not to discriminatory treatment in employment after a contract had been established. These rulings, decried by many in Congress, provided the impetus to pass a revision to the Civil Rights Act of 1964 that had been lingering in the legislature, stymied by partisan disagreement. Enacted as the Civil Rights Act of 1991, several amendments specifically reversed aspects of the Court's 1989 employment decisions.

Rewriting the *Hopkins* holding, Congress made employers liable if discrimination played any part in adverse employment decisions, allowing the employer's "same decision" defense to mitigate damages but not to serve as a defense against liability itself. This seemingly technical adjustment had important practical ramifications; even if a "same decision" defense limited the amount of money damages awarded for the injury of adverse employment decisions, a finding of liability would allow plaintiffs to recover attorneys' fees, noticeably increasing the fiscal feasibility of suing in mixed-motive cases.

Congress also dramatically reconfigured the types of relief available to successful plaintiffs in employment discrimination cases. Under the 1964 act, only equitable remedies were available, typically declaratory judgments (finding liability but awarding only nominal damages), injunctions (orders to cease and desist illegal acts or to remedy the discrimination, including by reinstating or promoting the plaintiff), and back pay. Equitable relief aims to make the injured parties whole, but it has defects as a deterrent or remedy for workplace discrimination. Often the victims do not want their jobs back, or restoring them by court order to already poisoned job positions would be untenable. Back pay was crimped by plaintiffs' obligation to mitigate damages by seeking other work, with the wages earned deducted from the amount owed by employers. Front pay, compensation for lost future income that would have been earned at the plaintiff's original job but for the discrimination, is sometimes available, such as when hostility or lack of an open position makes reinstatement impractical. But front pay is an uncertain remedy, and the Supreme Court did not explicitly rule that it was available in instances of sexual harassment until the 2001 case of *Pollard v. E. I. DuPont de Nemours & Co.*

The 1991 act added to this tool kit of remedies by authorizing compensatory and punitive damages in instances of intentional employment discrimination. Compensatory damages compensate victims for ancillary harms arising from the discrimination. After 1991, plaintiffs could recover for humiliation, emotional pain and suffering, physical distress, medical expenses, damage to professional reputation, and other economic and noneconomic injuries caused by employment discrimination. The purpose of making this relief available was to compensate victims more realistically for the wide-ranging injuries beyond immediate job harms that employment discrimination produces. The act also authorized punitive damages, essentially fines imposed on lawbreakers to punish them for their wrongdoing and to deter all employers from future discriminatory acts. In deference to business interests, especially small enterprises, Congress capped the amount of damages according to company size, ranging from a low of $50,000 for companies with 15 to 100 employees up to $300,000 for large companies with more than 500 employees.

This enhanced damages scheme was buttressed by the provision that either party in employment discrimination cases could obtain a jury trial on demand. Title VII had not afforded claimants a right to a jury trial, and most employment discrimination cases had been bench trials, with judges functioning as fact-finders. Plaintiffs are usually the ones who seek jury trials, reasoning that juries are more likely to favor employee-plaintiffs' claims, while judges are more likely to be sympathetic to employer-defendants. This estimate is based on demographics and life experiences. Judges, especially in the federal judiciary, are generally drawn from elite strata, tending to be disproportionately white, male, and older. They share backgrounds and business and social connections with employers, and they have typically acted as employers themselves in their capacities as partners or co-owners of law firms. These experiences and associations doubtlessly influence their perspectives and sympathies. Juries, in contrast, are drawn from pools reflecting the population, and virtually all jurors are or have been employees. Data seem to confirm attorneys' hunches: a study of job-related civil rights cases pegged plaintiff win rates at 20 percent in bench trials but 39 percent with juries.

The Civil Rights Act of 1991 thus upped the economic ante and improved the odds of plaintiffs prevailing in employment discrimination lawsuits. The impact of the legislation, although augmented by contemporaneous events such as the Hill-Thomas hearings, was immense and almost immediate. The average verdict in sexual harassment cases between 1988 and 1992 was $181,847, but for 1993, it was $250,000. The number of sexual harassment suits rose correspondingly, nearly doubling from 6,892 in 1991 to 12,537 in 1993, and increasing without abatement until the late 1990s. These statistics indicate that Congress achieved its objective of improving enforcement of antidiscrimination laws by increasing the incentives of individual plaintiffs to sue.

Proving Unwelcomeness

One of the more controversial issues in the aftermath of *Vinson* has been the unwelcomeness standard for finding that sexual conduct is harassment. The high court held that the test for harassment is not that the sexual conduct was involuntary but rather that it was unwelcome. This holding was tempered by the Court's allowing lower courts to decide what evidence to admit, including testimony about plaintiffs' dress and sexual fantasies. Critics charge that the unwelcomeness requirement has operated as a double-edged sword, often putting plaintiffs' character and behavior on trial alongside defendants.

Defenders of the unwelcomeness standard argue that it is necessary to ensure that consensual sex, for example, a relationship that later goes sour, does not become the basis of suits. Unwelcomeness distinguishes harassing behavior from conduct reflecting the sexual attraction that plays a role in day-to-day social interactions between men and women, including in the workplace. In *Vinson*, Meritor Bank and the government had argued that sexual behavior is natural, pervasive, and "legally neutral," making sexual conduct different from racial, religious, or ethnic slurs that are intrinsically offensive. This special character of sex requires an explicit welcomeness test to determine whether sexual banter and advances are innocuous flirting or malevolent harassment.

Following Rehnquist's injunction in *Vinson* that "the correct inquiry is whether respondent by her conduct indicated that the alleged sexual advances were unwelcome," EEOC policy guidance places the burden on the complainant to affirmatively communicate that such conduct is unwelcome and advises investigators to look for objective evidence of unwelcomeness. The guidance notes that a complainant's use of sexually explicit language does not necessarily negate a claim that she did not welcome sexual conduct, but it cites cases in which courts found such language to be evidence of willing participation in sexualized work environments or relationships. Adopting the definition of unwelcomeness developed by the Eleventh Circuit in *Henson v. City of Dundee*, most courts consider unwelcome any conduct that the employee regards as "undesirable or offensive" and "did not solicit or incite," although some substitute "invite" for "incite."

Critics note serious problems with treating unwelcomeness as "the gravamen of any sexual harassment claim," as Rehnquist described it. At a minimum, the requirement places the burden on the target rather than the harasser to establish whether the conduct is unwelcome or welcome, a weight falling on the less powerful party. Critics see proof of unwelcomeness as unnecessary and redundant; welcome harassment is an oxymoron. Racial, religious, or ethnic harassment is regarded as self-evidently unwelcome. The standard itself is vague, predictably and irresistibly shifting the spotlight from the defendant to the plaintiff, who is victimized again in court as her privacy is invaded by embarrassingly public examinations of her dress, sexual fantasies, language, mannerisms, and sexual history. Underlying these specific problems, critics contend, is a subtle but malignant masculinist perspective that views macho sexual aggressiveness as natural and universal, the workplace as a sexualized venue like others where men and women interact, and male sexual initiatives as innocuous and desirable unless clearly refused by females.

Proposals for altering the unwelcomeness requirement to remedy these faults range from simply eliminating the requirement altogether to substituting different standards. One suggested substitute would ask whether the conduct was "unilaterally imposed" rather than unwelcome, a test that would differentiate consensual behavior from harassment but focus on explicit consent while excluding evidence of supposedly implicit invitations for sex. Another approach, advocated by critic Mary Radford, proposes modifying the application of the requirement rather than abolishing it entirely. Retaining a sharp definition of welcomeness as solicited sexual conduct could avoid adopting implicit invitation as the standard and perpetuating the worn-out stereotype that when a woman says no, she really means yes. Focusing on explicit welcomeness would also prevent courts from shifting attention from specific behavior to whether the plaintiff is the kind of person who would generally object to such conduct, a broad inquiry that opens wide the plaintiff's lifestyle and personal history for judicial evaluation of her character.

Radford also proposes narrowing the scope of admissible evidence. Despite federal rules of evidence that allow judges to exclude evidence that is more prejudicial than probative and the extension of rape shield law to sexual harassment cases, excluding the sexual history of victims, the *Vinson* opinion's refusal to categorically rule out some forms of evidence in considering unwelcomeness and the lower courts' wide latitude in deciding relevance threaten to expose plaintiffs to wide-ranging examinations of their sexual attitudes and behavior. Plaintiffs' sexual conduct outside the workplace is of dubious relevance, and even at work, conduct beyond the interaction of plaintiffs and defendants has little bearing on the welcomeness of the alleged harassment. For example, a plaintiff's willingness to date another coworker has little probative value about her welcoming an invitation, let alone pressure, for a romantic relationship with the defendant. At the very least, limiting evidence about plaintiffs' sexual attitudes and behavior to information the defendants actually had knowledge of would guard against embarrassing intrusions into plaintiffs' privacy and focus on whether the defendants could have reasonably believed that their conduct was welcome.

Radford would also shift the burden of proof to defendants to show that their conduct was welcome, rather than requiring plaintiffs to prove unwelcomeness. Evidence of ambiguous reactions, such as merely mild, polite objections or silence, would not suffice to rebut the harassment charge without proof presented by the defendant that the plaintiff welcomed his conduct. This scheme of proof, corresponding with the allocation of burden in other discrimination claims, would not saddle sexual harassment targets with special requirements not borne by victims in other employment litigation.

"Sufficiently Severe or Pervasive": Whose Perspective Counts?

One phrase in the Court's *Vinson* opinion that raised as many questions as it answered was the requirement that to be actionable, sexual harassment must be "sufficiently severe or pervasive" to "alter the conditions of [the victim's] employment and create an abusive working environment." Judges have varied widely in their assessment of whether defendants' conduct was sufficiently severe or pervasive to constitute illegal sexual harassment. Despite a popular perception that telling an off-color joke at the water cooler or asking a coworker out socially is sufficient to incur a sexual harassment lawsuit, court records are replete with shocking misdeeds that hampered women's equal economic opportunities yet were dismissed as not severe or pervasive enough to be illegal. In one of the most egregious examples, *Rabidue v. Osceola Refining Co.*, the court found no hostile environment even though the workplace contained posters of naked and partially dressed women and a male employee customarily referred to "whores," "cunt," "pussy," and "tits." He called the plaintiff "fat ass" and stated that "all that bitch needs is a good lay." Despite a vigorous dissent, the majority held that this atmosphere had only a "*de minimis* effect" without seriously harming the plaintiff's psychological well-being.

A related issue is the perspective from which to assess whether sexual misconduct is "sufficiently severe or pervasive" to provide grounds for a lawsuit. *Vinson*'s adoption of the EEOC definition of sexual harassment ruled out the extreme subjectivity of some definitions (for example, sexual conduct that merely offends the plaintiff), but the problem remained: "sufficiently severe or pervasive" according to whose standards? Law often adopts the perspective of a hypothetical "reasonable person" to avoid subjectivity and hypersensitivity. A quandary for sexual harassment law, however, is engendered by evidence that men and women have divergent views about what conduct at work is reasonable and what is sexual harassment. A 1980–1981 study found that 67 percent of men would be complimented by a proposition from a female coworker, but only 17 percent of the women surveyed would be similarly flattered. Despite more recent analyses questioning the significance of male-female disparities in sexual harassment assessments, the worry arises that the "reasonable person" standard actually reflects the male perspective, even if stated more inclusively than the traditional "reasonable man" legal norm.

To guard against this problem, some jurist scholars have advocated substituting a "reasonable woman" or "reasonable victim" standard. In 1991, the Ninth Circuit Court of Appeals adopted a reasonable woman standard in *Ellison v. Brady.* Plaintiff Kerry Ellison sued her employer, the IRS, for failing to prevent what she considered sexually harassing behavior by fellow agent Sterling Gray. After having lunch with Gray once (a common practice in the office), Ellison complained that he pestered her with unnecessary questions and hung around her desk. When he asked her out for a drink, she declined, suggesting lunch the following week instead. When he asked her to lunch, she refused. Soon thereafter, Gray handed her a note reading: "I cried over you last night and I'm totally drained today. I have never been in such constant term oil [*sic*]. Thank you for talking with me. I could not stand to feel your hatred for another day." While Ellison was out of state for training, she received a three-page letter from Gray that included some odd passages: "I have enjoyed you so much over these past few months.

Watching you. Experiencing you from O so far away. . . . Don't you think it odd that two people who have never even talked together, alone, are striking off such intense sparks? . . . I will [write] another letter in the near future." Gray added, however, "I am obligated to you so much that if you want me to leave you alone I will." Do Gray's unaccepted but persistent invitations and strange notes constitute sexual misconduct "sufficiently severe and pervasive" to judge his behavior illegal sexual harassment? Or are his approaches to Ms. Ellison merely inept, annoying, and misguided attempts to woo a coworker?

The Ninth Circuit's majority believed that Gray's conduct was sufficiently severe or pervasive to sustain Ellison's suit, noting that conduct considered unobjectionable by many men may offend many women:

> We realize that there is a broad range of viewpoints among women as a group, but we believe that many women share common concerns which men do not necessarily share. For example, because women are disproportionately victims of rape and sexual assault, women have a stronger incentive to be concerned with sexual behavior. Women who are victims of mild forms of sexual harassment may understandably worry whether a harasser's conduct is merely a prelude to violent sexual assault. Men, who are rarely victims of sexual assault, may view sexual conduct in a vacuum without a full appreciation of the social setting or the underlying threat of violence that a woman may perceive.

Although recognizing the need "to shield employers from having to accommodate the idiosyncratic concerns of the rare hypersensitive employee," the court held that plaintiffs may sue when they allege conduct that a reasonable woman would consider sufficiently severe or pervasive to alter her work conditions and create an abusive working environment. Even though the reasonable woman standard might classify as illegal some behavior that harassers might not realize creates a hostile environment, to adopt a sex-blind reasonable person standard, the court determined, would be to accept a male-biased standard that ignores the experiences of women.

Critics reject this reasonable woman standard, beginning with the dissenting judge in *Ellison*, who found the standard ambiguous and at odds with the purposes of Title VII and preferred gender-neutral terms, possibly including "reasonable victim" or "reasonable target" in addition to "reasonable person." Critics note that women do not share a unitary perspective and charge that the "reasonable woman" standard may actually mask a white, middle-class, heterosexual perspective that neglects the experience of less-privileged women. Using this partial standard risks attributing to women certain innate viewpoints while neglecting male sexual harassment victims. Defenders of the reasonable person standard argue that it represents an objective and universal norm that is accessible to all judges and juries, employers and employees, and one that appeals to what humans hold in common.

Advocates of the reasonable woman standard warn that the objectivity claimed by the reasonable person norm cloaks a masculinist viewpoint. A reasonable woman standard would alert male judges and jurists that a reflex notion of reasonableness, defined through male experiences, is exactly what needs to be changed, and incorporating women's perspectives into the law would caution men sitting in judgment on claims made by female victims that they must apply standards other than their own gut intuitions. Professor Kathryn Abrams seeks to incorporate these criticisms into her defense of a reasonable person standard that would move beyond masculinist understandings of this term. She argues that the legal system's conception of a reasonable person must be distinguished from the average, flesh-and-blood person who embodies society's limitations as well as its common sense. The reasonable person must be considered the enlightened person, an abstract ideal that would inform judges and juries of the sexual inequalities still extant at work and in society, of the threat to women entailed in their sexualization — both directly and as a devaluation of women as workers — of the effects of sexual harassment on its targets and on the workplace, and of the realistic responses of women to sexual harassment. Such a revised notion of a reasonable person could provide achievable and generally applicable norms for judging sexual misconduct without bootlegging the perspectives and values of a sexist status quo into the legal standard. Another alternative formulation that seeks to avoid the either-or choice of reasonable person versus reasonable woman is the "reasonable victim" standard. This test judges the alleged harassment from the perspective of a reasonable person in the plaintiff's circumstances. Courts remain divided on which standard to use.

Although the Supreme Court has not spoken definitively on this issue, the debate has waned since *Harris v. Forklift Systems,* decided in 1993. Teresa Harris worked as a manager for Forklift for just over two years. Charles Hardy, the company's president, frequently insulted her and badgered her with unwanted sexual innuendos. On several occasions and in the presence of others, Hardy told Harris, "You're a woman, what do you know?" and "We need a man as the rental manager," and at least once he called her a "dumb ass woman." In addition to making lewd remarks about women's clothing, Hardy suggested that he and Harris "go to the Holiday Inn to negotiate your raise," asked her to retrieve coins from his pants pocket, and threw objects on the ground and asked Harris and other women to pick them up. After Harris complained to Hardy, he apologized and promised to desist, but when he made yet another demeaning sexual comment, Harris resigned. The trial court, although recognizing that Hardy's conduct "offended [Harris], and would offend the reasonable woman," refused to find that a hostile working environment existed because Harris's psychological well-being was not seriously affected.

The Supreme Court reversed this judgment, revisiting the issue of sexual harassment for only the second time, seven years after its initial landmark ruling in *Vinson.* The Court reaffirmed the "sufficiently severe or pervasive" requirement as taking "a middle path between making actionable any conduct that is merely offensive and requiring the conduct to cause a tangible psychological injury." Remarking that "Title VII comes into play before the harassing conduct leads to a nervous breakdown," Justice Sandra Day O'Connor, writing for a unanimous Court, asserted that harassment that does not seriously affect employees' psychological well-being "can and often will detract from employees' job performance, discourage employees from remaining on the job, or keep them from advancing in their careers." Holding that "so long as the environment would reasonably be perceived, and is perceived, as hostile or abusive, there is no need for it also to be psychologically injurious," the opinion fleshed out the meaning of "sufficiently severe or pervasive" by spelling out a two-pronged test: "Conduct that is not severe or pervasive enough to create an objectively hostile or abusive work environment — an environment that a reasonable person would find hostile or abusive — is beyond Title VII's purview. Likewise, if the victim does not subjectively perceive the environment to be abusive, the conduct has not actually altered the conditions of the victim's employment, and there is no Title VII violation." The *Harris* opinion, while admonishing the lower courts to look at "all the circumstances" to determine whether an environment is objectively hostile or abusive, listed several aspects of the allegedly harassing conduct that should be examined. These factors include "the frequency of the discriminatory conduct; its severity; whether it is physically threatening or humiliating, or a mere offensive utterance; and whether it unreasonably interferes with an employee's work performance." The Court recognized that "the effect on the employee's psychological well-being is, of course, relevant," but it concluded that although all relevant factors should be considered, "no single factor is required" to find a working environment hostile or abusive.

Elusive Agency Principles and Employer Liability

In *Vinson*, over the sharp objections of four justices represented by Marshall's concurrence, the majority refused to impose strict liability on employers for their supervisors' sexual harassment, but instead directed lower courts to "look to agency principles" in deciding employer liability. When turning to agency law for guidance in the years following *Vinson*, however, lower courts reached differing conclusions about how these principles applied in various situations. Because agents use authority delegated to them by their principals, agency law holds that principals are liable for the misdeeds of their agents who are acting within the scope of their employment. Principals are not responsible for their agents' misconduct when they are acting outside the scope of their employment unless, among other provisos, the agents relied on their "apparent authority" or were aided in accomplishing their misdeeds by the existence of the agency relationship. A consensus emerged that agency principles dictated that employers be held liable for quid pro quo sexual harassment by their supervisors and managers, as well as by themselves. Because this type of sexual harassment links sexual favors to job rewards or punishments, such as promotions, raises, transfers, discharges, or working conditions, the employer's authority is necessarily exercised in quid pro quo harassment. Supervisors may be on a "frolic" (the traditional term for acting outside employees' scope of employment) when making sexual advances, but they act within the scope of their duties when exercising delegated authority to penalize resistance to their overtures by denying job benefits.

But what if the rewards or punishments are merely threatened but never implemented? What if the victim submits out of fear, as Mechelle Vinson says she did, or if the supervisor fails to follow through? Courts were divided in their approach to these "submission" and "unfulfilled threat" scenarios. Some considered these to be quid pro quo sexual harassment, regardless of whether the rewards or punishments were actually forthcoming, and held the employers liable for their supervisors' misdeeds. Other courts treated this type of situation as creating a hostile environment and refused to impose strict liability on the employer.

In hostile environment sexual harassment cases, standards for employer liability varied more widely. Although variously phrased, the majority of courts tended to hold employers liable for sexually abusive workplaces created by the victims' coworkers only if the employers were negligent in allowing the offensive environment to exist. This standard was often stated as imputing legal liability to the employer only if it knew or should have known of the abusive environment and failed to effectively correct the problem. This standard balances opposing considerations: that the employer is not responsible for policing all the nonwork behavior of its employees, but that the employer owns and controls the workplace. So although the employer is not responsible for unauthorized, nonwork misdeeds of its employees, if targets complain or if these misdeeds pollute the workplace to the extent that the employer should have been aware of the problem and corrected it, the employer can properly be held financially liable to the victims of such an abusive work environment when the employer negligently fails to clean it up.

What is less apparent, however, is who bears the responsibility for compensating victims of hostile environments when the abuse is created not by coworkers but by company supervisors or managers. Should a higher level of responsibility apply, since the employer delegated authority to these miscreants? Or should employers be liable only if they negligently ignore or fail to remedy this supervisory misconduct that is outside of the harasser's duties? As with the problems of unfulfilled threats and submission, courts responded with divergent answers to these questions, leaving sexual harassment victims as well as employers uncertain about the extent to which employers were financially liable for monetary damage awards in these types of cases.

It was these unresolved dilemmas that the Supreme Court undertook to resolve in 1998 in a pair of cases involving issues of employer responsibility. The first, *Burlington Industries v. Ellerth*, involved Kimberly Ellerth, a salesperson for Burlington Industries for just over a year. She charged that midlevel manager Ted Slowik had sexually harassed her, most egregiously in three separate incidents when Slowik's comments went beyond his routinely "boorish and offensive" remarks and gestures and were construed by Ellerth as threats to deny her specific job benefits. On a business trip, Ellerth felt compelled to accept Slowik's invitation to the hotel lounge, but when his comments on her breasts were met with no encouragement, he admonished her to "loosen up" and warned, "You know, Kim, I could make your life very hard or very easy at Burlington." During a promotion interview, Slowik suggested that Ellerth was not "loose enough" and rubbed her knee. When she received the promotion, Slowik told Ellerth, "You're gonna be out there with men who work in factories, and they certainly like women with pretty butts/legs." On another occasion, Slowik allegedly asked her over the phone, "Are you wearing shorter skirts yet, Kim, because it would make your job a whole heck of a lot easier." Although Ellerth once told Slowik that a comment was inappropriate, she quit Burlington without informing any company official of these incidents. Although Ellerth's resignation followed a caution from her immediate supervisor to return customer calls more promptly, she had been promoted and had suffered no tangible retaliation, leaving Slowik's veiled threats unfulfilled. When Ellerth sued, the trial court granted summary judgment for Burlington on the issue of its liability, finding that the company neither knew nor should have known about Slowik's alleged misconduct. On appeal, the Seventh Circuit reversed, but without coming to a consensus on the rationale for holding Burlington liable.

The companion case, *Faragher v. City of Boca Raton*, involved a hostile work environment allegedly created by supervisory personnel. Beth Faragher worked part-time and summers for five years as a lifeguard for the Boca Raton Parks and Recreation Department. She claimed that two of her immediate supervisors created a sexually hostile atmosphere at the beach work site by subjecting her and other female lifeguards to "uninvited and offensive touching" and lewd remarks. Examples of unwanted touching ranged from hugging and patting Faragher on the buttocks to tackling her. One supervisor allegedly told Faragher, "Date me or clean toilets for a year," and on another occasion, he pantomimed oral sex. In addition to lewd comments, she claimed that the supervisors made disparaging remarks about women generally as well as about Faragher specifically. The city adopted a sexual harassment policy while Faragher was employed but never disseminated it to the lifeguard station. Although Faragher told a third supervisor about the crude behavior, she did not consider the conversation a formal complaint, and despite similar discussions with other female lifeguards, he never spoke with the harassing supervisors or higher authorities. After she resigned, Faragher sued the city for nominal damages of $1, costs, and attorney's fees.

The Supreme Court used *Ellerth* and *Faragher* as vehicles to clarify the rules of employer liability for sexual harassment, announcing the same holding in both opinions. The Court rejected imposing strict vicarious liability for all sexual harassment by supervisors. Calling *Vinson* the foundation on which we build today, the Court felt bound by *Vinson*'s holding that employers are not "always automatically liable for sexual harassment by their supervisors." That declaration could be considered "enhanced precedent," carrying implicit congressional endorsement of the Court's interpretation of Title VII, because in the years since the *Vinson* decision, Congress had failed to enact a different rule, even when it amended the law by enacting the Civil Rights Act of 1991.

Forgoing the usual categorization of sexual harassment as either quid pro quo or hostile environment, at least for the purposes of defining employer liability, the Court made "tangible employment action" the touchstone of employer liability. The Court described a tangible employment action as "a significant change in employment status, such as hiring, firing, failing to promote, reassignment with significantly different responsibilities, or a decision causing significant change in benefits." These decisions dictated different liability rules depending on whether the supervisor's sexual harassment included an adverse tangible employment action. In situations of submission or unfulfilled threats (*Ellerth*) or supervisor-created hostile environments (*Faragher*), when a supervisor's sexual harassment did not involve a tangible employment action, the defending employer could raise an affirmative defense to its own liability if it could prove by a preponderance of evidence two necessary elements: first, "that the employer exercised reasonable care to prevent and correct promptly any sexually harassing behavior," and second, "that the plaintiff employee unreasonably failed to take advantage of any preventative or corrective opportunities provided by the employer or to avoid harm otherwise." The opinions offered limited guidance on proving these elements, stating that although having an antiharassment policy with complaint procedures was not an absolute requirement, an appropriate stated policy should be taken into account when assessing the first prong. Furthermore, although proof of plaintiffs' failure to avoid harm was not limited to showing that they had failed to avail themselves of the employer's complaint procedure, "a demonstration of such failure will normally suffice to satisfy the employer's burden under the second element of the defense." Conversely, the Court announced a rule of strict liability for employers if the harassment involved a tangible employment action: "No affirmative defense is available, however, when the supervisor's harassment culminates in a tangible employment action."

Same-Sex Harassment

In 1998, the Supreme Court resolved another issue that had long plagued sexual harassment jurisprudence. Pre-*Vinson* judges initially resisted interpreting sexual harassment as a form of prohibited sex discrimination, holding that the discrimination occurred because the victim refused to grant sexual favors, not because she was a woman. This barrier to conceiving of sexual harassment as violating Title VII was overcome when courts began to reason that victims were targeted for sexual favors because they were desirable to the harasser, that is, because of their sex. This rationale could cover homosexual harassment based on sexual desire, but what if the target is the same sex as the harasser but the harasser is not homosexual and the harassment does not take the form of sexual advances? Lower courts faced with this question had rendered widely varying answers. In *Oncale v. Sundowner Offshore Services*, the Supreme Court delivered an authoritative decision on the topic.

Joseph Oncale worked for Sundowner on an offshore oil platform. He charged that several members of the eight-man crew, including his supervisor, forcibly subjected him to humiliating, sex-related mistreatment, physically assaulted him in a sexual manner, and threatened him with rape. Oncale complained that, while coworkers restrained him, his supervisor placed his penis on his neck and arm and on another occasion shoved a bar of soap between his buttocks when Oncale was showering. Oncale's complaints to management led to no remedial action, so he eventually quit, giving as his reason "sexual harassment and verbal abuse." Oncale's alleged tormentors did not select him, however, out of sexual desire but apparently because he was small and, in their eyes, "effeminate" or at least insufficiently "masculine."

Writing for a unanimous Court, Justice Antonin Scalia held unequivocally that same-sex harassment is actionable sex discrimination. Although he recognized that same-sex harassment was not the principal evil Congress intended to remedy with Title VII, Scalia found that the purpose of combating sex discrimination encompassed harassment if it involved discrimination "because of sex," even if the parties happened to be of the same sex. The critical issue was that the discrimination was "based on sex," regardless of the genders of the persons involved.

Justice Scalia dismissed the defendant's contention that recognizing liability for same-sex harassment threatened to turn simple male horseplay into a basis for legal action. He denied that prohibiting same-sex harassment would "transform Title VII into a general civility code for the American workplace," noting that "the statute does not reach genuine but innocuous differences in the ways men and women routinely interact with members of the same sex and of the opposite sex." Both same-sex and male-female cases are subject to the "severe or pervasive" standard, which assesses the severity of the misconduct not merely by the plaintiff's sensibilities but from the perspective of "a reasonable person in the plaintiff's position, considering 'all the circumstances.'" Moreover, Scalia averred, "common sense, and an appropriate sensitivity to social context, will enable courts and juries to distinguish between simple teasing or roughhousing among members of the same sex, and conduct which a reasonable person in the plaintiff's position would find severely hostile or abusive." For example, "[a] professional football player's working environment is not severely or pervasively abusive if the coach smacks him on the buttocks as he heads onto the field, even if the same behavior would reasonably be experienced as abusive by the coach's secretary (male or female) back at the office."

The *Oncale* decision confirms that harassment based on sex extends beyond misconduct based on sexual desire, but just how far the holding applies is not yet clear. The reasoning of the opinion implies that victims deserve protection if they are targeted not merely because they are men or women but because of the way they embrace their masculinity or femininity, but the outlines of legal protections against harassment aimed at nonconforming gender constructions deemed inappropriate by harassers remain obscure. A related issue is the extent to which gays and lesbians will be protected under the *Oncale* ruling. Lower courts have held that Title VII's prohibition on discrimination because of sex does not forbid discrimination because of sexual orientation, and although in the 1990s the Senate came within one vote of passing a bill banning discrimination against homosexuals in the workplace, Congress has not yet acted to make antigay employment discrimination illegal. Does *Oncale* mean that homosexuals being harassed by employers or coworkers because they fail to embody harassers' notions of proper gender models will now have a cause of action even if the harassers and targets are of the same sex? Lower courts are split on the question. Some interpret antigay harassment as based on sex because it targets "improper" gender constructions and thus is actionable under *Oncale*. Others find the harassment to be based on sexual orientation, not sex as biologically or socially defined, and thus not illegal under Title VII.

––––––

Legal developments since *Meritor Bank v. Vinson* have strengthened the law's protection against sexual harassment. New legislation has bolstered enforcement by increasing incentives for plaintiffs to sue. Courts have clarified legal standards in sexual harassment cases, sometimes extending the reach of protection. Other rulings arguably have diminished the force of sexual harassment safeguards. The meaning and significance of still other developments in sexual harassment jurisprudence, such as the employer liability rules promulgated in *Faragher* and *Ellerth* and potential protections of gays and lesbians from sexual harassment, will become clearer only over time, with the manifestation of agency and lower court interpretation and implementation of these rules and responses to these new standards. Innovations in related areas of law will also influence the course of sexual harassment law; the next chapter surveys these ancillary developments.

CHAPTER 6

Extensions and Retractions

Related Developments since *Vinson*

The future of legal efforts to combat sexual harassment depends not only on emerging precedents in Title VII cases but also on evolving legal doctrines in other areas. The relevance of some developments, such as legal standards applied to sexual harassment in education, is readily apparent, while others, such as courts' willingness to honor arbitration agreements, have a less direct, though significant, impact. This chapter surveys several related legal developments with potential implications for efforts to eliminate sexual harassment.

Sexual Harassment in Education

Title VI of the 1964 Civil Rights Act precluded racial discrimination in federally funded programs, but unlike Title VII, discrimination based on sex was not added to this section. To ensure equal opportunity in education, Congress passed Title IX of the 1972 Education Amendments, barring sex discrimination in educational programs funded with federal money. Title IX provided that "No person in the United States shall, on the basis of sex, be excluded from participation in, be denied the benefits of, or be subjected to discrimination under any education program or activity receiving Federal financial assistance." Like Title VII, Title IX prohibits "discrimination" without explicitly mentioning sexual harassment, but in a similar vein, courts, beginning with *Alexander v. Yale University* in 1977, and the agency charged with enforcing Title IX, the Office of Civil Rights of the Education Department, came to interpret Title IX's antidiscrimination provisions as encompassing sexual harassment.

Sexual harassment is a serious problem in schools at all levels, with some data indicating that its prevalence may surpass its frequency in the workplace. In a 1993 survey of eighth through eleventh graders conducted for the American Association of University Women, 85 percent of girls and 79 percent of boys reported that they had experienced some form of unwanted sexual behavior. Seventy-nine percent of this harassment was by other students. More than two-thirds had suffered from sexual jokes or gestures, 65 percent of girls and 42 percent of boys had been touched in a sexual manner, and 11 percent had been asked to engage in sexual behavior beyond kissing. *Seventeen* magazine's 1993 survey found that 89 percent of girls from nine to nineteen had been the targets of unwelcome sexual behavior, and 39 percent reported that the misconduct was daily. College students, too, are victims of sexual harassment, with some estimates suggesting that 50 percent suffer harassment by their professors.

The harm of this harassment in schools falls more heavily on female students. Girls were more likely than boys to have been repeatedly sexually harassed, and at younger ages. They were more likely to report feeling embarrassed, self-conscious, upset, or scared because of the harassment. Although almost all students who experienced harassment said that it distracted them from concentrating in school, girls felt the interference slightly more than boys. Twelve percent of boys but 33 percent of girls said that they were reluctant to speak in class or attend school after their harassment. Because harassment occurs most frequently between the sixth to ninth grades, its injurious impact is felt most keenly during a crucial period of development and at a time when girls begin to lag behind boys academically.

The Office of Civil Rights (OCR) enforces Title IX by receiving complaints and investigating or by initiating its own compliance reviews. If violations are discovered, the recipient of federal funds is notified of the problem and given a chance to achieve compliance voluntarily. Although the OCR can initiate proceedings to cut a school's federal funding or request the Justice Department to sue, such actions are rarely undertaken. Suits by victims of discrimination in education, including targets of sexual harassment, are not mentioned in the statute, and it was not until 1979 that the Supreme Court recognized a private right to sue. In *Cannon v. University of Chicago*, the Court implied a private right to sue under Title IX for a female student claiming that she had been denied admission to two private medical schools because of her sex. The Court reasoned that because it had been finding implied private rights to sue in several other statutes in the time frame during which Title IX was passed, Congress must have intended its silence on the subject to imply that a private individual as well as the OCR could enforce Title IX by suing in federal court.

In 1992 in *Franklin v. Gwinnett County Public Schools,* the Court extended this logic by recognizing a sexual harassment victim's right under Title IX to recover monetary damages for her injuries from a school system receiving federal funds. A high school student charged that since her tenth-grade year her coach-teacher had subjected her to sexual harassment escalating from sexually oriented conversations to pressure for sex to forced kissing to coercive intercourse. Although the school learned of this misconduct and of the teacher's harassment of others, the plaintiff complained that the administration took no action to stop it and even discouraged her from pressing charges. When the teacher resigned, the school dropped its investigation, and the student sued. The issue presented to the Supreme Court was whether a private plaintiff could recover monetary damages from a recipient of federal funds, given that the statutory remedy for violations of Title IX was the threat of loss of funding. The Court held that unless Congress expressly excluded a remedy normally available to plaintiffs, it must have intended for it to be available. Because Title IX does not explicitly bar pecuniary damages, this relief is not precluded. As Justice Antonin Scalia noted in his concurrence, since Title IX is silent on a private right to sue, it naturally is likewise silent on remedies available to private litigants.

What these cases left open was what plaintiffs had to prove to win monetary damages. The question of legal criteria for sexual harassment suits under Title IX was answered in a pair of Supreme Court decisions in 1998 and 1999, the first involving alleged harassment by a school employee, the second by a fellow student. In *Gebser et al. v. Lago Vista Independent School District* (1998), a student and her mother sued a teacher who led a book discussion group. The teacher allegedly made inappropriate comments to the students and began to direct his most suggestive remarks toward Gebser, an eighth grader at the time. Eventually the teacher kissed and fondled Gebser in her home, visiting her under the pretext of delivering a book, and the two began having sexual intercourse. The relationship continued into the next year, ending when a police officer discovered the two having sex. Gebser had never reported the relationship, but the parents of two other students had complained about this teacher's comments in class. In a five to four decision written by Justice Sandra Day O'Connor for the conservative majority, the Court held that school systems were not liable under Title IX for pecuniary damages for sexual harassment by an employee unless "an official who at a minimum has authority to address the alleged discrimination and to institute corrective measures on the recipient's behalf has actual knowledge of discrimination in the recipient's programs and fails adequately to respond. We think, moreover, that the response must amount to deliberate indifference to discrimination." Although O'Connor noted that the school system's failure to establish policies and procedures to prohibit sexual harassment and to facilitate the reporting and remedying of it violated OCR regulations, she did not believe that their absence amounted to actual knowledge and deliberate indifference.

Why would the Court erect a more formidable bar to holding schools legally liable for the sexual harassment of students by teachers than it had mandated for finding employers liable for the sexual harassment of employees by supervisors? Justice O'Connor explained the Court's more exacting liability rules by contrasting the statutory schemes of Titles VII and IX. In passing Title VII, Congress intended to compensate victims of discrimination, whereas Title IX's purpose was to protect participants in federally funded programs from sex discrimination. O'Connor's concern was to ensure that schools had adequate awareness that by accepting federal money they were leaving themselves open to legal liability. Actual knowledge of employee sexual misconduct rather than mere constructive knowledge ("should have known") and a response of deliberate indifference, recklessness rather than mere negligence, served as sufficient notice to the school system that it risked more than loss of funds by failing to protect program participants from sex discrimination. O'Connor also argued that Congress contemplated that Title IX, unlike Title VII, would be enforced primarily through administrative procedures promulgated by the funding agencies, which would pursue compliance through voluntary means before cutting off funds.

Writing for the four dissenters, Justice John Paul Stevens asserted that the majority opinion was unfaithful to Congress's purpose in enacting Title IX, which was to protect program recipients from sex discrimination rather than funds recipients from lawsuits. OCR guidelines on sexual harassment, as well as common-law agency principles, would impose liability on a district for the misconduct of an employee who was aided in accomplishing the harassment by the authority derived from the agency relationship, as is surely the case when teachers sexually harass their students. Hewing to these agency principles would "induce school boards to adopt and enforce practices that will minimize the danger that vulnerable students will be exposed to such odious behavior" and would place the risk of harm where it could most easily be borne and ensured against: on the district rather than the victim. Justice Ruth Bader Ginsberg agreed, adding that she would fashion liability standards for schools similar to those mandated for employers under Title VII in the 1998 companion cases *Ellerth* and *Faragher:* liability unless the employer could prove effective policies and remedies and the plaintiff's failure to make use of them.

The next year, the Supreme Court ruled on school liability standards in a case of a student sexually harassed by a fellow student. In *Davis v. Monroe County Board of Education*, LaShonda Davis, a fifth grader, was verbally and physically harassed on eight separate occasions over a six-month period by a classmate who eventually pled guilty to criminal sexual battery charges. LaShonda reported each incident to her teachers and to her mother, who also complained to teachers and eventually to the principal. In response to complaints by LaShonda and other girls in the class, teachers admonished the harasser and moved LaShonda's desk, but these measures failed to halt the torment. The school district did not have antiharassment policies or procedures and had not trained its staff to handle sexual harassment issues.

Again writing for a closely divided Court, but this time for a five-justice majority of the more liberal wing of the Court, O'Connor extended the *Gebser* standard by adding two other requirements for finding schools liable for student-to-student harassment. In addition to actual knowledge and deliberate indifference, the peer harassment must be so "severe, pervasive, and objectively offensive" that it "effectively deprives the victim of access to a federally funded educational opportunity."

The conservative justices joined a dissent by Justice Anthony Kennedy, who argued that Congress had not intended Title IX to make schools legally responsible for student-to-student sexual harassment because it prohibits only misconduct by funds recipients. Recipients lacked clear notice that they were liable for peer sexual misconduct, and the majority's decision upholding such possible liability violated federalist principles by infringing on issues traditionally left for state and local governments.

Commentators on *Gebser* and *Davis* criticize the Court for diluting protections for students. By requiring actual knowledge and deliberate indifference before a school can be held liable, the decisions provide a perverse incentive for school authorities to "look the other way" to avoid learning of sexual misconduct, and they certainly fail to encourage the adoption of policies and procedures to affirmatively prevent and remedy sexual harassment. Critics also charge that the Court's liability standards narrow the range of prohibited misconduct. Title IX prohibited program participants from being "subjected to discrimination" based on sex, but the Court's standards shield school systems from liability for discriminatory differential treatment unless it excludes or denies program benefits to victims. The ironic result of the Supreme Court's 1998–1999 decisions on employer and school system liability for sexual harassment is that the different rules adopted for Title VII and Title IX afford less protection to the nation's schoolchildren than to adult employees.

"He Can't Say That": Free Speech and Sexually Harassing Speech

A constitutional challenge to sexual harassment law that the Supreme Court has yet to address directly is the contention of a small band of legal scholars that prohibiting sexually harassing words and pictures violates the First Amendment's injunction that "Congress shall make no law . . . abridging the freedom of speech." Although quid pro quo and most hostile environment sexual harassment involves conduct or directly threatening words, these commentators argue that some verbal hostile environment harassment would be constitutionally protected speech. Only two federal district courts have squarely faced the issue, and both rejected the constitutional claim.

In *Robinson v. Jacksonville Shipyards*, a female welder faced a gauntlet of sexual and sexist comments, such as "women are only fit company for something that howls" and "there's nothing worse than having to work around women." The workplace was rife with sexual graffiti, some of it directed at plaintiff Robinson, including the message, "Lick me you whore dog bitch." Locker and working areas were also saturated with posters and pictures of nude or scantily clad women in suggestive or submissive poses, including a dartboard depicting a female breast and a nude poster captioned "USDA Choice." Male coworkers often made sexual remarks about the pictures, such as "I'd like to have some of that." When she complained to management, the response was unsympathetic; Robinson was told to be less sensitive and to "get over it." Indeed, management exacerbated the problem by distributing to the workers pornographic calendars promoting parts suppliers. When Robinson sued, the judge issued a sweeping injunction requiring the company to rid its workplace of "pictures, posters, calendars, graffiti, objects, promotional materials, reading materials, or other materials that are sexually suggestive, sexually demeaning, or pornographic" and to bar "sexually-oriented gestures, noises, remarks, jokes, or comments about a person's sexuality or sexual experience directed at or made in the presence of any employee who indicates or has indicated in any way that such conduct in his or her presence is unwelcome." The judge summarily rejected objections that this order violated free expression protected by the Constitution.

Critics offer several arguments to support their contention that barring verbal sexual harassment infringes on the First Amendment. Some criticisms maintain that prohibitions on verbal sexual harassment inevitably slip into inhibiting valid speech. One claim is that the definition of sexual harassment is so vague that speakers will practice excessive self-censorship out of caution because they cannot discern the boundaries of speech constituting illegal sexual harassment. Defenders of sexual harassment jurisprudence respond by noting that legal definitions are never mathematically precise and that the elements required to prove sexual harassment are both extensive and rigorous, differentiating, for instance, between merely offensive words and those "sufficiently severe or pervasive" to amount to illegal harassment. A second concern is whether the legal prohibition on sexual harassment is overly broad, banning constitutionally protected as well as illegal expression. The statement by Robinson's coworker that "there's nothing worse than having to work around women" or claims that "women can't do this job" might be abhorrent, but the First Amendment's function is to protect unpopular, even despicable speech along with more uplifting and worthy ideas. Hostile environments rarely consist of purely "political" views unaccompanied by threats and misconduct, and a 2001 survey of sexual harassment litigation found only one case based on objections to pornography and graffiti alone.

A third claim is that fear of sexual harassment suits chills free speech by encouraging employers to be overzealous in regulating the speech of their employees. The offending speech, after all, is not the employer's, which may not even value its sentiment or defend the right to self-expression, and the employer has little incentive to risk liability by failing to stop it. This type of "collateral censorship" privatizes censorship, with company managers substituting for government censors. Defenders of sexual harassment law, however, note that all restrictions on speech pose the danger of some collateral censorship and that, in the case of hostile environment prohibitions, that risk is minimal because they interdict only speech associated with properly prohibited conduct. Employers may defend employees' speech rights because of shared beliefs, or management might condone sexist expressions because it believes that a sexually hostile climate keeps male employees' morale high and perpetuates occupational segregation, which depresses wages. If employers restrict expression, they are in a better position than individual employees to tailor regulations to match the overall workplace atmosphere, because management can observe the workplace in its entirety, rather than from the partial perspectives of individual workers.

Finally, some critics maintain that verbal sexual harassment itself, no matter how appalling, is constitutionally protected from restrictions that are content and viewpoint based. Sexual harassment law is content based because it bans discrimination based on some factors, such as sex, but not others, such as political views; it is viewpoint based because it treats harassing speech as an evil that should be legally interdicted. Defenders of sexual harassment law offer a number of counterarguments. One is that prohibiting sexually harassing speech actually expands, rather than abridges, the amount of speech by preventing women from being silenced by harassment. Courts have typically not accepted this argument in hate speech cases, instead upholding the proposition that the First Amendment protects individual expression and not merely the aggregate amount of speech.

Another counterargument is premised on the constitutional protection of equality, embodied in the Fourteenth Amendment's equal protection clause. Because sexual harassment threatens equality, balancing these two constitutional values is necessary if some speech is infringed. Defenders of sexual harassment law claim that the scales favor some limitations on verbal sexual harassment; although sexual harassment is highly injurious to its victims, harassers are relatively unharmed by having their harassing speech repressed. On the positive side of the equation, harassing speech is generally not of great constitutional value: "lick me you whore dog bitch" contributes little to the search for truth in the marketplace of ideas, proclaim defenders of Title VII. Besides, restricting verbal harassment in employment and education leaves open alternative channels of communication outside of work or school.

Another approach balancing free speech and equality admits that sexual harassment law is content and viewpoint based but argues that these regulations survive the strict scrutiny the Court applies to such restrictions. The compelling interest behind sexual harassment law is equality, a key democratic value enshrined in the Fourteenth Amendment. The law is narrowly tailored and necessary to prevent sexual harassment. The restrictions are not aimed at merely sexist ideas but at workplace climates that create steep barriers to equal opportunity, and informal, private solutions have proved ineffective in removing these obstacles.

Another defense against free speech claims is that restrictions on verbal sexual harassment are justified by the captive audience doctrine. Although audience members can generally avoid unwanted verbal or visual expression by simply walking away or averting their eyes, the Supreme Court has ruled that when the audience is, in effect, held hostage to the speakers (for example, in the case of noisy demonstrations outside homes), some restrictions on expression are permissible. Workplaces are arenas that employees are not free to leave, at least if they value their jobs. More than physical restrictions, work is defined by relationships, especially the dependence of employees on employers, which inhibits the employees' choice of what expression to attend to or avoid. The "captivity" of workers is greater than the confinement of people in their own homes, justifying some protection from unwanted expression.

A final consideration is that most employees do not enjoy freedom of expression at work; the First Amendment protects free speech from being violated by government, not private employers. Free speech critics are defending a chimerical freedom, rights enjoyed by only a tiny minority of employees. This defense, however, skids dangerously close to implying that free expression in the workplace is of no constitutional value. Several legal scholars emphasize that workplace expression should be an area of heightened free speech concern. Especially in an era of increased isolation and social separation, workplaces are the most diverse arena of American life, the places we are most likely to encounter fellow citizens with different experiences and ideas. These scholars argue that the law not only should be wary of repressing speech at work but should actively seek to protect it, a policy they believe is compatible with sexual harassment protections.

Academic freedom adds special complications to hostile environments in the classroom, considerations illustrated in *Silva v. University of New Hampshire* (1994). The university disciplined a writing instructor for using sexually suggestive classroom examples that offended several students. The professor's statements were highly ambiguous and arguably valid teaching tools, although allegations of out-of-class improprieties buttressed the students' complaints. The instructor sued, winning reinstatement and compensation, but the incident raised specters of hostile environment claims as a threat to academic freedom. Teachers and the American Association of University Professors tend to define academic freedom as the right of instructors to be free from interference in their research, teaching, and intramural and extramural speech, as long as they exercise that freedom responsibly. Courts, however, tend to view academic freedom from a constitutional vantage point as the right of colleges and universities to determine their curricula and academic policies free from government dictates. Although the classroom context will continue to present close cases requiring sound judgment about whether controversial teaching techniques create hostile learning environments, defending truly abusive sexual harassment in the name of academic freedom distorts the doctrine beyond recognition. The American Association of University Professors has adopted a strong statement condemning sexual harassment by teachers and stating that harassment contradicts academic freedom. Whether viewed as a breach of professional responsibility outside the bounds of academic freedom or as academic misconduct violating policies that colleges and universities have a right, indeed a duty, to adopt, sexual harassment should not be tolerated in the guise of academic freedom.

Sexual Favoritism

A novel twist to sexual harassment is favoritism based on sexual or romantic relations between supervisors and employees. Can coworkers who are not privy to benefits or who object to workplace atmospheres poisoned by such "paramour" discrimination claim violations of Title VII? Are they in effect harassed because of sex, not by reason of their own gender or their refusal to have sex with a supervisor, but because of the sex a coworker is having with the boss?

There are good reasons for barring favoritism based on sexual relations between supervisors and their employees. Basing work decisions on private sexual relations unrelated to job performance is simply unfair. Many question whether romantic relations that form the basis of favoritism are really romantic; some suspect an inevitable element of coercion when power is so disparate, such as between supervisors and employees or teachers and students. The burdens of favoritism fall disproportionately on women, both because glass ceilings and sex-segregated occupations mean that women are often competing against other women for benefits distributed by men and because sleeping with the boss tends to reinforce stereotypes and further objectifies women workers as mere sex objects. But the narrower legal issue is whether Title VII's prohibition on sex discrimination covers this type of sexual misconduct.

King v. Palmer, a 1985 D.C. Circuit decision, held that a nurse was illegally discriminated against when she lost a promotion to a less qualified nurse who was having an affair with the doctor deciding the promotion. The issue of favoritism was never directly joined, however, diluting the opinion's value as precedent, and most courts have rejected claims that sexual favoritism is illegal employment discrimination. In *DeCintio v. Westchester County Medical Center* (1986), the Second Circuit rejected claims by male respiratory therapists that their supervisor discriminated by favoring his female paramour for promotion. Holding that "voluntary, romantic relationships cannot form the basis of a sex discrimination suit" under federal anti–sex discrimination law, the court concluded that the supervisor's conduct, "although clearly unfair, simply did not violate Title VII." Other courts analogize sexual favoritism to nepotism, which is also unfair but not illegal. The 1990 EEOC's Policy Guidance on Sexual Favoritism maintained that Title VII did not bar instances of preferential treatment based on consensual relationships: "An isolated instance of favoritism toward a 'paramour' (or a spouse, or a friend) may be unfair, but it does not discriminate against women or men in violation of Title VII, since both are disadvantaged for reasons other than their genders."

The EEOC guidance recognized, however, that liability could arise when the sexual relationship underlying favoritism was not consensual. Coworkers indirectly injured as a result of the discrimination targeted at another employee coerced into granting sexual favors could claim derivative quid pro quo harassment. Widespread sexual favoritism might also provide the basis for an implicit quid pro quo claim if it were sufficiently rampant to signify solicitation of sex for benefits. Both male and female employees could claim hostile environment sexual harassment if sexual favoritism was widespread in a workplace, whether or not any misconduct was directed at them and regardless of whether those granting the favors were coerced. The message of such a workplace environment would be that women are "sexual playthings" or that women must sleep their way to the top to advance, and men or women could object to such an abusive atmosphere if it met the severe or pervasive standard. Thus, although sexual favoritism is not per se illegal, courts and the EEOC have interpreted Title VII to encompass favoritism in some situations as constituting "reverse sexual harassment."

―――

Courting Disaster? Company Policies Regulating Consensual Relations among Employees

With Americans working longer hours and with a labor force approaching gender balance, the workplace increasingly spawns romantic relationships. Surveys reveal that romance and sex are pervasive in

American workplaces, with as many as one-third of all romantic relationships beginning in the workplace. Twenty-five percent of the respondents to an American Management Association (AMA) survey reported having at least one office romance, and of these, 33 percent of the men and 15 percent of the women said it was with a subordinate. Replies to an Internet survey indicated that 71 percent of respondents had dated a coworker, and among managers, 50 percent had dated a subordinate. A combined sample of studies found that 71 percent of employees had observed at least one romantic relationship at work, and 31 percent reported personal involvement in workplace liaisons. Estimates, though uncertain, gauge that as many as 33 to 40 percent of adults have had sex at work. One Los Angeles property manager confirmed that catching couples "in the act" has become almost an occupational hazard for night cleaning crews: "Everyone seems to have a story about an incident on a conference room table."

Many office liaisons are perfectly legitimate; the AMA poll found that 55 percent of office romances ended in marriage. Not all relationships, though, have such an amicable ending. A study of large companies found that 27 percent of sexual harassment claims originated in relationships gone sour. Prominent employment law attorneys estimate that 40 to 50 percent of their caseloads grow out of disputes that began as office romances. The cost to employers of broken relationships can be huge; one practitioner estimates that she settles ten to fifteen cases per year of superior-subordinate relations turned sour for over $500,000 each, with some settlements exceeding $1 million. Attempts at revenge or reconciliation can generate lawsuits stemming from failed romances, and coworker suits involving favoritism or alleged retaliation for complaints about office liaisons are other possible legal headaches accruing from romantic relationships at work. Skeptics question whether office relationships are really consensual when power differentials loom large. Others have noted problems of "unintended coercion"; even when the more powerful partner seeks a voluntary romantic relationship, the less powerful person may feel pressured. Other problems include lowered morale and productivity among coworkers as well as the involved couple. Employers worry that vengeful or jealous ex-partners will vent their rage at work, possibly adding to the rising tide of violence in American workplaces.

Although many organizations are considering policies on employee relationships, a 1998 survey found that only 13 percent of companies have written policies; another 14 percent rely on unwritten understandings about workplace romances. Only 12 percent of companies train managers to deal with such situations. One typology classified policies adopted by universities, finding a range of approaches that probably match the variations among company policies. Some policies discourage but do not forbid supervisor-subordinate relationships. Without totally denying the possibility of consensual romance between persons of different power and status, such policies are skeptical of these liaisons, judging them potentially coercive, exploitative, and, at a minimum, imprudent. Similar policies adopt aspirational standards, for example, relying on education and voluntary mediation to enforce the norms or creating a presumption that sexual relations are not consensual among power-differentiated persons. A more common policy forbids relations while a supervisory situation exists, such as while a faculty member is teaching or advising a student. Other policies combine both approaches, banning relationships when conflicts of interest exist and discouraging them in the absence of direct conflicts. To protect trade secrets or corporate images, some companies go beyond the workplace and attempt to police their employees' after-hours private lives, for example, by disciplining employees for fraternizing with individuals who work for competitors.

Despite the extensive problems arising from workplace romances, organizational policies regulating personal relations between employees, especially blanket prohibitions, predictably encounter objections. Employees may feel that their privacy or right to free association is infringed when the company assumes the role of "Cupid cop." Although some feminists maintain that unequal power undermines any possibility of consensual relationships, others claim that the incapacity argument, presuming that women in relationships with more powerful men lack the capacity to give effective consent, betrays a lack of faith in women's judgment and perception. Others worry about the threat to women's economic opportunities entailed in company policies aimed at preempting situations with the potential to breed sexual harassment or sexual relations, such as limiting out-of-town travel or proscribing accommodations in the same hotel or closed-door conferences. Sweeping policies are unpopular, with twice as many employees opposing as favoring broad prohibitions on employee romance, but more than half of employees polled said that it depends on the situation. The status of those involved in the relationship is key; one poll found that almost 80 percent agreed that companies can legitimately ban employees from dating their supervisors, but less than 10 percent thought that employers should be able to stop coworker dating. Most commentators recommend clear company policies that balance employee privacy and free association interests with the business interests of the employer.

Other Avenues of Legal Protection

Titles VII and IX are not the only laws that might be used as the basis of legal action against sexual harassment. Although generally less promising than these federal antidiscrimination statutes, other laws might, depending on the circumstances, provide protection against sexual harassment.

State and local government employees have been brought under the coverage of Titles VII and IX, but recent decisions by the Supreme Court may indicate its growing reluctance to allow states to be sued in federal courts against their will. The Court has interposed the Eleventh Amendment, which bars suits against states unless the state expressly waives sovereign immunity or injunctive relief is sought, as a bar to these suits, which typically ask for other forms of equitable relief and damages. State employees face major hurdles when suing their state government employers unless the state gives its permission.

State laws may offer more broadly available remedies for employees of private employers. Every state but Alabama and Mississippi has passed "little Title VIIs," human rights or antidiscrimination laws that forbid employment discrimination. Often these state laws cover businesses with fewer than fifteen employees, too small to be covered by Title VII. They may also provide for jury trials and a wider range of relief than Title VII provides.

State common law may also provide bases for sexual harassment suits. The particular claims could vary by the circumstances of the offense. For example, offensive touching could be the basis of a battery claim, while pinning the plaintiff in an uncomfortable position may constitute the common-law tort of false imprisonment. Intentional infliction of emotional distress is a typical tort claim when the plaintiff has been subjected to severe emotional distress, but the standards for proving this innovative claim are generally quite stringent, including that the offending conduct must be not merely offensive but outrageous, "exceeding all bounds usually tolerated by decent society."

Arbitration Agreements: The Privatization of Employment Law?

Evolving management practices, increasingly approved by the Supreme Court, jeopardize workers' rights by substituting arbitration for litigation as the vehicle for deciding employment claims. Many employers are now presenting prospective or current employees with agreements to arbitrate employment disputes as a condition of employment or consideration for promotions or other benefits. Alternative dispute resolution techniques offer clear advantages to courts, but as mechanisms to enforce workers' statutory rights, these private forums suffer from severe defects, and critics contend that they threaten to roll back decades of progress in protecting employees from sexual harassment and other abuses.

The Supreme Court has shown a growing disposition to uphold agreements to arbitrate and to find that parties who are unhappy with arbitration awards are precluded from suing in federal courts, even when statutorily protected rights were allegedly violated. In its 1974 *Alexander v. Gardner-Denver* decision, the Court held that a discharged employee claiming racial discrimination did not forfeit his right to sue because he had first sought arbitration, ruling that "the private right of action remains an essential means of obtaining judicial enforcement of Title VII." However, in *Gilmer v. Interstate/Johnson Lane Corp.*, it reached virtually the opposite conclusion. In that 1991 ruling, the Supreme Court relied on the Federal Arbitration Act's requirement that any written agreement to arbitrate disputes arising from a commercial contract "shall be valid, irrevocable, and enforceable" as long as the underlying contract is valid. The Court determined that the plaintiff had waived his right to pursue his age discrimination suit in court when he agreed, in procuring a position as a securities representative, to arbitrate any disputed employment claim or controversy between him and his employer.

In 1998, the Supreme Court ruled that a collective bargaining agreement to arbitrate contract disputes does not preempt the employees' right to pursue statutory claims in court unless the union-company contract contains a "clear and unmistakable waiver" of employees' right to sue. In 2001, the Court refused to interpret broadly a provision of the 1925 Federal Arbitration Act excluding from coverage "contracts of employment of seamen, railroad employees, or any other class of workers engaged in foreign or interstate commerce." The Court's decision in *Circuit City Stores v. Adams* means that for employees other than transportation workers, signing an agreement to settle employment by arbitration could forfeit the option of pursuing claims in court.

Although many legal questions remain unanswered, employers are clearly enamored of arbitration agreements. Only a handful of workplaces were covered by such agreements a decade ago, but a 1998 survey found that 20 percent or more of employers had adopted arbitration procedures. With unions representing less than 10 percent of the private workforce, arbitration agreements as a means of settling worker claims are becoming more widespread than union protection.

Arbitration proponents tout the clear advantages of this alternative to litigation, especially its accessibility, claiming that it is often cheaper, simpler, speedier, less formal, and generally easier to use. Arbitration decisions generally achieve acceptance and compliance. Arbitration decisions, as well as the proceedings, are usually confidential, sparing the parties potential embarrassment, and arbitration seems better suited than sharply adversarial litigation to preserving or restoring ongoing relations between the parties, such as an employment relationship.

Nonetheless, arbitration suffers from severe drawbacks when compared with litigating employee rights. Hearing officers in internal processes may lack impartiality, and outside arbitrators have interests that may incline them to favor employers. There may be serious due process defects; for example, limited discovery hinders employees' efforts to obtain information, which is largely in company hands, to support their claims. Arbitrator decisions may be inadequately justified or explained or may be unaccompanied by any written opinion, making appeals almost impossible. Although costs are frequently lower, arbitration awards are likely to be less lucrative than court-ordered damage awards, and some arbitration agreements require that employees alone pay arbitrators' fees. Secrecy that shields parties from public embarrassment also protects employers from public accountability and undermines the utility of arbitration awards as precedent, limiting their impact on wider workplace practices and policies.

Still, employees may benefit from the displacement of litigation by arbitration. With the high costs of lawsuits and the slim odds of winning, only about one out of every hundred claims is worth pursuing in court, and losing can be financially ruinous. Instead of a litigation system protecting only the rights of a few professional or mid-management employees with resources to sue and high salaries to support huge damage claims, cheaper, more accessible arbitration procedures promise lower-level workers the chance to recover their jobs and modest financial recompense. Conversely, the drawbacks of litigation, such as lengthy trials, expensive procedures, uncertain outcomes, and possibly massive damage awards, are precisely the horrors that give employment law its deterrent sting and help ensure that employers respect workers' legal rights. In an era of acute brand consciousness, fear of bad publicity as an inevitable by-product of lawsuits adds another crucial incentive for companies to abide by the law.

Employment law expert Katherine Van Wezel Stone suggests that in today's fluid workplaces, fair arbitral systems can be effective, but only if used in conjunction with, rather than as a substitute for, statutory rights backed by court protection. Sweeping compulsory arbitration agreements take employee protections "out of the public arena, away from public scrutiny and political accountability," replacing legal rights with "the variable, unpredictable, and invisible outcomes of private arbitration." Replacing the enforcement of employee rights by public law with a system of private contracts entered into by parties with vastly unequal bargaining power negates the fundamental aims of employment statutes and produces the ironic and bitter result, as Stone observes, that American workers have "more rights and less protection than ever."

Looking beyond Sexual Harassment Law

The effectiveness of sexual harassment law does not depend exclusively on the line of cases that evolved from the *Vinson* decision and its early forerunners; it is also affected by ancillary developments in the law. Congress greatly enhanced the legal campaign against sexual harassment by extending protections to students in federally funded educational programs, and court decisions have displayed variable tendencies in buttressing or weakening protections against sexual harassment or other violations of employees' rights. These legal developments cannot be considered apart from political and social trends and forces outside the legal system that may hold the vital key to determining the ultimate direction and efficacy of sexual harassment protections.

CHAPTER 7

Judging the Results
The Social Impact of *Vinson*

The social impact of Supreme Court decisions is controversial, and adding sexual harassment to the mix merely amplifies the controversy. Whether to use law to reform social mores and structures, the extent to which laws alter practices and patterns of society, and the benefits of legally restructuring social relations are all disputed issues. This chapter surveys information and debates about the effects of *Meritor Savings Bank v. Vinson* and related developments, leaving to the conclusion my reflections on the contemporary status of sexual harassment law and a discussion of the more general question of the law's potential for social reform.

Although no assessment of the impact of *Vinson* and its progeny can be definitive, if for no other reason than the battle against sexual harassment is an ongoing rather than a completed campaign, one predictable result of the Court's speaking on an issue is to heighten public attention. In shining the spotlight of press and public opinion on an issue, a Supreme Court decision may not finally settle the dispute so much as set in motion other influences that more decisively affect the outcome, possibly years later. The Supreme Court's agenda-setting role can be seen as a precondition for change, affecting which actors play leading roles in the resolution process. Supreme Court decisions also frame the terms of debate, and legal doctrines and concepts shape the way we think. Both by expanding the scope of involvement through increased visibility and by defining the terms of debate, Supreme Court decisions profoundly shape the politics of change.

Supreme Court rulings and American legal doctrines have international repercussions as well. As Margaret Crouch observes, "While the United States has led the world in recognition of sexual harassment as a phenomenon and development of the concept of sexual harassment, other countries have been quick to follow." A 1992 survey of twenty-three industrialized countries by the International Labor Organization found that only seven had statutes that specifically addressed sexual harassment, but judicial decisions in six others, including the United States, explicitly dealt with the offense. In most other nations, the law prohibited sexual harassment by implication as a violation of other legal strictures, such as unjust discharge, torts, or criminal law. Canada, Great Britain, and Australia have hewn most closely to the U.S. path, defining sexual harassment as sex discrimination. Other nations have enacted alternative approaches. Spain treats the offense as an invasion of privacy. France criminalizes sexual harassment but narrows the scope of the offense to include only quid pro quo harassment and to exclude harassment by coworkers. International organizations are another source of legal prohibitions. The United Nations, International Labor Organization, and European Community have condemned sexual harassment, and the UN's Commission on the Status of Women classified it as violence against women. Although Crouch finds that U.S. sexual harassment law has exercised widespread influence, she concludes that American law is more moralistic, with a tendency for some interpretations to emphasize sexual misconduct rather than gender discrimination. Alternative approaches de-emphasize gender, instead banning discrimination and sexual harassment as violations of employee rights and the dignity of all humans.

Legal Impact: Enforcing Sexual Harassment Law

Although expectations, and certainly hopes, are that authoritative statements by law-giving bodies will have a significant and salutary effect in curbing misconduct, assessing the effects of one case or of legal changes in general apart from other political, social, and economic factors is difficult if not impossible. *Vinson* has certainly been a central part of the combined changes that have transformed gender relations in the United States in recent decades, but its influence cannot be separated from other salient factors and events, such as the Hill-Thomas hearings, the gender gap in elections, new legislation, and the organizing and educational efforts of women's groups. Not surprisingly, statistical data measuring the direct impact that *Vinson* and sexual harassment law have had on sexually harassing conduct are lacking. Countervailing factors make increased reporting of incidents likely, even if the actual amount of misconduct has declined. Higher visibility doubtless raises awareness, encouraging more resistance, including complaints. Certainly sexual harassment has moved to center stage in our legal, business, educational, and political institutions as complaints have grown and highly publicized cases have captured the public's imagination and stirred whirling controversies about the efficacy and legitimacy of sexual harassment law in the post-*Vinson* era.

Charges of sexual harassment grew exponentially in the years after *Vinson*. The Equal Employment Opportunity Commission registered fewer than 10 charges per year before 1986; that year, the number catapulted to 624, climbing steadily to 2,217 in 1990 and to 4,626 in 1995. Since the mid-1990s, however, filings leveled off, with 4,783 filings in 1999, accounting for 6.2 percent of the almost 80,000 employment discrimination charges recorded by the agency. Combining EEOC charges and those filed with state fair employment practices agencies, a similar pattern occurs: 10,532 sexual harassment charges were filed in 1992, increasing by roughly 50 percent to 15,549 in the next five years, but growing slowly thereafter; 15,836 charges were filed with state and federal antidiscrimination agencies in 2000. Males are filing a growing proportion of the charges: 9.1 percent in 1992, and 13.6 percent in 2000. EEOC data do not report whether these charges were lodged against females or other males.

Agencies pursued 28.2 percent of these charges to "merit resolutions." Resolutions included finding reasonable cause to believe that discrimination had occurred, typically followed by attempts to conciliate the parties (successful in 3.1 percent and unsuccessful in 6.8 percent of the cases), negotiated settlements (10 percent of the time), or withdrawal with benefits (covering the 8.3 percent of cases in which the complaining party withdrew the charge upon receipt of the desired benefits). The average amount of compensation that agencies won for persons charging sexual harassment doubled from 1996 to 2000. In 1992, the aggregate amount of monetary benefits recouped was $12.7 million; charging parties received $54.6 million in 2000. Agencies closed 27.7 percent of the cases on various administrative grounds, including that the charging party withdrew the charge or failed to pursue the case. No reasonable cause to believe discrimination had occurred was determined in 44.1 percent of the cases, although the charging parties could bring private lawsuits despite being unsuccessful before the EEOC.

In federal courts, sexual harassment cases have been a substantial part of the colossal growth in employment lawsuits. The number of employment cases, most claiming discrimination, has increased more than 430 percent since the early 1970s. By 1996, there were 23,000 court cases alleging employment discrimination, double the number of filings in 1992, and the trend was for the number to increase by 20 percent annually. By 2002, the *Economist* reported that one out of five civil cases in the United States involved harassment or discrimination, compared with one in twenty a decade ago, and the Administrative Office of the Courts reported that employment discrimination cases were approaching 10 percent of the federal docket.

Sexual harassment lawsuits increased from fewer than 7,000 to about 18,000 during the 1990s. A study by Ann Juliano and Stewart J. Schwab uncovered 650 sexual harassment cases with reported opinions in the federal district and appeals courts in the decade after the *Vinson* decision. The authors recognize that by eliminating cases that did not result in a reported opinion by a judge, they are studying cases high up in the naming-blaming-claiming pyramid, possibly skewing their sample toward overrepresenting more serious and meritorious claims. Probably 95 percent of cases, like *Vinson*, settle out of court, and most court cases do not produce reported decisions. Nonetheless, the study yields the most comprehensive overview available of judicial enforcement of sexual harassment law after *Vinson*.

Partially reported demographic data indicate that males accounted for 5.4 percent of the plaintiffs. Plaintiffs tended to mirror the population in their marital and occupational status: most plaintiffs were blue collar (38 percent) or clerical (29 percent); professionals were slightly underrepresented, but managers were somewhat overrepresented, among plaintiffs. Eighty-nine percent had quit before suing. Individuals rather than government agencies, advocacy organizations, or class actions brought virtually all suits.

Mixed male-female workplaces accounted for about two-thirds of the cases, and about one-third involved mostly male workplaces. A negligible number of cases involved predominantly female workplaces. Almost one-fourth of the alleged misconduct occurred off-premises, although about half of these cases resulted from employment-related events, such as company parties. The remainder was divided almost equally between private socializing, such as after-hours drinks, and nonconsensual conduct, such as calls or visits to the victim's home. Most lawsuits were against private employers, but the federal government was the defendant in 4 percent of the cases and state and local governments in 23 percent (roughly twice the proportion of the labor force comprising these government employees).

About 70 percent exclusively charged hostile environment harassment; another 22.5 percent combined hostile environment with quid pro quo claims. Pure quid pro quo cases represented only 7.5 percent of the sample. Male-dominated workplaces were more likely to generate hostile environment claims. Clerical and blue-collar plaintiffs were more likely to complain of physical harassment (50 and 48 percent, respectively) than were professionals (38 percent) or managers (32 percent). Most sexual harassment was directed at the plaintiff specifically and was not based on comments about women in general or diffuse material such as pinups or posters (7 percent). Only 4 percent of the cases involved a single incident, and plaintiffs prevailed at a lower rate (35 percent) in these suits. Despite the passage of the Civil Rights Act of 1991, only twenty-nine of these cases from 1986 to 1996 were tried before juries (including only three of the thirty-three cases covered by the 1991 act). The authors detected a trend for judges to act as gatekeepers by dismissing plaintiffs' claims based on legal conclusions before airing factual contentions at trial. Only about one-third of the cases went to trial, but when they did, plaintiffs did significantly better before a jury than in a bench trial.

Female plaintiffs fared better than males, and blue-collar and clerical plaintiffs were more successful than professionals and managers. Plaintiffs' success rates rose if both supervisors and coworkers participated in the harassment, and greater numbers of harassers increased the likelihood of plaintiff victory. Plaintiffs were likely to prevail when sexual comments (57 percent win rate) or derogatory comments (59 percent) were directed specifically at them, although without some physical component to the harassment, plaintiffs' win rate fell to 45 percent. When companies had no formal sexual harassment programs or grievance procedures, plaintiffs won 71 percent of their cases. When plaintiffs had not complained, however, they lost almost 70 percent of the time. Overall, plaintiffs and defendants won about half the time in district court, but plaintiffs appealed more often, 74 percent of the cases; employers filed 18 percent of the appeals, and both parties appealed in 8 percent of the decisions. On appeal, plaintiffs and defendants were equally unsuccessful, each winning reversals in 27 percent of the cases.

During this period, plaintiff win rates rose from 40 percent in 1986, the year of the *Vinson* decision, to 55.2 percent in 1995. More recent data suggest that plaintiffs are winning 58 percent of the time and that employers have to pay about $100,000 in each case they lose. Jury awards averaged $250,000 in 1993, and the median award for compensatory damages in 1997 was $250,000. The median punitive damages award was $100,000 that year.

———

The Business of Sexual Harassment

With employers losing this kind of money, it is small wonder that most American businesses and organizations are beginning to treat potential sexual harassment liability with the utmost seriousness. As early as 1988, a survey by *Working Woman* magazine suggested a "transformation in corporate attitudes in the past decade. . . . Sexual harassment, once a feminist issue, has become a financial one." Since then, growing numbers of complaints and suits, new rules of employer liability, and bigger awards to successful complainants at the EEOC and in the courts have spurred employers to invest time, energy, and revenue to avoid sexual harassment liability.

Damage awards are merely the tip of the iceberg in calculating what sexual harassment costs employers. Even if ultimately successful, defending a sexual harassment lawsuit can easily cost a defendant $100,000 for each day of trial. In 1994, the average cost of sexual harassment liability was estimated at $600,000 if legal fees were included. Average settlement costs, although far lower, are estimated to range from $15,000 to $50,000, but attorneys practicing in this area report much higher figures, routinely running over $500,000 and often surpassing $1 million. Highly publicized class actions and suits by multiple plaintiffs in the late 1990s, although rare, resulted in huge payouts by large corporations. Mitsubishi Motors Manufacturing of

America settled claims brought by twenty-nine female employees for $9.5 million, only to have to pay an additional $34 million to settle a suit brought by the EEOC on behalf of other harassed employees. Wal-Mart paid $5 million, and Astra USA paid $10 million to resolve claims. Workplace consultant Kathleen Neville maintains that twenty claims are settled without publicity for each suit that comes to light. One magazine aimed at executives in the financial industry estimated that settling sexual harassment claims cost corporate America more than $1 billion during the five years after passage of the 1991 Civil Rights Act. More than 100 insurance companies now offer employment practices liability insurance to protect against legal costs, damages, and settlements arising from employment discrimination and harassment claims.

Sexual harassment has other hidden costs that soak employers for millions even before a complaint arises. The federal government estimated that it lost $189 million between 1978 and 1980 as a result of sexual harassment in government offices. In the late 1980s, *Working Woman* projected that the typical Fortune 500 corporation could expect losses of $6.7 million annually because of the by-products of sexual harassment, including absenteeism, lower productivity, health care costs, lower morale, and employee turnover. In addition to these internal costs, the external harm attributable to these public-relations fiascoes is not negligible. For example, 51 percent of the purchasers of Mitsubishi autos are women.

Employers are increasingly taking affirmative steps to guard against these legal and extralegal costs, a trend given new urgency since the Supreme Court clarified liability rules for supervisor sexual harassment in the *Faragher* and *Ellerth* cases in 1998. Unless adverse tangible employment decisions have been taken, employers can defend against liability if they can demonstrate that they acted reasonably to prevent and remedy sexual harassment, at least if plaintiffs failed to avail themselves of such means to avoid harassment. Sexual harassment consulting and training is a major growth industry. *Working Woman's* 1992 survey found that 81 percent of Fortune 500 corporations sponsored training, up from only 60 percent in the magazine's 1988 survey. The market for online training alone is estimated to be $150 million. Mitsubishi, in addition to paying out almost $44 million in settlement in two historic cases, paid former labor secretary and business consultant Lynn Martin and her three-person staff $2 million in consulting fees in a two-year effort to improve conditions at its Normal, Illinois, plant. Studies show that training is effective at improving understanding and attitudes, although less is known about its impact on behavior.

A 1981 survey of *Harvard Business Review* readers found that only 29 percent reported working in companies where management had issued statements to employees disapproving of sexual misconduct, but by 1992, 75 percent of the companies belonging to the American Management Association had anti–sexual harassment policies. Sociologist Lauren B. Edelman interprets the move toward formal organizational policies and due process rights for employees as a response to the civil rights laws of the 1960s, which created a normative environment calling into question arbitrary authority in the workplace. To retain legitimacy, management instituted explicit grievance procedures. In her sample, the number of companies with formal complaint procedures tripled in the two decades after the enactment of Title VII, led by larger companies. Other studies have found five- to tenfold increases in due process mechanisms in response to "the legalization of the workplace."

Sexual Harassment in the Political Realm

Sexual harassment seemed omnipresent in the most sensational political headlines of the 1990s. The decade opened with heated public debate sparked by televised hearings into Anita Hill's charges of sexual harassment against Clarence Thomas, President George Bush's nominee to the Supreme Court. If the Supreme Court's *Vinson* ruling set the stage for public awareness of sexual harassment, the Hill-Thomas hearings cascaded the controversial topic into almost every American living room. The decade closed with the impeachment of President Bill Clinton on charges stemming indirectly from what, standing alone, might have been dismissed as a dubious sexual harassment charge.

President Bush nominated Clarence Thomas to replace Justice Thurgood Marshall on the Supreme Court. Although both were African American, Thomas was his predecessor's ideological polar opposite, having been appointed by President Ronald Reagan to head the Education Department's Office of Civil Rights and the EEOC and to serve on the D.C. court of appeals. Controversial from the beginning, his nomination drew a seven–seven tie in the Senate Judiciary Committee. Before the nomination could win the expected approval of the full Senate, Anita Hill, a law professor who had worked for Thomas at both the OCR and the EEOC, agreed to testify about improper conduct by her former boss only after statements made confidentially to government investigators seeking information about Thomas's qualifications were leaked to the press. Hill charged that Thomas had initiated conversations with her about pornographic movies, bragged of his own sexual prowess, repeatedly pressured her to go out with him, and demanded reasons when she refused his social invitations. These incidents ceased before Thomas transferred to the EEOC, but after Hill, too, transferred to that agency, the misconduct began again. When she left the government, Thomas allegedly told her that "if I ever told anyone about his behavior toward me it could ruin his career."

Thomas denied all of Hill's allegations and objected to having his reputation besmirched. He likened the hearings to "a high-tech lynching" and proclaimed that "these are charges that play into racist, bigoted stereotypes." Although his accuser was African American and some of his chief backers were opponents of civil rights, many African American women were suspicious of white women's rallying around Hill, fearing that she had become a pawn in Washington power struggles in which they had little stake. Thomas's invocation of solidarity rallied support for his confirmation, with African American opinion shifting from 54 to 71 percent in Thomas's favor. Playing the "race card" put Democratic senators in a bind. Although inclined to oppose Thomas because of his conservative ideology as well as his mediocre qualifications (brief service on the appeals court and a "minimally qualified" rating by the American Bar Association), Democrats feared that the president would nominate a white conservative if Thomas were rejected, placing the onus on the Democrats for denying African Americans representation on the Court.

Republicans experienced no comparable restraints in defending their nominee by attacking Hill's credibility. Detractors questioned her motives, her honesty, and even her mental stability, both in the hearings and in the press. Most sharply challenged were her failure to come forward earlier and her decision to "follow" Thomas to the EEOC. Hill gave plausible answers: she had not come forward with public charges voluntarily but had simply responded honestly to questions during Thomas's FBI background check. Her failure to speak out earlier and her career moves typified decisions by ambitious, upwardly mobile professionals who choose to protect their career prospects at the cost of suffering sexual pressures in silence. Although a sample of 100 judges believed her charges to be more credible than Thomas's denials by a margin of 41 to 22 percent, with 37 percent unsure, one survey found public opinion tilted toward Thomas, 48 to 29 percent. Other polls described the public as skeptical that either witness was telling the whole truth, but people were inclined two to one to confirm Thomas because he deserved the benefit of the doubt. Public opinion split evenly on whether the committee had treated Hill fairly. On credibility, women as well as men favored Thomas over Hill during the hearings, by 46 to 31 percent, but within a year, opinion had shifted away from Thomas. A 1992 poll found that the public now believed Hill rather than Thomas by a margin of 43 to 39 percent, and women now supported Hill 46 to 36 percent.

The hearings failed to change a single committee vote; the full chamber's vote to confirm was fifty-two to forty-eight, the slimmest margin for a Supreme Court confirmation in the twentieth century. Two Republicans opposed their president's nominee, while Thomas garnered the votes of eleven Democrats, seven of whom represented southern states with crucial African American constituencies. The confrontational confirmation process registered strong reverberations at the grass roots. The women workers' advocacy group 9to5 reported that thousands called its Survival Hotline. Some callers felt that the hearings would discourage sexual harassment victims from speaking out by proving that harassers win when complaints rest only on the word of victims, but others believed that the public attention would be beneficial, throwing the spotlight on this "dirty little secret." Anita Hill commented, "The silence has been broken." In the three months after the hearings, sexual harassment charges filed with the EEOC jumped a phenomenal 70 percent. The number of sexual harassment lawsuits almost doubled from 1991 to 1993, the amount of damages awarded increased substantially, and some observers suggest that juries became less sympathetic to defendants in sexual harassment cases in the 1990s. The impact was not limited to this country, as complaints about sexual harassment increased around the world.

The hearings probably speeded passage of the previously gridlocked Civil Rights Act of 1991 and may have thwarted a veto by President Bush, who had opposed earlier versions. The 1992 elections, sometimes called "the Year of the Woman," reflected at least in part the mobilization of women's groups in angry if delayed reaction to the Hill-Thomas hearings. Although that label exaggerates women's progress toward equal representation in this single election, female membership in the Senate tripled from two to six, with a seventh added by a special election the next year. In the House of Representatives, the addition of seven women of color almost tripled their representation, and the total number of female members leaped from twenty-nine to forty-eight.

If 1991 was the "seismic year" for sexual harassment, the shock waves continued on Capitol Hill in the following years. In 1992, Washington Senator Brock Adams, a respected liberal Democrat and leading advocate for women, terminated his reelection campaign amidst accusations by eight anonymous women and one who publicly charged Adams with misconduct. A second 1992 scandal drew more notoriety when ten women charged Oregon Senator Bob Packwood, a progressive Republican, with sexual harassment in incidents stretching from 1969, his first year in the Senate, to 1990. The charges included several incidents of physical harassment, such as grabbing, fondling, and kissing female staffers. Packwood's initial denials turned into admissions that he had acted badly, but he refused to resign, claiming to be simply an "overeager kisser." As the Senate Ethics Committee and Justice Department began separate investigations, the charges escalated to include the unlawful acceptance of gratuities, misuse of campaign funds, perjury, and obstruction of justice. Packwood lost court battles to shield his personal diaries from subpoena. The intimate musings portrayed a potent if lurid mix of sex and power in which the senator writes of having "made love" with twenty-two staffers and lusting after seventy-five more. In May 1995, the Ethics Committee issued a 174-page report, finding probable cause that Packwood had abused his office. That September, Packwood resigned. Incidents that came to light were probably only the tip of the iceberg.

In a 1993 survey, one-third of the women working on Capitol Hill reported that they had been sexually harassed, and one-third of these women claimed that their harassers were members of Congress. Wanda Baucus, wife of Montana's senator, disclosed that two senators had harassed her. Only in 1995 did Congress fully extend coverage of all employment laws to employees of the legislature.

The executive branch, including the military and the president, did not escape the taint of scandal. At the 1991 Las Vegas convention of the Tailhook Association, a gathering of naval aviators, at least twenty-six women, including fourteen officers, were assaulted at the host hotel. Many women complained of having to run a gauntlet of up to 200 drunken men who groped, pinched, and fondled them; some were knocked to the floor and their clothes ripped off or removed. Initial complaints to superior officers were met with apathy; one admiral responded, "That's what you get when you go to a hotel party with a bunch of drunk aviators." After some of the complainants went public, the Pentagon finally launched an investigation. Its 1993 report found more extensive harassment but concluded that the 1991 convention did not differ significantly from previous Tailhook meetings. Despite stonewalling by most attendees and initially lackadaisical efforts to ferret out the wrongdoers, eventually six senior officers were reassigned, three admirals were censured, and another thirty admirals were reprimanded for failing to respond appropriately, but the chief of naval operations was allowed to retire with full benefits.

Other sexual harassment abuses in the military grabbed headlines in the 1990s. In 1996, at the army's Aberdeen Ordnance Center and School, female trainees complained about sexual abuse ranging from inappropriate touching to rape at the hands of their drill sergeants. After investigation, some fifty victims were identified, and a dozen drill instructors were punished with either prison sentences, including one for twenty-five years, or administrative discipline, including discharge. Four senior officers received letters of reprimand. Despite corrective actions, survey data confirm that the problem is not solved. The army's Sexual Experiences Questionnaire showed that 78 percent of women reported crude or offensive behavior in 1997, but 84 percent experienced such behavior in 2001; 72 percent reported sexist behavior in 1997, and 74 percent in 2001; 47 percent complained of unwanted sexual attention in 1997, versus 51 percent in 2001; 15 percent were the targets of sexual coercion and 7 percent of sexual assault in 1997, and 17 percent and 8 percent were the targets of such misconduct in 2001. A macho military culture and lack of critical mass of women, who constitute 15 percent of the armed forces, are factors contributing to the continuing problem. The strict military hierarchy is another obstacle to rooting out sexual harassment in the services. A 1982 army survey found that 43 percent of enlisted women said that their superiors offered favors in exchange for sex, an offer many felt unable to refuse, and a 1990 Pentagon poll discovered that 42 percent of the women who had experienced some form of sexual coercion or harassment identified superiors as their harassers. In 2003, allegations of rampant sexual assault and rape shook the Air Force Academy, where investigators unearthed fifty-six cases of rape or sexual assault since 1993, but at least an equal number surfaced when cadets began to go public with their charges. Some female cadets charged that officials compounded the problem by being unsupportive, discouraging complaints lest they reflect badly on the academy's reputation, and punishing victims who dared to file charges.

The 1990s ended with a sexual harassment scandal that reached the Oval Office itself, nearly toppling a sitting president. On May 6, 1994, Paula Corbin Jones filed a sexual harassment suit against President Bill Clinton, based on an incident that she said occurred when he was governor of Arkansas. Jones, a state clerical employee, charged that after a brief greeting at a convention at the Excelsior Hotel in Little Rock in 1991, the governor summoned her to his room. According to Jones, he exposed himself to her, asked her to "kiss it," but when she refused, said, "Well, I don't want to make you do anything you don't want to do." Clinton's lawyers argued that the president is entitled to limited immunity against suits for alleged private misconduct occurring before he assumed office, but in *Clinton v. Jones* (1997), the Supreme Court rebuffed his argument and refused to stay the suit until Clinton left office. The president's lawyers then moved for summary judgment, which Judge Susan Webber Wright granted in April 1998. Judge Wright held that even if Clinton had behaved as Jones charged, his conduct did not constitute actionable sexual harassment because Jones had suffered no job detriments and the alleged incident was insufficiently "frequent, severe, or physically threatening" to create a hostile working environment. Jones appealed, but the parties settled out of court in November 1998 for $850,000, with no admission of fault by Clinton.

Embarrassing as this lawsuit was, the major damage was indirect, leading to Clinton's impeachment by a torturous trail of legal technicalities. Jones's lawyers had amended her complaint to include a charge of sexual assault, claiming that Clinton had put his hand on Jones's leg. A recent change in the federal rules of evidence, backed by the president, made admissible similar acts of sexual assault to establish that the defendant had a propensity for abusing women. Relying on Rule 415, Jones's attorneys asked Clinton to name all the women other than his wife with whom he had had "sexual relations" while in public office. Judge Wright narrowed the scope but allowed discovery to proceed.

Tipped off by Linda Tripp, a confidante of White House intern Monica Lewinsky, about an affair between Lewinsky and the president, Jones's lawyers questioned Lewinsky and Clinton about a sexual relationship. They elicited denials under oath from both: a sworn affidavit from Lewinsky, and a January 17, 1998, deposition of the president in which he claimed not to have had "sexual relations" with Lewinsky. Tripp also informed independent prosecutor Kenneth Starr, who was investigating the Clintons' financial dealings in the Whitewater land transaction. Expanding the scope of his authority to explore this latest allegation of presidential misconduct, Starr threatened to prosecute Lewinsky unless she cooperated. News of the affair leaked to the press in January 1998, but Clinton denied having "had sex with that woman, Ms. Lewinsky." In August 1998, Clinton videotaped his deposition before the independent counsel's grand jury and then appeared on television to admit having an inappropriate relationship with Lewinsky. In September, Starr's report was released, describing Clinton's affair with Lewinsky in graphically salacious detail. Although Clinton's defenders charged that the report's emphasis on sex shored up a weak legal case, on December 19, the House of Representatives voted to impeach the president for perjury and obstruction of justice. On February 12, 1999, the Senate voted fifty-one to forty-nine, along partisan lines, not to convict.

The political fallout was widespread but unpredictably mixed. Support for Clinton among feminists and women's organizations varied significantly. Gloria Steinem argued that Clinton had consistently adhered to the "no means no; yes means yes" rule. Others questioned whether consent could be meaningful with power so glaringly imbalanced, suggesting that "the President of the United States knowingly and recklessly abused his power in taking advantage of a psychologically vulnerable, 'star struck' romantic half as old as he." Yet others feared that it was more paternalistic than feminist to reject the choice of a woman who had attained the age of majority and was a White House volunteer rather than a presidential employee. Public opinion tended to agree with former senator George McGovern that "it's Hillary's business, not mine." Although disapproving of Clinton's private behavior, most voters were satisfied with the country's peace and prosperity and bestowed high job approval ratings on the president. The Republican Congress suffered a stinging setback in the 1998 elections, prompting the resignation of Speaker Newt Gingrich, engineer of the 1994 "Republican revolution." Although Clinton's approval ratings remained high, disapproval of his personal behavior neutralized Al Gore's ability to capitalize on the administration's policy achievements by associating himself with the peace and prosperity of the two Clinton terms, costing him votes in the 2000 election.

———

Backlash

High visibility brought opposition as well as support for sexual harassment law. Representing a spectrum of reasons and views, the backlash ranged from mild efforts to curb what were seen as excesses or clear up vague points or unintended consequences to attacks on the whole regulatory enterprise as inherently pernicious.

For critics such as Professor Kingsley Browne, who employs an evolutionary psychology approach to sexual harassment, the attempt to legally interdict sexual harassment is not merely wrongheaded but also inevitably an exercise in frustration. If sexual harassment is caused by misunderstandings between men and women who have adopted differing sexual strategies flowing from eons of reproductive success, gender conflicts are inevitable and essentially "no fault." Although attempts to improve communication between men and women are laudatory, dragging the law into a biologically based "battle of the sexes" merits a contemporary version of Edmund Burke's classic rebuke to egalitarians: "You think you are combating prejudice, but you are at war with nature."

Several related criticisms of sexual harassment law implicitly build on this naturalistic perspective, even if they do not articulate its claim of biological roots. Critics of sexual harassment regulations are often particularly sensitive to perceived threats to an unvoiced but jealously guarded male "right of sexual initiative." These critics are wary of any restraints that might discourage or penalize males for making advances to females and want to protect the traditional, perhaps even natural, courtship patterns or, more bluntly, sexual strategies by which men search out female partners. Voicing an extreme variant of this viewpoint, Warren Farrell complains that prohibiting sexual harassment interferes with the traditional mode of male sexual initiative captured in Harlequin romances, aimed at working women (readers average twenty books a month): "A successful man pursuing a working woman, the working woman resisting, *the man overcoming her resistance*, and her being 'swept away.'" Once, he asserts, "the process of overcoming her barriers was called 'courtship.' Now it is called *either* 'courtship' *or* 'sexual harassment.'" Farrell maintains that while women enjoy complete discretion to define male initiatives as sexual harassment, men remain confused and vulnerable: "When it works, we call it a wedding and the woman's picture is in the paper; when it doesn't, we call it a lawsuit and the man's picture is in the paper." What galls Farrell even more is that women take indirect initiative by enticing men into making overt sexual advances. A woman can read *Cosmopolitan* for suggestions on how to dress and act to lure her prey into initiating romantic advances and, in the same magazine, get advice on how to sue her hapless coworker if she decides his "moves" fail to spark her interest.

These concerns have not been limited to criticisms but have been incorporated into the doctrinal fabric of sexual harassment law. For example, demanding that women prove unwelcomeness, admitting embarrassing proof of welcomeness, setting a high standard for severity or pervasiveness, and judging that standard from the perspective of a "reasonable person" can all be considered hedges against legal liability for men pursuing women at work. These doctrinal hurdles tend to preserve the traditional, and some jurists may fear unappreciated, role of men as initiators of sexual relations.

A related criticism faults sexual harassment law for attempting to sanitize workplaces, a social engineering project that courts are ill-equipped to undertake. *Rabidue v. Osceola Refining Co.*'s majority epitomizes this rejection of the law's purported mission. The court's opinion admitted that "it cannot seriously be disputed that in some work environments, humor and language are rough-hewn and vulgar. Sexual jokes, sexual conversations and girlie magazines may abound." But the court opined that the law was not "designed to bring about the magical transformation in the social mores of American workers." Sex and sexism are not confined to the workplace but permeate society. How could the atmosphere at Osceola's work site be judged illegally hostile "when considered in the context of a society that condones and publicly features and commercially exploits open displays of written and pictorial erotica at the newsstands, on prime-time television, at the cinema, and in other public places"? Implicitly adopting rampant sexism as the standard, the court trivialized the grotesquely raunchy environment at Osceola and treated the plaintiff's reaction, instead of the sexism, as outside the social norm. The court completely abandoned Title VII's purpose — to remove barriers to women's equal economic opportunity — and accepted social mores as natural, or at least the proper purview of the law. The court's analysis implicitly left women working in environments reflecting these sexist social values and customs with a simple choice: "lump it or leave it."

Against this backdrop of gendered sexual patterns, traditional courtship rituals, and social mores, critics complain that sexual harassment law is vague. This criticism solicits concern for innocent males whose harmless if sometimes maladroit flirtations unwittingly land them in a snare between changing and arcane legal doctrine and timeless social custom. Some expressions of concern sound eminently reasonable: "It's very tough for me to know what I can say and what I can't say. Without some definition, how is one to know?" Sexual harassment law, in common with law generally, is complex and lacking mathematical precision, but much post-*Vinson* jurisprudence represents courts' attempts to establish clear distinctions between grave and seriously injurious misconduct and frivolous workplace irritations. Much of the hyperbole of backlash, however, wildly mischaracterizes the actual state of the legal regulation of interpersonal relations in the workplace. As one vice president of personnel lamented, "a man would be afraid to speak to a woman in the office without first speaking to her lawyer." The putatively nebulous border between sexual pursuit and sexual harassment has men claiming to be afraid of "tripping into deep water," petrified that doing lunch could end in a "career-buster day."

Mythology about the "sexual minefield that is the modern workplace" reflects popular ignorance of the law and Americans' inflated ideas about rights at work, and sensationalized accounts of sexual harassment in the media feed these fears of legal liability for trivial breaches of etiquette. One oft-cited example of overreaction is six-year-old Johnathan Prevette's suspension for giving a female classmate a friendly kiss on the cheek, in an incident reported under headlines such as "Loose Lips," "Kiss and Yell," and "Peck of Trouble." Another is the infamous "Seinfeld" case involving a Miller Brewing Company executive who was fired supposedly for repeating a joke heard on the Jerry Seinfeld show the previous night, a discharge "more laughable than the TV episode itself." These stories are hardly representative of lawsuits brought by plaintiffs, much less judgments rendered by courts. Investigation generally reveals that these horror stories present misleading or at best partial accounts of the actual incidents. For example, the "suspended" six-year-old's punishment was limited to an in-school suspension that separated him from his class for one day, causing him to miss an ice cream party. Nevertheless, this moderate penalty for "bad touching" under the school's general conduct code — the school had no sexual harassment policy — stirred a national furor, fueled by a media blitz that included appearances by Johnathan's parents on CNN, the *Today Show*, and *NBC News* and a press conference where his mom wore a "Kiss Me Johnathan" button. The fired manager in the Seinfeld case did not simply repeat a slightly off-color joke from TV but rather badgered his former subordinate about it, had previously been accused of sexual harassment by his secretary, and was fired for poor management and poor judgment, not for sexual harassment. The sanctions meted out in both instances were discipline administered under organizational rules, not sexual harassment law, and the Miller manager sued the company and won $26 million.

Media-fed caricatures have taken their toll in the public mind. In a 1998 poll, 80 percent of men and women agreed that false reports of sexual harassment were common. Fifty-seven percent of men and

52 percent of women believed that "we have gone too far in making common interactions between employees into cases of sexual harassment," and a 1997 survey of executives found that 89 percent worried about being sued for sexual harassment. Popular images are remote from workplace realities: "Only a tiny proportion of office come-ons result in harassment complaints," noted a recent article, and only 9 percent of these rare complaints lead to formal proceedings.

Doubtlessly, efforts to eliminate sex discrimination and harassment risk going overboard in a society influenced by a strongly puritanical heritage. F. M. Christensen captures the prudishness of American attitudes when he writes, "The fact that a type of behavior as harmless and as natural for human beings as talking about sex would be treated as a crime reveals something deeply perverted in this culture." Yet to suggest that sexual harassment law criminalizes "talking about sex" is misleading. This inaccurate view of sexual harassment law fits a broader pattern of accepting only elemental gains for women (for example, the basic concept of equal rights for women) while distancing those gains from feminism itself. Many now deplore the most egregious forms of sexual harassment, that is, the "sledgehammer harassment" of quid pro quo sexual coercion, while perceiving efforts to eradicate hostile environments of "personal remarks, off-color jokes, and ogling" common to many workplaces as "going too far" and attacking the "rights of men." The very banality and pervasiveness of this "dripping tap" harassment reinforce the view that efforts to reform it are futile assaults on social patterns that appear natural or, at least, "normal."

Sexual harassment law is not immune to valid criticisms; for example, there is Jeffrey Rosen's complaint that amended evidentiary Rule 415 unfairly exposes the sexual histories of accused offenders, which raises genuine concerns that sexual harassment law, if not applied cautiously, can expose legitimately private affairs to the "unwanted gaze" of government supervision. But the backlash against sexual harassment law has been fueled by the broader backlash against government programs and regulations that culminated in the conservative climate of the 1980s and 1990s. With even "liberal" Democrat Bill Clinton declaring that "the era of big government is over," the public was receptive to charges that government had overreached its properly limited authority by tackling the social problem of sexual harassment and that such efforts represented Big Brother–like "snoopervision" of essentially private relations in private workplaces.

False conceptions of antidiscrimination law as creating "special rights" for protected groups also undermine public support for reforms. Although the language of some opinions may imply that prohibiting discrimination "because of sex" offers special protection for women, the law clearly protects men as well as women against sexual harassment, coverage that men increasingly utilize. Lack of trust in women, however, by both courts and the public, feeds suspicions that women bring the ostensibly unwanted sexual attention on themselves and cannot be counted on to report only cases of true harassment and not be thin-skinned and easily offended, or perhaps simply vindictive.

Race further complicates the social problem of sexual harassment, in ways that may be linked, however tenuously, to backlash. African American and other minority women are disproportionately likely to be targeted as victims of sexual harassment and are more likely to file complaints or sue about sexual harassment, although underreporting seems more predictable. African American women have played a prominent role in bringing sexual harassment to the forefront and in its eventual prohibition. The public is aware of Anita Hill's race, but less well known is that many plaintiffs in the pioneering cases were African American. These early plaintiffs not only were women of color but also typically held working-class positions: Paulette Barnes, payroll clerk; Margaret Miller, proofing machine operator; Diane Williams, Justice Department employee; Rebekah Barnett, shop clerk. Bank teller Mechelle Vinson was also African American, as were a number of other individuals who figured prominently in her sexual harassment suit: Sidney Taylor, her manager and alleged harasser; Judge John Garrett Penn, the federal district court judge who tried the case; Judge W. Spottswood Robinson III, who wrote the court's opinion for the D.C. Circuit court of appeals; and of course, Justice Thurgood Marshall, who penned the Supreme Court concurrence arguing for stricter employer liability.

Several explanations have been offered as to why women of color are especially frequent targets for sexual harassment. Catharine MacKinnon has suggested that race is a marker for vulnerability; harassers generally choose less powerful victims, and women of color, like young, divorced, lower-paid, clerical or blue-collar women, have less power in American society, making them more susceptible as targets. Kimberle Crenshaw traces the roots of current heightened abuse to slavery, a system that institutionalized forcible access to black women. Sex offenses against black women were minimized, even justified, by dominant myths and stereotypes, especially that African American women were sexually voracious and indiscriminate. Sexual harassment of African American women involves an added racist dimension to the abuse, explaining the overrepresentation of black women as targets.

This "racialization of sexual harassment" also reveals its true nature as "intentional discrimination that is insulting, threatening, and debilitating," destroying the illusion that it is merely unappreciated flattery or awkward, perhaps boorish, social overtures. Racialization may be linked to backlash. Historically, the legal system equated lack of chastity with lack of veracity. Because women of color were assumed to be unchaste, they were also denied credibility. Adding race to the mix of sexual harassment may help explain why targets of sexual abuse are so often greeted with skepticism by the legal system and the public when they step forward to confront their harassers.

Failure to Avail: Law versus Reality?

One factor limiting the achievements of *Vinson* and its successors is that much of the burden to resist sexual harassment remains on individual victims to complain and seek redress through their organizations' grievance procedures, press administrative charges, or ultimately file lawsuits. The Supreme Court's twin 1998 employer liability cases, *Faragher* and *Ellerth*, attempted to engineer legal and economic incentives that encourage organizations to take proactive steps to prevent sexual harassment before it occurs or, at least, to remedy it as soon as incidents happen. Roughly stated, employers may have a defense if they provide serviceable policies and procedures against abuse, and victims risk forfeiting their legal remedies unless they reasonably avail themselves of these or alternative means to combat sexual harassment.

The obligation placed on victims to report their harassment contrasts markedly with most victims' responses to sexual harassment. Most sexual harassment targets, as many as 90 to 95 percent, do not report the problem to their employers. Contrary to popular conceptions of men as more assertive and rights conscious, men may be even less likely to take formal action; one survey found that only 7.8 percent of men experiencing same-sex harassment and 3 percent of males claiming harassment by females took formal action. The law and reality appear to be on a collision course.

Why don't victims report their sexual harassment? Judges, as well as many jurors and the general public, readily perceive this failure as unreasonable, but nonreporting is quite understandable when viewed from the victim's perspective. Dominant ideology may immobilize victims. They may simply not recognize, or name, the behavior as sexual harassment, or they may consider it a personal problem to be solved by individual initiative. Victims may subordinate their interests to those of the organization or minimize the problem to avoid conflict, perhaps interpreting the misconduct as a misunderstanding. They may view their harassment as a minor annoyance or conclude that it is inevitable. About a quarter of all victims blame themselves. Many are ashamed, and others are simply so sickened by the situation that they are unable to make any effective response.

Victims validly fear that they will not be believed. The ideology of "exit" underestimates the barriers and costs of escaping the situation. Viewing harassment through a lens of "choice" encourages victims to retreat and puts resisters in a double bind: if they report the harassment, they are troublemakers; if they submit, they must have "wanted it." Sensing that the dominant culture still distrusts women's reports of sexual abuse, victims must anticipate that they will be exposing themselves, as well as their harassers, to skepticism, disbelief, investigation, criticism, ostracism, public humiliation, and further vexation if they have the temerity to blow the whistle on their harassers. Many victims fear the consequences of public accusations not only for themselves but also for their loved ones.

Reporting can entail tangible economic or career consequences. Three-quarters of victims have legitimate fears of retaliation. One study found that 24 percent of victims who complained were fired, and another indicated that a majority of complainants were eventually discharged. Short of termination, victims who complain experience psychological abuse, poorer evaluations and other types of lost benefits, and social ostracism. Beyond discharge, the employer may withhold letters of recommendation, harming prospects for future jobs. Many victims conclude that complaining is tantamount to committing career suicide. Balanced against these grave risks, many victims are likely to perceive few tangible benefits in reporting harassment. Many place little trust in the employer, which, after all, allowed or at least failed to prevent the harassment. And victims may lack faith in the employer's ability or will to remedy the harm of harassment. One survey found that only 20 percent of women believed that complaints were dealt with justly, although 70 percent of personnel managers believed that complaints were resolved appropriately. Organizations sometimes employ a "double discourse" on reporting sexual harassment: although the official policies and procedures discourage harassment and facilitate reporting, a "hidden transcript" of scuttlebutt supplements the official documents, deterring targets from taking formal action.

Lack of complaint, however, does not mean lack of response. Although studies show that between a quarter and a half of all victims "ignore" the problem, that term may obscure an active decision to try to endure the harassment in the hope that it will dissipate or to temporize while assessing what, if anything, to do about it. Another 25 percent respond "mildly." Such responses may include treating the harassment as a joke, answering with humorous or diversionary retorts, or voicing polite requests to stop the behavior. Many victims simply try to avoid the problem or the harasser. Probably 10 to 20 percent seek a transfer or quit altogether. Few — 2 percent, according to one study — seek legal advice, and of those who register charges with the EEOC, only 1 percent follow through with lawsuits.

Despite these bleak realities, the law and the public generally do not empathize with nonreporting. At trial, the case's circumstances look radically different from when the harassment actually occurred. By trial time, the victim is legally represented and protected, the vague dimensions of the original problem have been clarified, and any penalties for going public have been exacted. Reporting, in other words, appears eminently reasonable, but the victim has already crossed many bridges since the harassment occurred. Then, the conduct likely was ambiguous, and the victim needed to retain her job and perhaps her working relationship with the harasser. Reporting procedures may be unclear, the outcome highly uncertain, and the risks formidable. Temporizing or alternative responses likely appear reasonable, while reporting seems daunting. Although enforcement must rely on complaints, since prevention is not foolproof, to require reporting simultaneously with the initial harassment removes effective hope of relief for most victims.

Joanna L. Grossman has criticized the new Supreme Court rules on employer liability for shifting the focus in analyzing employer liability from the acts of the employer's agent — that is, the harasser — to the employer's own actions and those of the sexual harassment target. Practically, the *Faragher-Ellerth* rules subvert strict liability and substitute negligence standards. This emphasis could be salutary in stimulating preventive efforts by employers, but it abandons Title VII's goal of compensating victims for its other goal of deterrence. Lower courts, Grossman finds, are interpreting the new rules to give employers a free pass on liability unless their own actions are inadequate. Just as the common law allowed dog owners to escape strict liability until after their dogs had taken a first bite (giving owners notice of the problem), the *Faragher-Ellerth* rule creates a safe harbor for employers that establish reasonable policies and procedures because the "first bite" of sexual harassment is "free."

This stance heightens the centrality of determining what is "reasonable" to expect from sexual harassment victims in terms of availing themselves of avenues of reporting or otherwise resisting harassment. Charitably viewed, the Supreme Court's approach to employer liability is an attempt to structure the legal rules to motivate both employers and victims to be more aggressive in their efforts to eradicate sexual harassment. In the long run, this strategy may prove to be less willfully naive than it appears, judged on past social realities. Although studies document that mandating reporting puts the law at odds with reality, social reality is not static. New employer policies, procedures, and training may make a difference in reporting rates if targets come to believe that they have a right to be free from harassment and that available remedies can realistically stop the harassment. Research in the 1990s suggested that reporting could be expected to increase, and fragmentary evidence supports this hypothesis. A Canadian study found that disseminating antiharassment policies by means ranging from posters to pamphlets to presentations both encouraged women to respond assertively to harassment, including filing complaints, and resulted in fewer incidents of harassment. Jill Kriegsberg suggests practical and philosophical reasons to support a reporting requirement: "Pushing women to report instances of sexual harassment should also be encouraged from a feminist standpoint. It is important for women to be proactive against this problem and by speaking out against such behavior, women send a message that such conduct is not and should not be accepted." Although everyone concerned with eradicating sexual harassment has a stake in changing the reality of nonreporting, it is unclear whether the heavy burdens of reporting can be borne by individual victims absent an organized political response.

In a society that displays a marked penchant for turning political issues into legal disputes, legal clashes often assume epic political proportions. When private plaintiffs such as Mechelle Vinson go to court to protect their interests and to assert their putative rights, they invariably pull courts into broader social controversies. Although ostensibly performing the limited function of applying the law to resolve disputes between individual parties by relying on the conservative technique of following precedent, courts sometimes make decisions that send shock waves of change reverberating throughout society. The story of *Meritor Savings Bank v. Vinson* and its aftermath illustrates how deeply involved the Supreme Court and lower courts have been in the evolution of gender relations, leading to some of the most striking social changes of the late twentieth century. And widely varying assessments of the role played by the law and courts in these and other changes demonstrate how vigorously contested that involvement has been.

CONCLUSION: LAW AND SOCIAL CHANGE

Definitive assessments of Supreme Court decisions are hampered by a dearth of empirical research, the difficulty of controlling for the effects of other factors that can influence outcomes, and especially longitudinal data tracking effects over time. Moreover, not even landmark Supreme Court rulings are the final word in resolving social conflicts, but merely one word in an ongoing social dialogue involving the voices of many participants. *Vinson* was preceded by much labor in the trenches by feminist advocates and attorneys, as well as the passage of an antidiscrimination statute by Congress more than two decades before the Court heard the case. The decision, far from settling all the legal questions about sexual harassment, initiated a process of further litigation and legislation that filled in gaps and clarified many issues, but also left open many questions.

This case, originating in a conflict at work between Mechelle Vinson and Sidney Taylor, has reverberated remarkably across the American landscape since the Supreme Court spoke less than two decades ago. The legal system has devoted huge attention and resources to the eradication of sexual harassment. The economic impact has been massive, as organizations have devoted money and energy to combating the scourge of sexual harassment through more active policies and programs. Scandals involving sexual harassment have rocked our government, affecting all three branches and tarring the reputations of many prominent politicians, including a president of the United States.

Efforts to end sexual harassment and the corollary crusade against discrimination have been important components of government efforts that have dramatically reshaped the climate and procedures in many organizations, forcing them to be more formal and self-conscious about due process and employee rights. A Brookings Institution study of the fifty greatest government achievements of the past half century ranked reducing workplace discrimination the fifth highest achievement overall. Ranked by a survey of historians and political scientists, reducing workplace discrimination was voted fourth in terms of importance of the problem, third in difficulty of the objective, and twentieth in success achieved.

The battle against sexual harassment has not been limited to harassment at work. Title IX has extended protections to education. Measures against sexual harassment have resonated in other arenas beyond schools and workplaces. Addressing street harassment of women has depended more on the attitudinal and cultural transformations achieved by *Vinson* and other sexual harassment law than on formal enactments. Sexual harassment has crept into clergy-penitent, lawyer-client, doctor-patient, and other professional relationships in which clients' dependency creates vulnerability to exploitation. Abuses have sparked lawsuits in these helping professions. Landlord-tenant and other housing-based relationships, reflecting women's disabilities in the housing market because of unequal social roles in families and workplaces, have also provided a wedge of vulnerability that facilitates sexual harassment. Despite successes, much remains to be done.

With such a complex and controversial issue, touching so many areas of gender relations and daily life, conflicting opinions on the changes achieved by legal reforms come as no surprise. The attorneys who participated in *Vinson* tend to rate highly the significance of the case. John Meisburg, Vinson's original attorney, affirms, "In thirty-one years of legal experience, this is the top — the most important thing I ever did." The bank's attorney Bob Troll feels fortunate to have argued the case through every level of the court system, judging the experience "a once-in-a-lifetime thing for a lawyer." And these attorneys' retrospective assessments are also quite positive. Troll, who is pleased that the particular points of law that were paramount to the bank were grounded in traditional legal principles, reflects more broadly that the decision was "an advancement of social concerns" and furthered "the interests of average people." Meisburg, a devout Christian, sees divine intervention in the course of events, leading to what he calls "a landmark case, a victory for women." Vinson attorney Pat Barry, though recognizing the distance women must still travel in the quest for equality, believes that this case contributed to building a society where "women can feel safe, walk around freely, and be secure in their bodily integrity." Having women gain these rights "will only help this world," because "how women are treated is a benchmark of the civility and advancement of a society."

More mixed evaluations come from academics and critics. Some researchers, such as Dana Kaland and Patricia Geist, suggest that, alone, "legal and organizational efforts to eliminate harassment and to provide assistance to victims have done little to reduce the frequency of cases or experiences with it." In contrast, even Jeffrey Rosen, a critic of the excesses of sexual harassment law, praises sexual harassment jurisprudence: "Anyone who has joined the workforce in the past generation has benefited from the heightened sensitivity to sexual harassment, sensitivity that has helped men and women work together with greater civility, equality, and mutual respect." Martha Chamallas suggests that sexual harassment law is a "feminist intervention into law that has affected the cultural meanings of interactions between men and women in the workplace, even when the new meanings have not translated into legal victories." Perhaps the last word on the impact of sexual harassment law should go to Catharine MacKinnon, whose 1979 book provided some of the first words on the subject. Writing in 2002, she observed, "As women's pain broke through public silence, their resistance to sexual abuse became articulated as a deprivation of their entitlement to equality, and social movement became institutional change generating further social movement." The result has been, she concluded, that "the development of law against sexual harassment, and its transformation from private joke to public weapon, is one of the more successful legal and political changes women have accomplished."

A Chicken-and-Egg Problem?

A venerable debate asks whether law can reform society. Historically, social reformers have turned to law to restructure social patterns. From Prohibition to school desegregation to environmental regulation, activists have sought to enlist laws in their efforts to transform social structures and practices. In the battle to eliminate sexual harassment, new legal rules prohibiting such sexual misconduct resulted from the confluence of the civil rights movement, which prevailed on Congress to pass Title VII of the Civil Rights Act of 1964, and the women's movement, which not only played a little-noticed role in adding sex discrimination to Title VII but also was the main impetus for persuading courts that sexual harassment constituted illegal sex discrimination under Title VII. Activists perceive many advantages in using law as a tool of reform, one being that law puts the power of the state behind reform. But the power of law does not rest primarily on physical coercion; law bestows legitimacy and carries the weight of morality. Even though skeptics doubt that law can change attitudes, law can regulate behavior, and evidence indicates that when constrained to act within legal mandates, people adjust their attitudes to conform with their behavior rather than tolerate the cognitive dissonance of inconsistency. Recognizing that social structures, including laws, shape individuals, activists see little realistic hope for progress by relying exclusively on individual "conversion" unless it is accompanied by structural reforms.

Skeptics resist using law to reform society. Critics are especially wary of the role of courts as agents of change, fearing that activist lawyers will sacrifice the interests of their clients for the sake of wider impact. Others stress the antimajoritarian nature of courts, especially unelected and life-tenured federal judges, and the elitist bias of the whole legal system in opposing "social engineering" imposed "top down" by law. More fundamentally, skeptics question the efficacy of law, arguing that law does not produce social change but instead reflects it. If new laws are enacted, even if they purport to modify social structures, old attitudes will render these structural changes meaningless because of lack of compliance, lack of enforcement, static interpretations, or other techniques to contain the legal changes. Law, powerless to effectuate reform unless social forces have already set change in motion, merely codifies social change.

When posed as an either-or choice, the debate assumes a chicken-and-egg quality: social reforms need new law to produce effective social changes, but how can laws change unless the social forces that law mirrors change first? Reformulating the debate helps escape this stalemate and sheds more insight on the issue. First, examining the complexities of the terms used to pose the question allows greater precision in analyzing the issue. Second, transforming the question from an either-or to a conditional one facilitates more accurate assessment. Instead of asking whether law can reform society, the question becomes, under what conditions can law achieve social reform?

Asking a Better Question

Martha Minow disaggregates some of the overgeneralizations that sometimes muddle the "law and social change" debate by reexamining the terms of the debate. "Law" should not be equated with a "big-case" approach; limiting the examination to the impact of a high-profile case or even to the Supreme Court as an institution likely underestimates the potential for law to foster change. For example, when Gerald Rosenberg examines signal decisions such as *Brown v. Board of Education*, posing the question of whether the Supreme Court is dynamic or constrained, he finds that reliance on the Supreme Court offers only "hollow hope" for producing effective societal reforms. But as sexual harassment demonstrates, change stems not from a *Meritor Savings Bank v. Vinson* alone; other Supreme Court rulings, lower court decisions, statutes, legal advocacy, scholarship, and activism intertwine with the landmark decision to determine the meaning and impact of the legal change.

The Supreme Court has limits that are characteristic of courts generally. Courts passively take cases brought to them; they cannot actively initiate policies to solve problems they perceive as needing attention. The cases are, by and large, disputes between private individuals or parties, and courts' ability to set general rules or policies is limited by their duty to do justice in the particular cases before them. Courts lack extensive research capacities, especially on social, economic, or political issues beyond the legal questions presented. And of course, courts lack extensive enforcement mechanisms such as large budgets, bureaucracies, or constabulary. For the implementation of their decisions, courts must rely on the executive branch or, more typically, on voluntary compliance by society. As a rule, courts are better suited to redress harms to individuals than to make general policy to remedy social problems, although obviously court decisions have wider deterrence effects.

Skeptics correctly fault courts as policy innovators; courts are designed to determine the legality of measures, not their desirability as policy. The law itself is often framed in terms that may not adequately address the interests of the less powerful; for example, in sexual harassment law, requirements such as unwelcomeness, severity or pervasiveness, the reasonable person standard, and the mandate that plaintiffs use company procedures may dilute legal protections. Yet law can help bridge the gap between current realities and future ideals by educating and expanding conventional wisdom rather than merely embodying inherited prejudices. And the task of schoolmaster devolves on more than the nine justices of the Supreme Court. Community institutions such as battered women's shelters or community patrols, as well as legal advocacy that goes beyond standard lawsuits to include impact legislation, legislative advocacy, grassroots organizing, media campaigns, and direct activism, amount to an "alternative legal regime" that extends the reach of the "law" far beyond the court system.

Where researchers look for "social" change must likewise be expanded. Moving beyond policy and the public sphere, law's ability to affect everyday life in private venues instills it with a "culture-shifting capacity." If legal developments have a diffuse yet intimate impact, the social change may be more mundane than dramatic, but the effects may flow deeper and be sustained longer. The social meaning of *Vinson* is still being shaped in thousands of American workplaces.

This insight also suggests broader conceptions of "change." At a minimum, change must be recognized as a process, not simply an end result, and that process is not always linear or direct. Studies of legal changes have, for example, discovered "sleeper effects," with impacts occurring only after long years, perhaps generations, and sometimes producing results quite ancillary to the original intent. New Deal policies encouraging African American home ownership bore unexpected fruit decades later when home owners in the 1960s led challenges to disenfranchisement because they were less subject to eviction threats than tenants were. Some progress may come not from legal innovations but from the backlash against them. The *Brown* decision, for example, may have given impetus to eventual school desegregation beyond its direct results; the ugly segregationist reaction so outraged the nation that the resistance "boomeranged," producing political support for civil rights legislation that desegregated schools. Unintended consequences are a hallmark of political life. If Representative Smith's motive in sponsoring the amendment that added "sex" to the statute's ban on employment discrimination was to sink the bill, his tactics backfired, with unforeseen but widespread repercussions.

Although passing legislation can serve as a symbolic substitute for real change, half measures may have a domino effect by increasing people's desire for more change, sensitizing them to grievances, and fostering a sense of entitlement that produces more assertion of rights, even beyond the actual rights guaranteed by the law. Mechelle Vinson's dogged pursuit of her mistaken belief that she had a quid pro quo claim resulted in the Supreme Court's recognition of hostile environment sexual harassment. Even ineffective legal change can lead to real reform if the law's inadequacies stimulate reformers to escalate their efforts to win more meaningful victories. Sleeper, boomerang, and domino effects all suggest that change should not be seen exclusively as a direct result of reform, but must be recognized as following more complicated, less predictable paths.

Beyond taking account of the complexities of the terms of the law and social change debate, another way to escape the horns of either-or positions is to reformulate the question as a conditional, asking, under what circumstances can law achieve social change? Numerous studies of civil rights law have documented that the successes achieved differed in various contexts and according to numerous factors. Rather than simplistic either-or answers, researchers have found that the better answer to whether laws produce important social progress is, "it depends," and they have tried to specify the circumstances on which change depends. Michael McCann's study of the comparable worth movement, for example, discovered that accompanying political struggles conditioned the achievements won by legal battles for women's pay equity. Only when a political movement fought for and was reciprocally stimulated by efforts to redefine legal standards were these attempts successful in making women's wages more equal.

This case study confirms the theoretical insight that change strategies that exclusively target either social structures or individual attitudes are inadequate for achieving lasting reforms. Sustained success requires changing structures and people simultaneously. Movements against unjust conditions, such as the civil rights movement, succeed when they transform society's laws and institutions and people's hearts and minds simultaneously. Mobilization also played a prominent role in struggles against sexual harassment. The women's movement played such a critical role — first in bringing sexual harassment under the law's coverage, and then, especially in response to the problem's high profile in the 1990s, in ensuring that early legal mandates were enforced and extended. In the long run, continuing progress will depend not only on evolving legal doctrine but also on women and their allies in the workplace mobilizing against sexual harassment.

Back to Basics: Rethinking the Harm of Sexual Harassment

Two developments in legal doctrine hold contradictory potential for the long-term results of sexual harassment reforms. On the one hand, legal scholarship rethinking the basic premises of sexual harassment jurisprudence presents the opportunity to extend and tailor the law to make its impact more powerful and effective. On the other hand, secular trends in the laws governing employment threaten to leave isolated employees with inadequate protection of their workplace rights achieved only after long years of political struggle.

Recently, feminist legal scholars have subjected the goals of sexual harassment law to searching reexamination. Classifying the focus of scholarship by periods, Kathryn Abrams suggests that early writings concentrated on establishing why sexual harassment was not simply wrong but also illegal sex discrimination. This focus was followed by scholarship seeking to clarify what conduct constituted the offense. After *Vinson*'s ruling recognized a legal cause of action for sexual harassment, attention shifted to defining the elements of the offense required to fashion coherent and enforceable sexual harassment claims. Recently, she notes, "the new jurisprudence of sexual harassment" has come full circle, asking why sexual harassment is illegal and once again examining the harms that make sexual harassment a proper problem for legal interdiction.

Anita Bernstein promotes replacing reasonableness as the standard for workplace harassment with respect, imposing on others the duty to refrain from treating people as a means to an end, humiliating them, or denying their personhood and self-conception. Sexual harassment violates the "respectful person standard"; the harm of sexual harassment is the failure of respect and the attack on targets' dignity that offends, humiliates, and denies their equal human status. This reformulation shifts attention away from individual fault toward workplace climate and conditions that foster incivility and disrespect, frustrating the equality of economic opportunity sought by Title VII. Arguing that reconceptualizing the harm of sexual harassment avoids the victim-blaming that sometimes creeps into current thinking, Bernstein emphasizes employers' actions rather than targets' reactions, stressing employers' duties to protect employees' dignity and create work sites where individuals can flourish.

Katherine Franke criticizes prevalent conceptions of sexual harassment for misdiagnosing the problem as motivated by sexual desire and misdirecting enforcement to a barring of sexual expression from the workplace. Although sexual harassment is a mechanism for sexually subordinating women, Franke argues that the harm is even broader; sexual harassment is a "technology of sexism," a means of constructing gender identities of men and women in conformity with "fundamental gender stereotypes: men as sexual conquerors and women as sexually conquered." The harassment of men as well as women "perpetuates, enforces, and polices a set of gender norms that seek to feminize women and masculinize men." Sexual harassment discriminates because it both enforces gender boundaries and systematically orders gender hierarchy by devaluing conventional femininity.

Vicki Schultz advocates de-emphasizing the sexual aspects of sexual harassment and linking it more firmly to economic inequality. Asserting that "the real issue isn't sex, it's sexism on the job," she argues that sexual harassment law should concentrate on conduct that consigns people to gendered work against their advantage or aspirations. The law's characteristic "desire-dominance paradigm" is underinclusive, too narrow in its attempts to weed out sexual harassment. By recognizing only sexual misconduct, it ignores nonsexual harassment of women by denying them training, information, or learning opportunities; denigrating their job performance; isolating them from support networks; requiring sex-stereotyped tasks beyond the duties of the job; and taunting, pranks, and hazing. But whether or not the harassment of women takes a sexual form, it discriminates on the basis of sex by enforcing gender boundaries at work that limit women's access to desirable jobs and skills. The desire-dominance approach can also be overbroad, tempting some courts to try to sanitize the workplace and suppressing some sexual expression that is merely offensive but not a barrier to women's equal economic opportunities.

{ *Conclusion* }

Schultz recommends a competence-centered paradigm that conceives of harassment as functioning to shape jobs and people along gendered lines in order to retain favored work and competence as masculine-identified turf. Recognizing the centrality of competence in maintaining male dominance at work and elsewhere, Schultz's alternative paradigm identifies the harm of harassment as undercutting women's sense and image of competence by defining "their very womanhood as the opposite of what it takes to be a good worker." This approach redirects the focus of sexual harassment law to the core problem, which is conduct that serves a "gender-guarding, competence-undermining function" and that "polices the boundaries of the work and protects its idealized masculine image — as well as the identity of those who do it."

Abrams favors a pluralistic account of sexual harassment, one that is sensitive to the workplace context but that recognizes that the problem is not limited to employment. She favors expanding the focus to encompass gender centrally, and not sexuality exclusively, because sexual harassment encompasses a "surprising range of dynamics through which hierarchy can be implemented." Although sexual harassment produces sexual objectification as well as economic marginalization, the principal harm inflicted is "constraints upon personal agency," denying especially women "the capacity to put together the disparate elements of self — biological being, gendered subject, worker, sexual actor — to create a particular contingent whole in a particular context." Sexual harassment is discrimination because it "structures the workplace as a site of male control and masculine normative primacy, where men and women are shaped in accordance with conventional norms of masculinity and femininity," creating a workplace embodying a sex and gender hierarchy.

These attempts at rethinking sexual harassment law differ among themselves and are not without criticisms and alternative proposals. On the one hand, Linda LeMoncheck maintains that "sexual harassment is about sex because it is about how sexuality can empower some and disempower others; the sexual harassment of women by men is the relegating of women as a class to an inferior status by sexualizing women." On the other hand, Rosa Ehrenreich would abolish the requirement of proving that harassment was "because of sex." In her account, the harm of harassment does not hinge on sex. "The workplace harassment of women is wrong not because women are women, but because women are human beings and share with all other human beings the right to be treated in the workplace with respect and concern." Ehrenreich would ban any harassment of less powerful workers as discrimination violating Title VII. The "new jurisprudence of sexual harassment" of Abrams, Bernstein, Franke, and Schultz, however, seeks to retain the focus on sexual harassment as gender discrimination while broadening its purview beyond the limits of sexual misconduct. These approaches can better encompass same-sex harassment and expand the range of prohibited harassment to include misconduct that is not specifically sexual in nature. In concentrating attention on the harassment and its harm, these scholars encourage lifting the burden of victim-blaming from targets and restoring the onus of enforcement on harassers and employers, which are in a better position to correct discriminatory conditions. By reconceptualizing the harm of sexual harassment as creating and maintaining gender inequality, they simultaneously enlarge the sweep of the law and sharpen its focus. Although this recent theorizing is responsive to criticisms of sexual harassment law, such rethinking promises to reinvigorate rather than dilute sexual harassment doctrine and garner wider support for continuing reform.

"Flexibilized" Work and Individuated Workers

Unfortunately, other long-term trends in employment law augur less well for employees. Rather than law specifying fair terms and conditions of employment, the American approach to regulating employment has emphasized private bargaining between employers and individual employees or employee groups whose rights to organize are protected by the 1935 National Labor Relations Act (NLRA). Although legislation and court rulings, primarily since the 1960s, have strengthened individual employee rights, 90 percent of American employees work "at will." This gives employers incredible power and generally unconstrained discretion to control their employees' work lives *unless* a provision of law specifically forbids their action. The two simple but consequence-laden words "you're fired" demarcate one of the most significant power differentials in American society, and the rapidly globalizing economy has reinforced the advantages of huge corporate employers. Yet fewer workers are unionized today that when the NLRA was passed during the depression, with less than 10 percent of the private workforce organized.

With a goal of redistributing power to workers, the NLRA was possibly "the most radical law ever passed by Congress," but the retrenchment of workers' rights to organize independently and bargain collectively began soon after its passage. A process of "deradicalization" by court rulings and legislative amendments weakened workers' ability to organize and made strikes less effective bargaining weapons. A telling indication of judicial reshaping of labor law is manifest in cases involving employee voice in the workplace, always a central concern in organizing campaigns. Reversing direction from earlier decisions, in 1981 the Supreme Court reinterpreted the NLRA requirement that employers bargain with unions about certain company decisions, severely curtailing the influence that unionized workers had over matters affecting their employment prospects. The Court ruled in 1980 that faculty at Yeshiva University were managers, not employees whose right to organize was protected under the NLRA, precisely because these professors exercised considerable power in formulating university policies. The implicit message to American workers was that if they organize, they risk losing their voice in company decisions, and if they have an audible voice, they might forfeit their right to organize.

Ironically, this judicial trend was happening amidst a great hue and cry from management about employee involvement in decision-making. From Japanese-style quality circles to semiautonomous teams, employers were experimenting with "employee empowerment," "worker participation," and "flattening hierarchies." Most restructuring to "democratize the workplace," however, was created, structured, and maintained at management's sole discretion. The combined thrust of labor law and management practices, then, amounts to enhanced opportunities for employees' involvement in workplace decisions, as long as their voices are not independently protected by the strength of organizations created by themselves rather than their bosses.

Although employees' collective voices have received less legal protection, since the 1960s, laws and court decisions have added protections for individual workers. These laws provide valuable rights against some of the worst forms of abuse that have blemished American workplaces, such as discrimination because of an individual's race, sex, religion, age, or disability, but they do not directly promote employees' voice at work. These laws should properly supplement, not supplant, legal protection of the right to self-organization, but as the percentage of the workforce represented by unions has declined precipitously, not surprisingly, the number of individual employees filing lawsuits has climbed. Particularly in a globalized economy, when the mobility of capital, the restructuring of organizations, and the "flexibilization" of work have tilted the balance of power even more decisively toward corporate management, the act of individual workers taking their employers to court seems unlikely to protect workers against the inevitable insecurities created by fluid work and organizations, let alone represent employees' interests in company decisions. And with the recent movement to substitute arbitration for litigation as the preferred means of resolving employment disputes, even these statutorily protected individual rights may be undermined by moving them from public courts to private arenas of justice.

Limiting Rights through Law

In isolation, without the support of organization, sexual harassment law conceived of as individual rights is vulnerable to retrenchment. Historical experience with other legal reforms, such as labor law, school desegregation, and environmental protection, suggests that without popular pressure, courts may offer slim hope for sustaining the progress of social change. Three obstacles in particular threaten the long-term viability of continued advances against sexual harassment.

One danger of judicial deradicalization resides in the possibility that paternalistic judges will apply egalitarian laws in a protectionist fashion. The puritanical shadings that tinge some sexual harassment decisions may reflect this nation's cultural heritage, but American reliance on courts to protect workers, largely absent the employee organization common to many democracies, may contribute to paternalism. Depending on the good graces of the perhaps enlightened but elite judiciary makes law vulnerable to the limits of its benevolence, and judges have imposed thresholds limiting the reach of statutory prohibitions, exemplified by the judge-made "severe or pervasive" requirement. Schultz argues that sexual paternalism bestows its protection only on women who are deemed by male judges "to possess the purity that renders them deserving of protection." Even middle-class white women favored by judges' biases may forfeit their protection by deserting the domestic sphere and entering unsuitable workplaces. The unwelcomeness requirement and its evidentiary correlates, as well as various reasonableness standards incorporated into the elements of sexual harassment claims and defenses, illustrate how courts may refuse protection to plaintiffs who are not considered "good victims." Focusing on the sexual aspects of misconduct misleads judges into protecting women's sensibilities and "virtue," while neglecting sexual harassment as a practice thwarting women's equality at work and in other social spheres.

A second problem with conceiving of sexual harassment individualistically is the potential snare of interpreting the law from a "perpetrator's perspective." Analyzing the record of employment discrimination law, Alan Freeman argues that effective social change requires adopting a victim's perspective, a framework rooted in concrete historical experience and endorsing rules aimed at structural discrimination rather than timeless, abstract norms. Its primary impetus is results, so it would shape legal rules that promise to work realistically to end discrimination. But judges tend to contain change by embracing the perpetrator's perspective. This stance emphasizes eradicating the misconduct of wrongdoers engaged in prejudicial practices rather than systemic social change. With its focus on specific, intentional actions by lawbreaking individuals rather than objective social conditions, its central concern is the fault of the perpetrator. Ignoring broader historical and social considerations, it uses legal principles such as intent and causation to place blame and the burden of remedying discrimination on the particular perpetrators, excusing everyone else and society at large from any responsibility for solving the problem. Rather than preventing or solving social problems, the perpetrator's perspective provides remedies targeted to identifiable victims who are offered compensation as relief.

From the beginning, sexual harassment law has exhibited both perspectives, and *Meritor Bank v. Vinson* blended these contradictory elements. Declaring hostile environment harassment illegal recognized that harassment is not limited to individual misconduct aimed at lone victims but rather forms a structural barrier to women performing and benefiting from their work. Adopting the unwelcomeness rather than the involuntariness standard acknowledged that contextual constraints can deny victims realistic options for resisting harassers' demands. Conversely, the Court's unwillingness to exclude evidence of the victim's dress and fantasies reflects the perpetrator's perspective, which focuses on fault and limits relief to "worthy victims." The Court's refusal to adopt strict employer liability tends to limit responsibility for the problem and its solution to identifiably guilty individuals. In other words, the Court's opinion was progressive and furthered social change in recognizing and making illegal a serious, widespread, and long-standing social ill, but at the same time, the rules it laid down for assigning legal responsibility for rectifying the problem limited its impact by emphasizing individual fault rather than institutional responsibility for producing more sweeping progress against sexual harassment.

This mixed perspective has continued to characterize the law of sexual harassment. To the extent that the *Faragher-Ellerth* liability standards place the burden of curing the problem on employers' shoulders and encourage positive steps toward prevention, these rules adopt a victim's perspective, with stress on achieving real change. The affirmative defense, however, embodies the perpetrator's perspective in its emphasis on employers' and victims' fault, casting the problem in terms of penalties for intentional misconduct and relief for responsible victims. The *Gebser* and *Davis* liability rules under Title IX evince the perpetrator's perspective even more clearly, spotlighting individual wrongdoing while shielding schools from the burden of correcting intolerable systemic conditions. By concentrating on punishing violators and compensating victims, courts limit the power of sexual harassment law to cure unhealthy social conditions and foster Title VII's goal of genuine equality of economic opportunity regardless of sex.

Putting Power behind Rights

Solving a social problem such as sexual harassment requires a collective and organized political response. The courts and law play a vital part in the process. Without *Vinson* and the countless decisions that followed, sexual harassment would not be the timely topic it is in American companies and organizations, fewer Americans would be sensitive to their rights and responsibilities in dealing with their coworkers, and sexual harassment would not have rocked American public life for much of the 1990s. Law has provided a "public classroom," helping Americans use their "sociological imagination" to connect their "personal troubles" with "public issues." Still, if new, more egalitarian norms and conditions are going to seep into every American workplace in the foreseeable future, more is required than courts trying to enforce them from afar. Genuine progress toward gender equality requires organized efforts at the grass roots.

Unions are vital to reforming workplaces, but alone, they will not suffice to end sexual harassment. Historically, unions have too often been bastions of male power at the work site. More progressive leadership and more diverse membership, now composed of 48 percent women, doubtless put many unions on the right side of the sexual harassment issue today. But with many companies now "union-free" and union membership rolls shrunken, even when unions devote energy to sexual harassment issues, their influence is diminished.

In a workforce that is increasingly gender balanced, expanding employee involvement might contribute to more equitable working conditions and less sexual harassment. Without legal protections for employee voice, however, the efficacy of participation in remedying workplace harassment and other unjust conditions is problematic. Although scholars have proposed legally sanctioned works councils similar to those in other democracies, the prospects of legislating guaranteed employee participation in workplace decisions are dim.

A better prospect for the immediate future lies in organizations such as 9to5 (the National Association of Working Women), the National Organization for Women, the Coalition of Labor Union Women, and Women Employed. The strategies pursued by 9to5 hold particular promise for combating sexual harassment because they center on organizing women in the workplace. Founded in the late 1970s and popularized by the movie *9 to 5*, the group is one of the leading advocates for women's issues in the workplace. Although an affiliated Local 925 operates as a traditional collective bargaining agent where employees have voted to unionize, in most areas, 9to5 functions as a women's network and support group, offering support, training, and advocacy for women employees. A hot line tells women with work-related problems where to get help; sexual harassment is one of the callers' leading complaints.

The organization also has a history of successful coalition building with sympathetic and like-minded groups advocating for employee rights and interests. Although sexual harassment is a problem that harms primarily women, men are victims too, perhaps increasingly so. The new jurisprudence is rethinking sexual harassment in broader terms that make clearer the widely shared stakes in eradicating the problem, and gender inequality at work is related to other forms of inequality and oppression. These linkages provide opportunities for cooperation and coalitions. Ultimately, although women must play central roles in any crusade against sexual harassment, many men, too, should join these efforts, especially if the goals of the movement include vindication of equality, opportunity for development, and voice for all employees, as well as the liberating potential of expanding gender definitions and loosening constraints.

If sexual harassment remains a critical problem at work, workplace issues derive their prominence from the centrality of work in our individual and social lives. Work provides not only a foundation for individual development but also a keystone for democracy. Cynthia Estlund calls the workplace a "satellite of the public sphere," one of the few arenas where people actually discuss matters of common concern in a society that treats citizens as passive consumers. These discussions, often explicitly political or policy oriented, assume more importance as other public spaces atrophy in an increasingly privatized society. Even narrowly focused workplace discussions may produce "spillover" political benefits if workers, educated and practiced in participating in decisions at work, acquire citizenship skills and interest in taking part in public decision-making. Estlund notes that as social segregation spreads, work, more than other American institutions, brings together people of diverse backgrounds and experiences. So when employees discuss issues, they are more likely to encounter different perspectives than during similar discussions held in other social settings. And as Schultz, Abrams, and others note, work shapes resource distributions, behaviors, habits, identities, and attitudes that influence patterns and structures throughout society. Elim-inating sexual harassment would remove a major barrier to more just workplaces. The struggle against sexual harassment is situated locally in offices, stores, schools, and factories, but its reform potential has global reach.

CHRONOLOGY

1964	Civil Rights Act of 1964 passed. Title VII prohibits employment discrimination based on sex as well as race, color, national origin, or religion.
1972	Equal Employment Opportunity Act strengthens and extends coverage of Civil Rights Act of 1964.
	Title IX of Education Amendments prohibits sexual harassment in federally funded education programs.
September 9, 1974	Mechelle Vinson begins working at Capital City Federal Savings and Loan Association.
1974	*Barnes v. Train* plaintiff loses in first sexual harassment suit in federal court.
1975	Term *sexual harassment* is coined in Ithaca, NY.
1976	*Williams v. Saxbe* is first federal court decision holding that sexual harassment is prohibited employment discrimination under Title VII.
September 22, 1978	Vinson files federal lawsuit against Sidney Taylor and Capital City.
November 1, 1978	Vinson simultaneously is discharged and resigns.
November 22, 1978	Vinson files sexual harassment charges with the EEOC.
1978	Lin Farley publishes *Sexual Shakedown.*
1979	Catharine MacKinnon publishes *Sexual Harassment of Working Women.*
February 26, 1980	*Vinson v. Taylor:* Judge Penn finds for defendants Taylor and Capital City; dismisses Vinson's lawsuit.
November 10, 1980	EEOC issues *Guidelines on Discrimination Because of Sex,* including guidelines on sexual harassment.
1980	Movie *9 to 5* starring Jane Fonda, Lily Tomlin, and Dolly Parton.
1981	*Bundy v. Jackson:* D.C. court of appeals holds hostile environment to be sexual harassment.
February 16, 1982	Oral arguments in *Vinson v. Taylor* before D.C. court of appeals.

January 25, 1985	*Vinson v. Taylor:* D.C. court of appeals reverses Judge Penn's judgment for defendants and remands to district court for hearings consistent with its opinion.
May 14, 1985	*Vinson v. Taylor:* D.C. court of appeals denies request for rehearing en banc, drawing dissent from Judge Robert Bork.
October 7, 1985	Supreme Court grants writ of certiorari in *Vinson v. Taylor* (renamed *PSFS Savings Bank v. Vinson*).
March 25, 1986	Oral arguments before Supreme Court in *Meritor Bank v. Vinson.*
March 28, 1986	Supreme Court justices meet in conference to discuss *Vinson.*
June 19, 1986	Supreme Court announces judgment in *Vinson,* affirming appeals court's reversal and remand to district court and recognizing hostile environment sexual harassment as illegal employment discrimination under Title VII.
1991	*Meritor Bank v. Vinson* settles out of court on secret terms.
	Civil Rights Act of 1991 provides for jury trial and compensatory and punitive damages in employment discrimination claims.
	Ellison v. Brady, Ninth Circuit Court of Appeals adopts reasonable woman standard.
September 1991	Women harassed at navy fliers' Tailhook convention.
October 1991	Senate Judiciary Committee hearings air charges that Supreme Court nominee Clarence Thomas sexually harassed Anita Hill.
November 1992	Senator Bob Packwood accused of sexually harassing female staffers and others; eventually resigns from Senate.
1992	"Year of the Woman": number of women in Congress jumps from thirty-one to fifty-four.
1993	*Harris v. Forklift Systems:* Supreme Court issues its second ruling on sexual harassment, holding that proof of psychological injury is not required to make a case of sexual harassment.

1994	Paula Jones sues President Bill Clinton for alleged sexual harassment while he was governor of Arkansas.
December 1998	President Clinton impeached by House of Representatives for alleged misconduct stemming from affair with White House intern Monica Lewinsky. Senate fails to find Clinton guilty of the charges.
1998	*Faragher v. Boca Raton* and *Burlington Industries v. Ellerth:* Supreme Court clarifies rules for employer liability for supervisor-created hostile environment sexual harassment.
	Oncale v. Sundowner Offshore Services: Supreme Court holds same-sex sexual harassment is prohibited by Title VIII.
	Gebser v. Lago Vista Independent School District: Supreme Court announces liability standards for employee harassment of students under Title IX.
1999	*Davis v. Monroe County Board of Education:* Supreme Court announces liability standards for peer sexual harassment of students under Title IX.
2001	*Pollard v. E.I. DuPont de Nemours & Co.:* Supreme Court allows claims for front pay in sexual harassment suits.

Alexander v. Gardner-Denver, 415 U.S. 36 (1974)

Alexander v. Yale University, 459 F.Supp. 1 (D. Conn. 1977)

Barnes v. Costle, 561 F.2d 983 (D.C. Cir. 1977)

Barnes v. Train, 1974 U.S. Dist. LEXIS 7212; 13 Fair Empl. Prac. Cas. (BNA) 123 (D.D.C. 1974), *rev'd sub nom. Barnes v. Costle*, 561 F.2d 983 (D.C. Cir. 1977)

Brown v. Board of Education, 347 U.S. 483 (1954)

Bundy v. Jackson, 641 F.2d 934 (D.C. Cir. 1981)

Burlington Industries, Inc. v. Ellerth, 524 U.S. 742 (1998)

Cannon v. University of Chicago, 441 U.S. 677 (1979)

Circuit City Stores, Inc. v. Adams, 532 U.S. 105 (2001)

Clinton v. Jones, 520 U.S. 681 (1997), *dismissed on remand*, 990 F.Supp. 657 (E.D. Ark. 1998), *appeal voluntarily dismissed*, 161 F.3d 528 (8th Cir. 1998)

Corne v. Bausch & Lomb, Inc., 390 F.Supp. 161 (D. Ariz. 1975)

Davis v. Monroe County Board of Education, 526 U.S. 629 (1999)

DeCintio v. Westchester County Medical Center, 807 F.2d 304 (2nd Cir. 1986)

Ellison v. Brady, 924 F.2d 872 (9th Cir. 1991)

Faragher v. City of Boca Raton, 524 U.S. 775 (1998)

Franklin v. Gwinnett County Public Schools, 503 U.S. 60 (1992)

Gebser et al. v. Lago Vista Independent School District, 524 U.S. 274 (1998)

Gilmer v. Interstate/Johnson Lane Corp., 500 U.S. 20 (1991)

Great American Federal Savings and Loan Association v. Novotny, 442 U.S. 366 (1979)

Harris v. Forklift Systems, Inc., 510 U.S. 17 (1993)

Henson v. City of Dundee, 682 F.2d 897 (11th Cir. 1982)

King v. Palmer, 778 F.2d 878 (D.C. Cir. 1985)

Lochner v. New York, 198 U.S. 45 (1905)

Meritor Savings Bank, FSB v. Vinson, 477 U.S. 57 (1986)

Miller v. Bank of America, 418 F.Supp. 223 (N.D. Cal. 1976)

Monge v. Beebe Rubber Co., 114 N.H. 130 (1974)

Moose Lodge No. 107 v. Irvis, 407 U.S. 163 (1972)

Oncale v. Sundowner Offshore Services, Inc., 523 U.S. 75 (1998)

Patterson v. McLean Credit Union, 491 U.S. 164 (1989)

Pollard v. E. I. DuPont de Nemours & Co., 532 U.S. 843 (2001)

Price Waterhouse v. Hopkins, 490 U.S. 228 (1989)

Rabidue v. Osceola Refining Co., 805 F.2d 611 (6th Cir. 1986)

Robinson v. Jacksonville Shipyards, 760 F.Supp. 1486 (M.D. Fla. 1991)

Rogers v. E.E.O.C., 454 F.2d 234 (5th Cir. 1971)

Silva v. University of New Hampshire, 888 F.Supp. 293 (D.N.H. 1994)

Tomkins v. Public Service Electric & Gas Co., 422 F.Supp. 553 (D.N.J. 1976)

Vinson v. Taylor, 1980 U.S. Dist. LEXIS 10676; 23 Fair Empl. Prac. Cas. (BNA) 37, *rev'd* 753 F.2d 141 (D.C. Cir. 1985), *hearing en banc denied*, 760 F.2d 1330 (D.C. Cir. 1985), *aff'd sub nom. Meritor Savings Bank, FSB v. Vinson*, 477 U.S. 57 (1986)

Wards Cove Packing Co., Inc. v. Atonio, 490 U.S. 642 (1989)

Williams v. Saxbe, 413 F.Supp. 654 (D.D.C. 1976)

BIBLIOGRAPHICAL ESSAY

The literature on sexual harassment in law, social sciences, and women's studies is vast, so this essay is necessarily limited to directing readers' attention to only a sampling of the books and articles used to narrate the story of this litigation. Several general works are especially recommended. Margaret A. Crouch, *Thinking about Sexual Harassment* (New York: Oxford University Press, 2001), provides the best multidisciplinary overview of the topic. *Sexual Harassment: Issues and Answers* (New York: Oxford University Press, 2001), edited by Linda LeMoncheck and James P. Sterba, assembles a diverse and digestible collection of articles and documents, while Ellen Bravo and Ellen Cassedy, *The 9to5 Guide to Combating Sexual Harassment* (Milwaukee: 9to5 Working Women Education Fund, 1999), offers a readable, practical discussion. Anne C. Levy and Michele A. Paludi, *Workplace Sexual Harassment* (Upper Saddle River, N.J.: Prentice-Hall, 1997), provides a concise primer.

Sources used in chapter 1 include the following: On women and work: Vicki Schultz, "Life's Work," 100 *Columbia Law Review* 1881 (2000); Teresa Amott and Julie Matthaei, *Race, Gender, and Work* (Boston: South End Press, 1996). On feminism: Barbara Ryan, *Feminism and the Women's Movement* (New York: Routledge, 1992). On the 1964 Civil Rights Act: Charles and Barbara Whalen, *The Longest Debate: A Legislative History of the 1964 Civil Rights Act* (New York: New American Library, 1985); Robert C. Bird, "More than a Congressional Joke," 3 *William and Mary Journal of Women and Law* 137 (1997).

Chapter 2 draws from a wide array of sources on its diverse topics. Among the few histories of sexual harassment are Kerry Seagrave, *The Sexual Harassment of Women in the Workplace, 1600–1993* (Jefferson, N.C.: McFarland, 1994), and Stephen Morewitz, *Sexual Harassment and Social Change in American History* (San Francisco: Austin and Winfield, 1996). *Sexual Shakedown: The Sexual Harassment of Women on the Job* (New York: McGraw-Hill, 1978), by Lin Farley, was critical in putting sexual harassment on the public agenda, and Catharine A. MacKinnon's *Sexual Harassment of Working Women* (New Haven, Conn.: Yale University Press, 1979) had untold legal impact. Articles in Shereen G. Bingham, ed., *Sexual Harassment as Discursive Practice* (Westport, Conn.: Praeger, 1994), shed light on hegemony and the significance of naming sexual harassment. William O'Donohue, ed., *Sexual Harassment: Theory, Research, and Treatment* (Boston: Allyn and Bacon, 1997), surveys social scientific research, including studies by Louise F. Fitzgerald et al. and James E. Gruber. On ideological reactions to sexual harassment, see Holly B. Fechner, "Toward an Expanded Conception of Law Reform," 23 *University of Michigan Journal of Law Reform* 475 (1990); Martha R Mahoney, "Exit: Power and the Idea of Leaving in Love, Work, and the Confirmation Process," 65 *Southern California Law Review* 1283 (1992).

The primary sources for chapters 3 and 4 are the records and briefs of this case at the district court, appeals court, and Supreme Court levels of the litigation, supplemented by news accounts and by personal interviews whenever possible. The files of Justices Brennan and Marshall are located in the Library of Congress.

Among the outpouring of writing on sexual harassment and the law since *Vinson* tapped in chapter 5 are Rebecca Hanner White, "There's Nothing Special about Sex: The Supreme Court Mainstreams Sexual Harassment," 7 *William and Mary Bill of Rights Journal* 725 (1999); B. Glenn George, "The Back Door: Legitimating Sexual Harassment Claims," 73 *Boston University Law Review* 1 (1993); Francis Achampong, *Workplace Sexual Harassment Law* (Westport, Conn.: Quorum Books, 1999). On unwelcomeness: Casey J. Wood, "Inviting Sexual Harassment: The Absurdity of the Welcomeness Requirement in Sexual Harassment Law," 38 *Brandeis Law Journal* 423 (2000); Mary F. Radford, "By Invitation Only: The Proof of Welcomeness in Sexual Harassment Cases," 72 *North Carolina Law Review* 499 (1994). On the reasonable person standard: Leslie M Kerns, "A Feminist Perspective: Why Feminists Should Give the Reasonable Woman Standard Another Chance," 10 *Columbia Journal of Gender and Law* 195 (2001); Kathryn Abrams, "The Reasonable Woman: Sense and Sensibility in Sexual Harassment Law," in LeMoncheck and Sterba. On employer liability: Jill Kreisberg, "Employers and Employees Beware," 6 *Cardozo Women's Law Journal* 153 (1999); Joanna L. Grossman, "The First Bite Is Free: Employer Liability for Sexual Harassment," 61 *University of Pittsburgh Law Review* 671 (2000). On same-sex harassment: Steven L. Willborn, "Taking Discrimination Seriously: Oncale and the Fate of Exceptionalism in Sexual Harassment Law," 7 *William and Mary Bill of Right Journal* 677 (1999).

In chapter 6, for education and Title IX, see Kristen Safier, "A Request for Congressional Action," 68 *University of Cincinnati Law Review* 1309 (2000); Karen E. Edmondson, "*Davis v. Monroe Board of Education* Goes to College," 75 *Notre Dame Law Review* 1203 (2000). Eugene Volokh offers numerous free speech challenges to sexual harassment law, including "What Speech Does 'Hostile Work Environment' Harassment Law Restrict?" 85 *Georgetown Law Journal* 627 (1997). Defenders of sexual harassment law against this challenge include Cynthia L. Estlund, "Freedom of Expression in the Workplace and the Problem of Discriminatory Harassment," 75 *Texas Law Review* 687 (1997), and Deborah Epstein, "Can a 'Dumb Ass Woman' Achieve Equality in the Workplace? Running the Gauntlet of Hostile Environment Harassing Speech," 84 *Georgetown Law Journal* 399 (1996). Lisa M. Woodward, "Collision in the Classroom: Is Academic Freedom a License for Sexual Harassment?" 27 *Capital University Law Review* 667 (1999), brings the argument into the classroom. On favoritism: Michael J. Phillips, "The Dubious Title VII Cause of Action for Sexual Favoritism," 51 *Washington and Lee Law Review* 547 (1994); Michael J. Levy, "Sex, Promotions, and Title VII," 45 *Hastings Law Journal* 667 (1994). On consensual relations and company policies: Gary M. Kramer, "Limited License to Fish off the Company Pier," 22 *New England Law Review* 77 (2000); Sherry Young, "Getting to Yes: The Case against Banning Consensual Relationships in Higher Education," 4 *American University Journal of Gender and Law* 269 (1996). On arbitration: Alexander J. S. Colvin, "The Relationship between Employment Arbitration and Workplace Dispute Resolution Procedures," 16 *Ohio State Journal on Dispute Resolution* 643 (2001); Theodore J. St. Antoine, "Mandatory Arbitration of Employee Discrimination Claims: Unmitigated Evil or Blessing in Disguise?" 15 *Thomas M. Cooley Law Review* 1 (1998); Katherine Van Wezel Stone, "Mandatory Arbitration of Individual Employment Rights: The Yellow Dog Contract of the 1990s," 73 *Denver University Law Review* 1017 (1996).

Among the sources tapped in chapter 7 are Ann Juliano and Stewart J. Schwab, "The Sweep of Sexual Harassment Cases," 86 *Cornell Law Review* 548 (2001); Rosemarie Skaine, *Power and Gender* (Jefferson, N.C.: McFarland, 1996); Deborah Zalesne, "Sexual Harassment Law: Has It Gone Too Far, or Has the Media?" 8 *Temple Policy and Civil Rights Law Review* 351 (1999); Wendy Pollack, "Sexual Harassment: Women's Experience vs. Legal Definitions," 13 *Harvard Women's Law Journal* 35 (1990); Jeffrey Rosen, *The Unwanted Gaze: The Destruction of Privacy in America* (New York: Vintage Books, 2001); Alison M. Thomas and Celia Kitzinger, eds., *Sexual Harassment: Contemporary Feminist Perspectives* (Bristol, Pa.: Open University Press, 1997); Kimberle Crenshaw, "Demarginalizing the Intersection of Race and Sex," in Katherine T. Bartlett and Rosanne Kennedy, *Feminist Legal Theory* (Boulder, Colo.: Westview Press, 1991); Martha Chamallas, "Writing about Sexual Harassment: A Guide to the Literature," 4 *UCLA Women's Law Journal* 37 (1993).

On law and social change discussed in the conclusion, see Martha Minow, "Law and Social Change," 62 *University of Missouri at Kansas City Law Review* 171 (1993); Gerald Rosenberg, *Hollow Hope: Can Courts Bring about Social Change?* (Chicago: University of Chicago Press, 1991); Michael W. McCann, *Rights at Work: Pay Equity Reform and the Politics of Legal Mobilization* (Chicago: University of Chicago Press, 1994); Alan Freeman, "Antidiscrimination Law," in David Kairys, *The Politics of Law* (New York: Pantheon, 1990). For an overview of and cites to the recent rethinking of sexual harassment law, see Kathryn Abrams, "The New Jurisprudence of Sexual Harassment," 83 *Cornell Law Review* 1169 (1998).

INDEX